Coorg

STORIES AND ESSAYS

C.P. Belliappa has written extensively about Coorg (officially known as Kodagu), covering the history of the land and its people. His writings encompass the affairs of its erstwhile kingdom, which went on to become a British-administered territory, followed by being a tiny model state in the Indian Union post-Independence and, finally, its present-day avatar as a district in Karnataka after the States Reorganisation Act of 1956. In this collection of stories and essays, Belliappa has delved deeper into antiquity, covering a wide range of topics relevant to understanding the ethos of Coorg. His other books are *Tale of a Tiger's Tail & Other Yarns from Coorg*, *Nuggets from Coorg History*, *Victoria Gowramma: The Lost Princess of Coorg* and *Tongue of the Slip: Looking Back on Life with Humour*.

Coorg

STORIES AND ESSAYS

C.P. BELLIAPPA

RUPA

Published by
Rupa Publications India Pvt. Ltd 2023
7/16, Ansari Road, Daryaganj
New Delhi 110002

Sales centres:
Prayagraj Bengaluru Chennai
Hyderabad Jaipur Kathmandu
Kolkata Mumbai

Copyright © C.P. Belliappa 2023
All photographs courtesy the author.

The copyright for the individual photographs rests
with the respective owners or photographers.

While every effort has been made to trace copyright holders and
obtain permission, this has not been possible in all cases; any omissions
brought to our attention will be remedied in future editions.

The views and opinions expressed in this book are the authors' own and
the facts are as reported by him which have been verified to the extent possible,
and the publishers are not in any way liable for the same.

All rights reserved.
No part of this publication may be reproduced, transmitted,
or stored in a retrieval system, in any form or by any means,
electronic, mechanical, photocopying, recording or otherwise,
without the prior permission of the publisher.

P-ISBN: 978-93-5702-185-2
E-ISBN: 978-93-5702-188-3

First impression 2023

10 9 8 7 6 5 4 3 2 1

The moral right of the author has been asserted.

This book is sold subject to the condition that it shall not, by way of
trade or otherwise, be lent, resold, hired out, or otherwise circulated,
without the publisher's prior consent, in any form of binding
or cover other than that in which it is published.

To my father and all the freedom fighters from Coorg

CONTENTS

Preface ix

PART I
COORG OF YORE

1. Ancient Dolmens in Coorg 3
2. Recorded History of Coorg in Brief 8
3. Blast from the Past 20
4. A Unique Shrine and the Tipu Sultan Connection 23
5. A Guesthouse for the British 27
6. The Rage of a Raja 33
7. Elephant Hunt by Lingarajendra 37
8. Saga of the Somayanda Family 41
9. Lord William Bentinck's Visit to the Ooty Club and Declaration of War on Coorg 44
10. Remembering Sir Mark Cubbon 49
11. The Thirteen Wives of Chikka Veerarajendra of Coorg 53
12. Dewan Chepudira Ponnappa 58
13. The Three Germans in Coorg 63
14. Coorg-Born First World War Hero 69
15. Subedar Chepudira Thimayya 75
16. A Century Old Convent School in Coorg 80
17. The Commissioner's Wife 84

PART II
THE VICTORIA GOWRAMMA PAPERS

18. Queen Victoria's Favourite Goddaughter: Princess Victoria Gowramma of Coorg	91
19. The Art and Creative Journey of Victoria Gowramma	99
20. Historical Connections	102
21. Gangamma: The Other Forgotten Princess of Coorg	108
22. Rediscovering Princess Victoria Gowramma	113

PART III
FREEDOM, INDEPENDENCE, AND MERGER

23. The Freedom Movement in Coorg	127
24. C.M. Poonacha's Role in the Freedom Movement	137
25. The Constitution of India	151
26. States Reorganization and Merger of Coorg with Karnataka	156
27. Post the Reorganization of Indian States	168
Appendix	182
Acknowledgements	251
Bibliography	252

PREFACE

This compendium of essays on Coorg (officially known as Kodagu) draws from and builds on my earlier books: *Nuggets from Coorg History* and *Victoria Gowramma: The Lost Princess of Coorg*. Many stories from the distant and not so distant past of Coorg have been steadily recovered as long forgotten and shelved materials are discovered in family attics and digitized archives. This wealth of historical information is now accessible online.

One of my areas of interest that I have explored in this anthology is how the freedom movement manifested in Coorg and the subsequent events that led to its merger with Karnataka. Nearly 70 years later, this continues to be a contentious subject. Many of its inhabitants find it difficult to reconcile the fact that Coorg, which was a Part 'C' state, lost its statehood in 1956. The Karnataka government's benign neglect of Coorg has highlighted this grievance. For a dispassionate interpretation of these momentous events, I have allowed the written records to speak for themselves. I hope they shed some light on what has become a very heated discourse. The final debate in the Coorg Legislative Assembly to pass a resolution on the merger of Coorg with Karnataka, in accordance with the States Reorganisation Commission report, was held on 6 December 1955. I have reproduced this interesting debate verbatim (see the Appendix).

This book is divided into three parts: Part I: Coorg of Yore, Part II: The Victoria Gowramma Papers and Part III: Freedom, Independence, and Merger.

- **Part I** chronicles the history of Coorg. It is a preamble with prehistoric accounts, which have fascinating details. It also explores the relatively better documented Haleri Lingayat dynasty (1600–1834) followed by the British rule (1834–1947) and provides glimpses of the enormous changes Coorg has undergone, particularly since the seventeenth century.
- **Part II** reports the exciting events following the publication of my book *Victoria Gowramma: The Lost Princess of Coorg*. I must mention Dr Nima Poovaya-Smith, Senior Research Fellow, School of Fine Arts, History of Arts and Cultural Studies, University of Leeds, UK, who invited me to several music and dance performances depicting the life of Victoria Gowramma, the lost princess of Coorg, and the Maharaja of the Punjab Duleep Singh.

One of the important outcomes of the publication of my book was the connections I established with a number of descendants of Chikka Veerarajendra, the last raja of Coorg, and his daughter Victoria Gowramma. When my book was launched in London in 2010, to my delight, one of the attendees was Anne Phillips, a great-great-granddaughter of Lieutenant Colonel John Campbell and his first wife Margaret Matthew. Lieutenant Colonel Campbell married Victoria Gowramma after the demise of his first wife. Phillips was most helpful in uncovering many details about Victoria Gowramma, including sharing a number of rare photographs of her and her daughter Edith Victoria. This interaction was instrumental in helping me locate the direct descendants of Victoria Gowramma, now living in Australia. Thanks to Dr Poovaya-Smith, I also got an opportunity to meet and interact with David Lascelles, eighth Earl of Harewood, a direct descendant of Queen Victoria.

Researching the story of Victoria Gowramma was

an incredible adventure. I was able to unearth important documents and photographs especially from the archives of *The Times*. I have reproduced several of the archived materials that I used to reconstruct the long-forgotten story of Victoria Gowramma.

- **Part III** is devoted to events that took place in Coorg during the freedom struggle and the political developments of that momentous era. As mentioned earlier, the details of the merger of Coorg with Karnataka in 1956 is covered in this section. My father, C.M. Poonacha, was a prominent freedom fighter from Coorg. Through his personal experiences, I have attempted to contribute to the narratives of the selfless service of the countless men and women from every corner of the subcontinent to the cause of freeing India from the colonial yoke. After Independence, my father was an important figure in both state and national politics, occupying key positions in both arenas. I have covered some of the historical events in which he was involved in this part of the book.

It is my fervent hope that this collection of stories and essays on Coorg will help future researchers who wish to delve deeper into the history of this extraordinary land with its distinctive history, traditions and culture.

PART I
COORG OF YORE

1

ANCIENT DOLMENS IN COORG

Coorg is a pristine stretch of hilly terrain in the lush Western Ghats of India. Copious monsoon rains and fertile soil have made it one of the most thickly forested areas in India. It is home to not only elephants and tigers but also a wide range of flora and fauna.

The earliest popularly known inhabitants of this forested land are the Kodavas or the Coorgs. The Kodavas, with their long military history, are different in more than one way from most South Indians. When the British annexed Coorg in 1834, they recognized the fighting capabilities of the Kodavas and classified them as a martial race and even formed a Coorg Regiment later. This tradition of being a warrior race continues till date. Although the total population of Kodavas is less than 200,000, a disproportionately large number of high-ranking officers in the defence forces of the country come from this community. Athletic by nature, they have excelled on several physically challenging fronts, especially in the game of hockey. Many hockey players who have represented the country in the Olympics and other international tournaments belong to this community. Many Kodavas are internationally accomplished in several other sports as well. Kodavas have distinctive features, unique customs, attire and cuisine. The British were intrigued by the enigma of the Kodavas and came up with several theories about their origin. However, none of them have been substantiated.

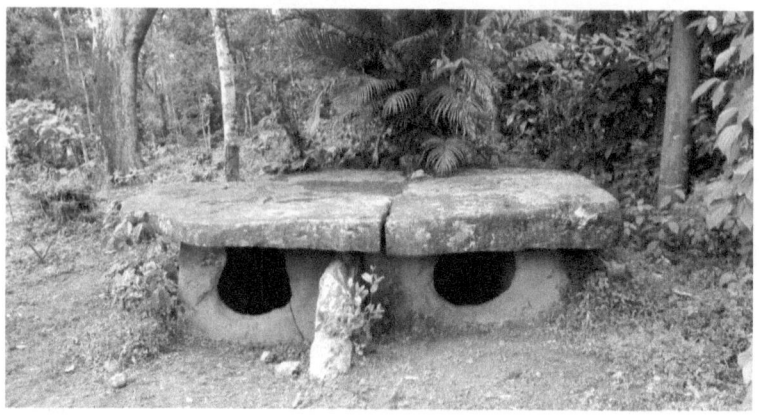

Figure 1: Ancient dolmens in Diveen Muthanna's estate, Virajpet, Coorg.
Source: Author's collection

Besides the mystery about its original inhabitants, Coorg is home to prehistoric stone structures, popularly known as dolmens. Such ancient dolmens have also been found in other parts of peninsular India. Intriguingly, these primitive megaliths resemble the Alemannic tumuli found in Germany, France, Switzerland and a few other European countries. Although the real purpose of these stone structures is unclear, it is now generally accepted that dolmens were used as memorial landmarks, portal tombs or markers of territorial boundaries.

It is estimated that the dolmens in Coorg and other parts of peninsular India are over 3,000 years old and belong to the Megalithic period.[1] Though these strange megaliths had been around for thousands of years, the local inhabitants had not

---

[1] Vahia, Mayank N., Srikumar M. Menon, Riza Abbas and Nisha Yadav, 'Megaliths in Ancient India and their Possible Association to Astronomy', *Proceedings of the the 7th International Conference on Oriental Astronomy*, Japan, September 2010, https://tinyurl.com/5eejv95d. Accessed on 13 February 2023.

studied or explored them. It is quite possible that people were generally wary of mysterious structures and feared antagonizing some spirit or the other by being inquisitive. The German missionary Reverend Hermann Mögling, who spent many years in Coorg, was the first to prise open a dolmen in 1856. He found it on land belonging to Alamanda Somayya in Armeri village while clearing the area to build a makeshift church. He found several well-crafted earthenware objects of different shapes and sizes buried inside. Some of these objects were miniatures resembling children's toys. They also contained soil, ash, beads, grains and bones.[2]

In 1868, Lieutenant Mackenzie, the assistant superintendent of Coorg, was intrigued to find these shadowy stone dolmens while clearing a wooded area near Virajpet.[3] Soon after, some better-preserved dolmens were found in the northern parts of Coorg—Madapur, Kushalnagar and Somwarpet. The superintendent of Coorg at the time, Captain Robert Andrews Cole, took a great deal of interest in exploring these megaliths and systematically recorded his findings. Earthenware, iron implements, arrowheads and spears were discovered in some of these dolmens. The earthenware found in these dolmens is now displayed in the Government Museum at Bangalore (now Bengaluru). The most remarkable of them is an elegantly shaped three-legged vase, which demonstrates that this ancient community was quite artistic. Reportedly, some of the earthenware even has simple patterns in elementary colours. However, none of them are glazed. It was found that some of the dolmens had already been opened, probably by tomb raiders of yore looking for valuables.

---

[2]Richter, Georg, *Manual of Coorg: A Gazetteer of the Natural Features of the Country and the Social and Political Condition of its Inhabitants*, B.R. Publishing, Delhi, 1870.
[3]Ibid.

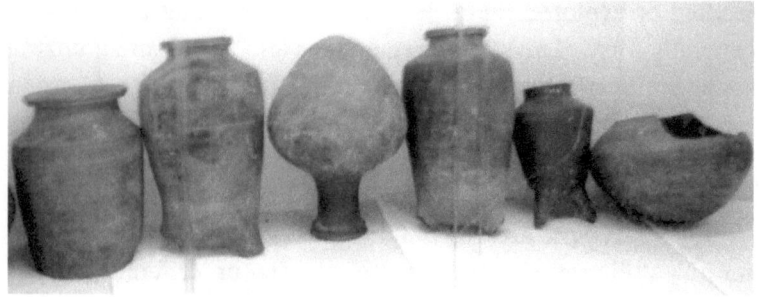

Figure 2: Clay pots found inside the Cairns at the Government Museum, Bangalore.
Source: Author's collection

My own search for these relics ended thanks to my friend, Kumbera Sharu Subbaiah, who guided me to some of the best-preserved dolmens in south Coorg. They are located in a private coffee estate near Virajpet, belonging to Palecanda Diveen Muthanna's family. Over several generations, they have preserved a few of the dolmens. According to Diveen, their property had many of these ancient structures and over time the crumbling stones from these dolmens were used for construction and other such activities in the process of starting their coffee plantations. It is highly likely that these were the same dolmens discovered by Lieutenant Mackenzie in 1868. Remnants of some of the megaliths are still strewn all over the estate. Interestingly, this entire area is popularly known as Pandavapare because it is believed that Pandavas, from the epic Mahabharata, built these mysterious stone structures. The British wryly mention in their records that the locals invariably attributed anything inexplicable to their epics.[4]

From the findings of Reverend Mögling, Captain Cole and

---

[4]Ibid.

Lieutenant Mackenzie, it was concluded that these megaliths were probably ancient dolmens. Reverend Georg Richter in his *Gazetteer of Coorg*[5] and Benjamin Lewis Rice, who was the director of public instructions, Mysore (now Mysuru) and Coorg, in his publication *Mysore & Coorg, A Gazetteer*[6] compiled in 1878 for the Government of India, concur with the findings. They state that the construction of these dolmens is quite disconnected from the life, customs and history of the present inhabitants of Coorg and that there is no evidence of any relationship or common ancestry with the people who constructed these structures. The mystery as to who these ancient people were remains unsolved.

The dolmens found in Coorg are of two types: single or double chambered. Those in the estate of Palecanda family are double chambered with stone dividers in between. They have two irregular, oval-shaped apertures nearly two feet in diameter to access each of the chambers. The double chambered dolmens are about ten-feet long, six-feet wide and four-feet high. The stone slabs used are solid pieces with a rough finish, which the British describe as 'rude construction'.[7] It is curious that the openings of all the dolmens face east.

These megaliths, though modest, are as intriguing as those at Stonehenge and Easter Islands. A scientific archaeological study could shed more light on these interesting relics left behind by our predecessors from a distant past.

---

[5]Ibid.
[6]Rice, Benjamin Lewis, *Mysore and Coorg: A Gazetteer Compiled for the Government of India*, Mysore Government Press, 1878.
[7]Fergusson, James, *Rude Stone Monuments in All Countries: Their Age and Uses*, John Murray, London, 1872.

2

RECORDED HISTORY OF COORG IN BRIEF

Most of the early accounts of Coorg are essentially drawn from oral history, grounded in myths and legends. Ninth and tenth century inscriptions found in several parts of the Deccan region include vague references to Coorg. Benjamin Lewis Rice, an archaeological researcher, conducted an extensive study and recorded his findings in his seminal publication: *Coorg Inscriptions: Epigraphia Carnatica*[8], first published in 1886. Coorg is variously mentioned in these inscriptions as Kodinadu, Kudakam, Kudamalainadu, Kodaga-malenadu, Kodi-adagu etc. These names, in South Indian languages, describe a region or settlement in the mountains and are believed to refer to present-day Coorg.

It is inferred from these inscriptions that Coorg as well as many of its neighbouring areas were under the suzerainty of successive South Indian dynasties, such as the Western Gangas, Pandyas, Cholas, Kadambas, Chengalvas and Hoysalas. After the fall of Hoysala rule in the fourteenth century, Coorg came under the control of the Vijayanagar Empire. In the sixteenth century, after the fall of the Vijayanagar Empire, Coorg was independently ruled by local chieftains called *Nayakas* or *Palegars*, until the advent of the Lingayat rajas of the Haleri dynasty.

---

[8]Rice, Benjamin Lewis, *Coorg Inscriptions: Epigraphia Carnatica*, Mysore Government Press, 1886.

The reign of the Haleri rajas began in early seventeenth century when Veeraraja, a minor Lingayat prince from Ikkeri in present day Shimoga district, ventured into the then-inhospitable province of Coorg with a fire in his belly to establish a dynasty of his own. Veeraraja initially posed as a *Jangam*, a Lingayat priest, and gained the confidence of the feuding Nayakas as an arbitrator and astrologer. In time, he took advantage of the hopelessly divided Nayakas by skilfully pitting them against each other and ultimately took control of Coorg, establishing the Haleri dynasty. This saga of a Lingayat with his small band of supporters tactically taking over Coorg has many parallels with how a clutch of British traders managed to wrest control over the Indian subcontinent by the mid-eighteenth century.

According to another unsubstantiated narrative, there were two powerful Kodava Nayakas who sought Veeraraja's counsel on a dispute. Veeraraja supposedly advised the duo to reconcile their differences so that they could come together and decide on one of them becoming the king of Coorg. The two Nayakas, daggers drawn at each other, turned down the suggestion and unanimously requested Veeraraja to be the king of Coorg, since he had a royal lineage. This line of thinking conformed to the universal belief held in those days that only the 'blue-blooded' had the divine right to sit on a throne.

Over the years, Veeraraja's successors considerably extended their empire. His grandson, Mudduraja, a popular ruler, brought most of Coorg under his rule by forging alliances, including matrimonial ones, with the Kodavas. On the other hand, Mudduraja's son, Siribai Veerappa Raja, ruthlessly eliminated the remaining, already weakened, Nayakas. Thus, the Haleri dynasty established firm roots in Coorg by 1700.

Around 1736, Hyder Ali, through trickery and deceit, deposed the Wodeyars, his erstwhile employers, to become the de facto ruler of neighbouring region of Mysore. By then, the East India Company had learnt the advantages of territorial acquisition to boost their trading activities. Hyder Ali and later his son, Tipu Sultan, controlled most of the southern parts of India and were formidable opponents of the British in the Deccan region. The East India Company had been well-established in the nearby region of Malabar. Tipu Sultan and the British soon clashed. Both the opponents saw Coorg as a strategic geographic area for their defensive and offensive activities. Hyder Ali and Tipu Sultan had a fragile hold over Coorg from 1780 to 1791. This period was extremely agonizing for the people of Coorg.

After the demise of Lingaraja (the grandson of Mudduraja) in 1780, his sons—Dodda Veerarajendra (the heir apparent), Appajiraja and Lingarajendra (also referred to as Lingaraja II)—were imprisoned by Tipu Sultan in the old fort at Periyapatna. In their quest to subdue and break the spirit of the Kodavas, who were fighting in the Haleri Raja's stead while he was imprisoned, Hyder Ali and Tipu Sultan committed grave atrocities against them. Using the false promise of peace, Tipu Sultan treacherously captured tens of thousands of unarmed men, women and children (nearly 80,000 according to some records)[9] and made them walk all the way from Coorg to Srirangapatna. Many perished on the way. He brutally converted the survivors to Islam. Tipu Sultan's atrocities in Coorg, Mangalore (now Mangaluru) and Kerala are well documented. There are documents where he gloats about his conquests, massacres and forcible conversions. To this day, Tipu Sultan is a much-hated figure in Coorg. In a daring operation in 1788, loyal Kodavas and Vokkaligas, led by Hombale Nayaka and

---

[9]Richter, Georg, *Manual of Coorg: A Gazetteer of the Natural Features of the Country and the Social and Political Condition of its Inhabitants*, B.R. Publishing Corp., Delhi, 1870.

a Muslim man named Ismail Khan, rescued the three princes from the fort in Periyapatna. Over the next three years, with help from the Kodavas, Dodda Veerarajendra reclaimed his kingdom.

In 1790, the East India Company proposed to sign a friendship treaty with Dodda Veerarajendra to fight their common enemy: Tipu Sultan.[10] Dodda Veerarajendra readily agreed, and the Kodavas were eager to avenge Tipu Sultan's brutal assaults on Coorg. This alliance successfully vanquished Tipu Sultan in the fourth and final Anglo-Mysore War of 1799.

These wars against Hyder Ali and Tipu Sultan had decimated the population of Coorg. Thus, Dodda Veerarajendra invited Hindus, Christians, Jains and Muslims from neighbouring areas to repopulate his kingdom. He founded the town of Virajpet in 1792, where these migrants were given land and other amenities. Their descendants continue to live in large numbers in and around the thriving town of Virajpet.

Dodda Veerarajendra stabilized Coorg. During his reign, people enjoyed relative peace and were able to pursue agriculture and trade without threats of war. However, despite being considered a hero of the Haleri dynasty, he grew despotic with age. He was distraught at not having a male heir to the throne. He feared conspiracies against him and his four daughters, born to his favourite wife Mahadevamma. Suspecting his younger brothers of treason, he ordered their assassination. His ruthless Siddi assassins brought him Appajiraja's head. However, Lingarajendra, his other brother, escaped decapitation when Dodda Veerarajendra changed his mind in the nick of time. Several of his close aides and dewans were executed because he suspected them of plotting against his rule. Some of the disaffected Kodava commanders hatched a plot against

---

[10]Mögling, Herrmann, *Coorg Memoirs: An Account of Coorg and of the Coorg Mission*, Wesleyan Mission Press, 1855.

him when they found out that their Raja had lost his mental equilibrium. Alerted to the conspiracy, Dodda Veerarajendra set up a trap for the conspirators. When the rebels entered his fort in Madikeri, Dodda Veerarajendra had the gates closed, capturing nearly 300 plotters and ruthlessly massacring them.

With his paranoia getting worse, Dodda Veerarajendra trusted no one. His health suffered and he feared he might not live much longer. In his desperation, he sought the help of the British to ensure that his eldest daughter Devammaji ascended the throne after his demise. He made large investments in the form of promissory notes with the British for his daughters' financial security after his demise. Before his death, Dodda Veerarajendra left a valuable narration of history of the Haleri Dynasty known as *Rajendranamme*. When he died in 1809, the 10-year-old Devammaji became the queen of Coorg with Sode Raja Basavalingaraja (husband of Dodda Veerarajendra's daughter, Rajamma, from his first wife) acting as the regent.

Lingarajendra schemed to replace Sode Raja, an outsider, and become the regent to the young queen. Within a year, Lingarajendra manipulated the British and the Kodava dewans and usurped the throne. He promptly declared his son, also named (Chikka) Veerarajendra, as the heir apparent.

Lingarajendra's rule lasted from 1811 to 1820. He maintained cordial relations with the British. With the elimination of Tipu Sultan, there was no threat of war, which led to agriculture and trade flourishing. Lingarajendra introduced a system wherein the taxes levied on his citizens were based on the fertility of the land. Towards the end of his reign, Lingarajendra became autocratic and surrounded himself with sycophants. He became intolerant of any form of criticism. His cold-blooded murder of senior dewan Chowrira Appanna, whose support had ensured his ascension to the throne, appalled his subjects. Likewise, the killing of the respected Brahmin Subarasaiah shocked the people of Coorg. In repentance for killing a Brahmin (a crime for which it was believed he would languish in hell), Lingarajendra built the Omkareshwara Temple in Madikeri to appease the spirit of Subarasaiah. However, no such act of atonement was done for Chowrira Appanna.

Lingarajendra was succeeded by his immature and overindulged 18-year-old son Chikka Veerarajendra in 1820. He depended on the advice of his childhood playmate Kunta Basava, who started as a kennel keeper of Lingarajendra and was known for his crude and ruthless conduct. He was elevated to be the principal dewan of the young Raja. Chikka Veerarajendra brought his downfall upon himself by disregarding the wise counsel of his other three elderly and judicious Dewans: Chepudira Ponnappa, Apparanda Bopanna and Laxminarayana.

There was an implacable, mutual hatred between Dewan Kunta Basava and the Kodavas. He instigated Chikka Veerarajendra to commit grave atrocities against the Kodavas, including the dreaded 'Kuthi Nasha', wherein the entire patrilineal sides of families were eliminated. The young Raja feared that Devammaji, his cousin who was dethroned by his father, would be assisted by the Kodavas to replace him on the throne of Coorg. Feeling extremely insecure, he, with help from Dewan Basava, eliminated the daughters of Dodda Veerarajendra.

Chikka Veerarajendra's next target was his sister, also named Devammaji, and brother-in-law, Chennabasappa, who he suspected of plotting to dethrone him. The couple barely escaped being slain and sought refuge with the British in Mysore.

Chikka Veerarajendra continued his predecessor's policy of humouring the British. The British had considered Coorg to be one their protectorate ever since they had signed a friendship treaty with Dodda Veerarajendra in 1790 to fight

Tipu Sultan. They had been keeping an eye on Coorg and receiving reports of the excesses of Chikka Veerarajendra and Dewan Kunta Basava. When the former demanded that his brother-in-law and sister be handed over to him, the British Resident in Mysore, James Archibald Casamajor, refused. In 1833, two Indian officers, Dara Seth and Kullapally Karunakaran Menon, who worked for the British in Calicut (now Kozhikode), Kerala, were sent to Madikeri to meet Chikka Veerarajendra and gather first-hand information about the situation. An infuriated Chikka Veerarajendra imprisoned both the emissaries of the British. This was the beginning of serious hostilities between the East India Company and the Raja of Coorg. While Dara Seth was released, Chikka Veerarajendra held Menon hostage and demanded Chennabasappa and Devammaji be handed over to him in exchange. Menon warned the Raja not to antagonize the British. In Menon's famous words: 'The British had the capacity to raise troops which could outnumber the trees in Coorg.'[11]

By then, the British received intelligence that the Kodava dewans, Chepudira Ponnappa and Apparanda Bopanna, had had enough of the erratic and bloodthirsty rule of Chikka Veerarajendra who continued to listen only to his psychopathic Dewan Kunta Basava. Dewans Ponnappa and Bopanna, whose loyalty to the Haleri rajas had been unswerving (they had served both Dodda Veerarajendra and Lingarajendra), felt betrayed and insulted. This was heightened by the general discontent in the kingdom. The Raja was getting increasingly alienated from the people. Finally, after insistent warnings by the British to release Menon went unheeded, Lord William Bentinck, who was the governor general at the time, declared war on Coorg on 15 March 1834.

---

[11]Belliappa, C.P., *Nuggets from Coorg History*, Rupa Publications, 2008.

Recorded History of Coorg in Brief 15

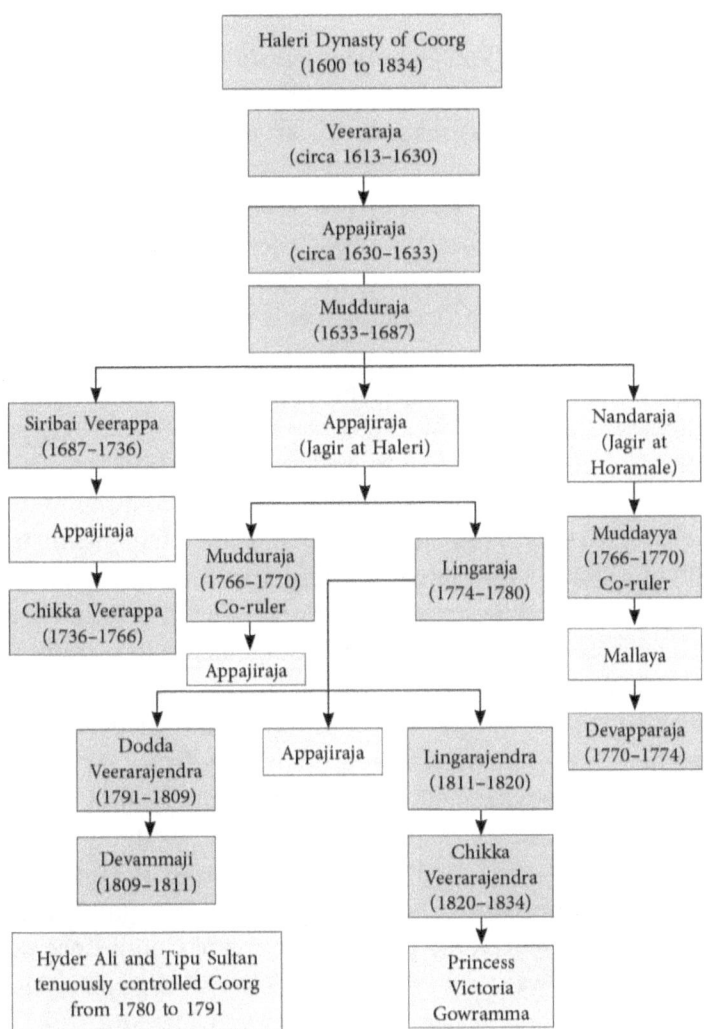

Figure 3: A family tree of the Haleri Dynasty of Coorg.

Source: Mapped by the author based on information sourced from: Richter, Georg, *Manual of Coorg: A Gazetter of the Natural Features of the Country, and the Social and Political Condition of Its Inhabitants*, B.R. Publishing Corp., Delhi, 1870.

Disgusted with the Raja's behaviour, the two Kodava Dewans, Ponnappa and Bopanna, remained neutral during the conflict. The British got the opportunity they had been waiting and launched a four-pronged attack on Coorg in early April 1834. They marched into Madikeri Fort on 7 April without much resistance, though they lost a few officers and men in isolated skirmishes with the loyal troops of the Raja. Chikka Veerarajendra had no option but to surrender. He was deposed and stripped of his throne, crown and most of his wealth. He was exiled to Vellore along with his 13 wives. A year later, Chikka Veerarajendra and his family were permanently banished to Benares (now Varanasi). Thus, the nearly 230-year-long rule of the Haleri dynasty came to an ignominious end.

It is to the credit of the resilient Kodava community that two centuries of Lingayat rule did not see Lingayatism take root in Coorg. Tipu Sultan's attempts at forcing his religion were also strongly resented and resisted. The British and some of the European missionaries used subtle means to spread their faith which, too, did not find favour among the Kodavas who remained steadfast worshippers of nature and their ancestors. They have, however, over a period, gradually adapted their beliefs to be accommodated under the broad umbrella of Hinduism. Though the influence of priests is minimal, Kodavas practise and follow the Hindu religion. The priests in the numerous temples in Coorg are Brahmins. Kaveri, the river goddess, and Igguthappa have been the presiding deities of Coorg since time immemorial. It was quite common for Kodavas to go on arduous pilgrimages to holy places like Benares and Mathura.

By 1852, the exiled Chikka Veerarajendra had seven sons and four daughters. He shrewdly befriended some of the British in Benares and managed to get permissions from the hard-nosed Governor General Dalhousie to visit England along with his favourite daughter Gowramma, whom he wanted raised as a Christian and given Western education. The father and daughter sailed to England in March 1852 and spent the rest of their lives in that country.

Chikka Veerarajendra's real purpose behind visiting England was to recover the funds that his uncle Dodda Veerarajendra had invested with the East India Company on behalf of his daughters. After the suspicious demise of the four daughters, he asserted himself as the only surviving beneficiary and filed a legal suit against the Company in the Chancery Court, London, for the release of the appropriated assets. After unsuccessfully fighting the case for seven years, he died a broken man in 1859.

In a happy twist of fate, within a few years of the British rule beginning, people in Coorg found their living conditions vastly improved. Threats of war disappeared and peace dawned on the troubled land. With the introduction of education, streamlined administration, improved infrastructure, better agricultural practices and the opening up of coffee estates, the economy of Coorg multiplied manifold. The British allowed the identity of Coorg to remain intact and administered the province under a chief commissioner who reported to the governor general.

There was a symbiotic relationship between the British and the people of Coorg. However, by the 1930s, the freedom movement took firm roots in Coorg as well. Sensing radical changes in India, especially after the Jallianwala Bagh massacre of 1919 in Punjab, many British coffee planters started selling their estates to locals and returning to the United Kingdom (UK). However, some of the plantation owners wanted to retain their estates while also going back to the UK. They merged their estates and formed a company named Consolidated Coffee

Limited in 1922. One of the prominent members of this company was Ivor Bull[12], a progressive and far-sighted individual, who was also a First World War veteran. He joined the company in 1929 and rose to the position of managing director. Being in tune with the Swadeshi Movement at the time, he converted Consolidated Coffee Limited from a sterling to a rupee company in 1943, making it one of the first British companies to become a rupee company in India.

Bull continued as the managing director of Consolidated Coffee Limited and lived in Coorg until 1954. He greatly contributed to the growth of the coffee industry and was instrumental in the formation of the Coffee Board of India and in the establishment of the Central Coffee Research Institute. He enthusiastically helped and advised private coffee planters in scientific cultivation. Bull is rightly considered to be the father of the Indian coffee industry.

In an interesting episode, during the Quit India movement in 1942, a group of school children marched to the head office of Consolidated Coffee Limited in Pollibetta, Coorg, shouting slogans against British rule. Among the group was a young boy named Koothanda P. Uthappa. Bull came out of his office, met the demonstrators cordially and interacted with them. When one of the boys offered him a Gandhi cap, he readily accepted and donned it to show his solidarity with the freedom movement. This way, he won many hearts. Uthappa later joined Consolidated Coffee Limited and rose to the position of executive director of the company when it was subsequently acquired by the Tata group and renamed Tata Coffee Limited in the 1990s.

The people of Coorg earnestly contributed to the freedom struggle. Many national stalwarts of the freedom movement

---

[12]Bull, Ivor, *Coffee Memories*, Coorg Planters' Association, Centenary Souvenir, 1979.

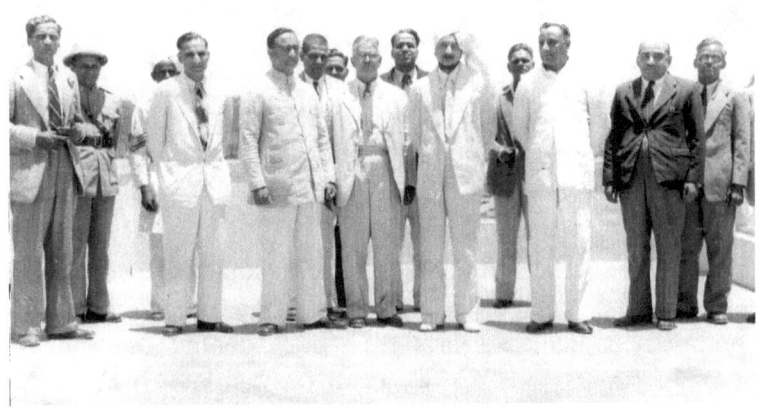

Figure 4: C.M. Poonacha, chief minister of Coorg, with dignitaries, circa 1954.
Source: Author's collection

visited Coorg and encouraged the local people. Part III of this collection details the freedom struggle in Coorg (see p. 125).

After Independence, Coorg was administered by an elected District Board from 1946 to 1952, comprising 24 members, with Ketolira Chengappa as the first Indian chief commissioner. From 1952 to 1956, Coorg was classified as a Part 'C' state, again with a chief commissioner. The 'Tiny Model State', as it was known, had a Legislative Assembly of 24 members.

In 1956, Coorg was incorporated into the Vishal Mysore state (renamed Karnataka in 1973), in accordance with the States Reorganisation Act (more on this in Part III).

3

BLAST FROM THE PAST

Just a stone's throw from the historic Nalknad Palace in Coorg is a private coffee estate belonging to the Apparanda family, appropriately named Palace Estate. The family, descendants of Dewan Apparanda Bopanna, runs a well-known homestay whose members are custodians of unique relics from the past.

The family possesses hundreds of cannon balls, each weighing about 5 kg, with diameters ranging between 3–5 in. This arsenal from the past is aesthetically arranged (see figure 5) in the garden in front of their 125-year-old house, overlooking the verdant Western Ghats. Prakash, one of the brothers, gave me the historical background of their family and how his grandfather found these cannon balls while scouting for new areas to cultivate coffee.

Having researched and written *Nuggets from Coorg History*, a book on the history of Coorg, in 2008, the sight of the array of cannon balls made me recall a compelling historical vignette that took place

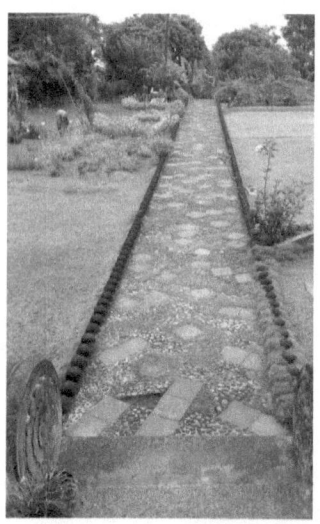

Figure 5: Cannon balls lining the cobbled path passing through the garden of Apparanda Prakash.

Source: Author's collection

in 1795. The Raja of Coorg at the time—Dodda Veerarajendra—with the able support of the Kodavas, had fought valiantly to regain most of his lost domain from Tipu Sultan. Having re-established his dynasty after a break of 11 years, he completed the construction of a modest palace deep in the safety of a forested area in Nalknad in 1795.

During one of the attacks on Coorg, Tipu Sultan's army was decisively trounced by the Coorg army. As the Sultan's soldiers beat a hasty retreat, they left behind a large cache of arms and ammunition. The abandoned arsenal consisted of several cannons and cannonballs, apparently supplied to Tipu Sultan by his French allies.

Despite continuing to live under the threat of Tipu Sultan, Dodda Veerarajendra was in a celebratory mood. He was happy that his new abode kept his family safe. Propitiously, there was a bumper crop of paddy in his domain that year. So, he planned an extravagant celebration of Puthari, the harvest festival. Sticking to tradition, Dodda Veerarajendra harvested the first sheaf of paddy in the presence of his dewans, family and subjects late one evening under the full-moon sky. To commemorate his victory over Tipu Sultan, he had the cannonballs they had captured shot into the forest as the fresh harvest was ceremoniously brought to his newly built palace. Firing salvos of cannonballs into the forest was a spectacular sight that everyone present enjoyed. Later, all the officials and village folk were treated to a special feast known as *Thombarada Oota* prepared in the palace kitchen.

Dodda Veerarajendra made celebrating Puthari an annual ritual during his reign, which lasted from 1791 to 1809. However, Lingarajendra, his brother and successor, discontinued the practice. He not only found it wasteful but also thought that the deafening blasts from the cannons disturbed the wildlife in the area. Lingarajendra was very fond of hunting and did not want the animals to move away from his hunting grounds. During his rule, he returned to the tradition of the Kodavas, firing a single shot into the full-moon sky with a muzzleloader at the time of the ceremonial harvest of paddy. This custom is practised even today with a shotgun being fired on the day of Puthari.

These cannon balls lay in the forest for more than a century until they were discovered by the Apparanda family sometime in the early twentieth century while clearing the area to plant coffee. However, the cannons used to fire this ammunition are not to be found in the area or in the premises of the Nalknad Palace. There are a few cannons in Madikeri Fort, which are likely the ones used by Dodda Veerarajendra and were probably moved by the British when they annexed Coorg in 1834.

The sight of hundreds of cannon balls now adorning the garden of the Apparanda family is quite unique. The family must receive due credit for preserving these artefacts and an interesting piece of history of Coorg.

4

A UNIQUE SHRINE AND THE TIPU SULTAN CONNECTION

Palangala, a remote village in Coorg, still retains its pristine environment despite the creeping urbanization. Palangala has a special significance for me, since my mother's family is from there. As children, we used to visit our maternal grandparents and, I have pleasant memories of this village bestowed with pristine natural beauty.

One of my many happy memories there is of a Spartan shrine atop a mountain named Malethirike. My grandparents' house is located at the foothills of this mountain. My parents were devotees of this shrine and it was an annual ritual for us to visit the temple during our summer vacation. The only way to get to this temple in those days was by walking through the thick, wooded mountain terrain. We used to set out early in the morning, and my father used to insist that we walk barefoot and on an empty stomach. It was an arduous, over a kilometre-long walk along a winding, beaten path. We even used to face leeches and other creepy crawlies on our way up. By the time we reached the top, we used to be ravenously hungry. However, we had to wait until the *pooja* was over to be served the *prasad*—delicious rice *payasa* prepared by the priests.

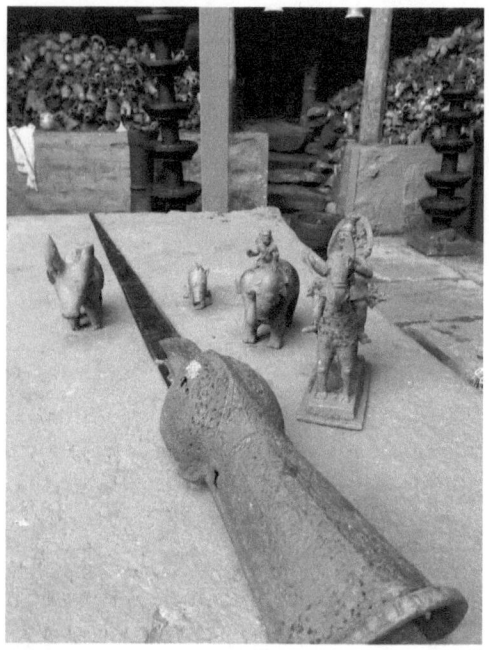

Figure 6: The sword handle in Malethirike Temple.
Source: Author's collection

One of the interesting stories connected with this shrine is related to the attack by Tipu Sultan's troops during the late eighteenth century. The Kodava warriors were outnumbered and unable to stop the marauders. They hid in the forest and prayed for divine intervention. Their prayers were answered, and according to lore, swarms of rock bees descended on the troops and chased them down the ghats. Evidence of this attack exists in the form of remnants of an old sword, which may have been abandoned by the attacking soldiers. The handle (see figure 6) with the protective guard is all that is left of this weapon. A devotee has added a blade to the sword handle.

We recently revisited Malethirike, which now has a reasonably motorable road to the top. The shrine is still serene and peaceful, with a spectacular view of the Western Ghats. Legend has it that the Pandavas spent part of their *ajnathavasa*—incognito phase—here. Lord Shiva is said to have appeared to the Pandavas in this shrine. It is a temple for Shiva, Parvathy and Ganesha. Three uneven stones atop an open, tree-covered platform represent the three deities.

This is the sanctum sanctorum. There is no structure around it. The priest succinctly described it as: 'The sky is the roof of this temple, the mountains are the walls, trees are the adornments, and the birds provide the music.' There is a pond nearby that has perennial crystal-clear, potable spring water. The priest was friendly and obliging and allowed me to take photographs of the vestige of the sword left behind by Tipu Sultan's soldiers more than two centuries ago.

Another interesting story related to this shrine is that of St Anne's Church in Virajpet, which was first built in 1792 during Dodda Veerarajendra's reign, who welcomed the Christians displaced by Tipu Sultan.[13] According to the priest in the temple, when the church was under construction, the spire kept collapsing every time it was built. The Italian architect was at a loss. A local Brahmin advised the architect to make an offering of a bell at the Malethirike Temple to overcome the problem. The architect, though highly sceptical, followed this advice as a last resort. He was amazed when the spire stood steady at the first subsequent attempt. Even now, devotees make vows and offer bells at this unique temple. The surroundings of the temple are also festooned with bells.

---

[13]Richter, Georg, *Manual of Coorg: A Gazetteer of the Natural Features of the Country and the Social and Political Condition of its Inhabitants*, B.R. Publishing Corp., Delhi, 1870.

Devotees who make vows at the temple also offer earthenware figurines. There are piles of figurines of horses, cows, dogs and humans that have been offered at the temple over the centuries.

The priest insisted we stay and receive the prasad after the pooja. We took in the divine beauty of nature as the priest went about conducting the various rituals. He rushed in and out of the kitchen where he was preparing the payasa. Savouring the delicious payasa brought back happy memories of my earlier visits to this beautiful shrine.

5

A GUESTHOUSE FOR THE BRITISH

The strategic friendship treaty signed between Dodda Veerarajendra and the East India Company in 1790 to fight their common enemy Tipu Sultan resulted in Coorg not only being an ally but also a quasi-protectorate of the British. A token, annual tribute of two elephants was gifted by Dodda Veerarajendra and his successors to the East India Company.

After Tipu Sultan's downfall in 1799, Mysore came under British control, even though the Wodiyars had been reinstated. Around 1795 to 1801, Dodda Veerarajendra built a guesthouse exclusively for his frequent British visitors. It was located amid an orchard of fruit trees not too far from the Madikeri Fort. A watercolour painting by artist John Johnson is the only image that provides a realistic picture of this imposing structure. In the sketch, Madikeri Fort can be seen in the background. Unfortunately, there are no traces left of this grand building today.

There are several mentions of the guesthouse in the writings of British visitors who were attracted to the thickly forested region of Coorg for wild-game hunting. The Coorg rajas, Dodda Veerarajendra, his brother Lingarajendra and Lingarajendra's son Chikka Veerarajendra went to great lengths to humour the British. Elaborate hunting expeditions were organized for their British guests. This well-appointed accommodation provided all the comforts the Europeans were accustomed to.

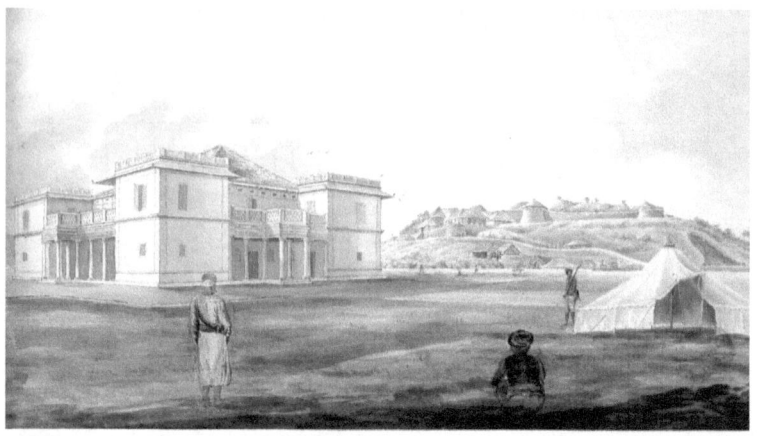

Figure 7: A watercolour painting of the Coorg Raja's guest house for the British artist John Johnson, circa 1815.

Colonel (later General) James Welsh visited Coorg in 1811, during Lingarajendra's rule, for a hunting trip. In his, book, *Military Reminiscences*, he vividly describes the building where he was accommodated:

> On the 19th of March 1811, having heard much in praise of the sport in Coorg, and being at leisure for such a trip, I set out from Bangalore, having a letter of introduction from the Honourable Arthur Cole, Resident at Mysore, and in company with Lieutenant W. Williamson, a young man of my own corps, both a keen and hardy sportsman as well as a very agreeable companion...
>
> I must now describe our own habitation, built on a small island, surrounded by paddy ground, now dry for the sole accommodation of Europeans. It is a large square, having a hall in the centre, a large covered-in verandah all round it, and four bedrooms projecting at the angles of the verandah, all on an upper story, the lower rooms

serving for the guard, attendants, storerooms etc. It stands on a square of seventy feet, the verandah having thirty-eight glass windows, with venetian blinds outside. The bedrooms have sixteen windows, and the hall eight glass doors; every part being neatly furnished, in the English style, with beds, tables, card-tables, writing boxes, chairs, chandeliers, settees etc. etc. And there is an old butler of my Vellore friend Colonel Ridgway Mealay, and a dozen active servants, who very speedily produced an English breakfast or dinner, served up on handsome Queen's ware, with every kind of European liquor; and what is even still more extraordinary, the cook bakes good bread![14]

Another early reference to this building can be found in Lieutenant P. Connor's book, *Memoirs of the Codugu Survey*:

It is a handsome building consisting of two stories; the form that of a centre with four turrets at the angles; it is in every way after the European model, both as to architecture and furniture; nor has anything been forgotten necessary to render it quite complete in those particulars; a regular establishment of servants is kept up expressly for it, and every care taken to anticipate the wants and provide for the convenience of the traveller who is treated with the most liberal hospitality.[15]

Yet another visitor was William Jeaffreson, a guest of Chikka Veerarajendra in 1830. He spent 22 memorable days in Coorg along with his colleague Captain Hill. Dr Jeaffreson wrote about the guesthouse in lofty words in his book *Coorg & Its Rajahs*:

---

[14]Welsh, James, *Military Reminiscences*, Smith, Elder, and Company, London, 1830.
[15]Connor, P., *Memoirs of Codugu Survey*, Central Jail Press, Bangalore, 1870.

Upon our arrival at the palace we were presented to the Rajah, who received us in the most cordial manner, assuring us that, like his ancestors, he entertained a particular regard and esteem for Englishmen.

The interview concluded, we were conducted to a garden outside the palace, in which the wildness of Indian mountain scenery was agreeably contrasted with the elegancies of modern horticulture. There we found a splendid bungalow, fitted up for our accommodation, with every possible convenience.

Round this residence grew flowers of the richest hues and the sweetest perfume, while trees, laden with delicious fruit, among whose branches perched wild birds of the brightest and most variegated plumage, cast over us their agreeable shade.

Near this bungalow was a tank, made of black marble of the highest polish and most elaborate workmanship, in the center of which rose a fountain, throwing up jets of water so clear and pellucid that hundreds of large and beautiful fish might be seen disporting in the basin, or else darting about in every direction after their prey. This tank was the favourite resort of the Rajah who was wont to visit it daily, at noon. Standing beside it, he would ring a small gold bell, he carried in his hand, and, at its tinkling, all the fish collected together at one spot, anxiously waiting for their food (young frogs, parched peas etc.), which an attendant threw to them from a basket.

In another part of the garden was an immense black marble stand, of pyramidal form, along the five front steps of which were arranged hundreds of bleached skulls of elephants, being the *Spolia Opima* of the chase.[16]

Dr Jeaffreson was sent to Coorg in 1830 by the British governor of Bombay, Sir John Malcolm, on Chikka Veerarajendra's request, to treat the Raja for a rare disease. However, the Raja, who was 26 years old at the time, had already recovered by the time Dr Jeaffreson arrived in Coorg. Chikka Veerarajendra extended his hospitality to the affable doctor with spectacular hunting expeditions and lavish entertainment during his stay. This generosity was highly appreciated by Dr Jeaffreson whose *spolia opima* included valuable elephant tusks, tiger claws, pelts, horns, etc. The Raja and the doctor remained good friends and corresponded with each other. When the Raja was exiled to Benares and later during his sojourn in England, Dr Jeaffreson met him and helped him in various ways in his attempts to recover the investment his uncle, Dodda Veerarajendra, made with the East India Company. Dr Jeaffreson authored the book, *Coorg & Its Rajas*, published in London in 1857. However, he wished to remain anonymous. In place of the name of the author, the book mentions the following line: 'By an Officer Formerly in The Service of His Highness Veer Rajunder Wadeer, Rajah of Coorg.'[17] Dr Jeaffreson received a retainer from Chikka Veerarajendra for his assistance. He records that the British administration dealt with the last Raja of Coorg unfairly by accusing him of crimes he had never committed. He further states that the Raja's subjects had been happy and had loved the Raja.

After the British annexed Coorg in 1834, this guesthouse was, surprisingly, neglected and abandoned. The British officers preferred to live within the safety of the Madikeri Fort. By 1860s,

---

[16]Jeaffreson, William, *Coorg & Its Rajahs*, John Bumpus, London, 1857.
[17]Ibid.

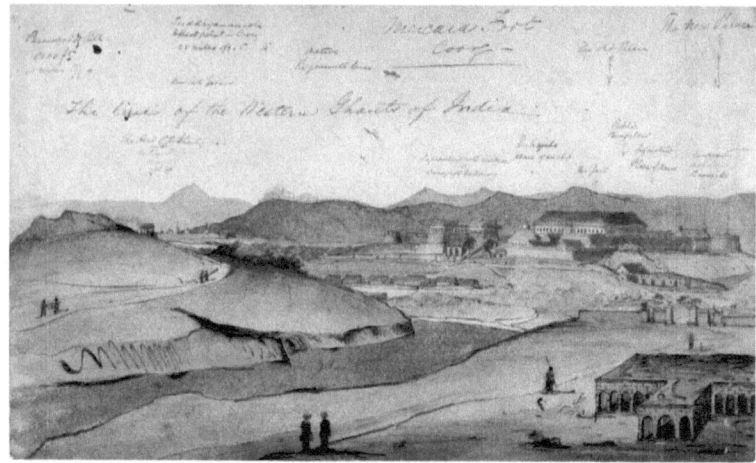

Figure 8: Pen and ink painting giving a panoramic view of Madikeri by an unknown artist, circa 1850.

the then 50-odd-years-old building was in ruins. It is likely that the wooden roof had leaked, deteriorating the condition of the building and making it unliveable. The crumbling edifice can be seen in the foreground in a rare pen-and-ink sketch by an unknown artist, apparently merging several features of Coorg with the landmarks in Madikeri.

In 1862, 64 Kodava elders approached the British government for assistance in constructing a boarding house for boys at the newly established Madikeri Central School. They suggested using the site of the guesthouse for the boarding house and requested to use the material from the collapsed building for constructing it. The British agreed and the boarding house was built by 1871 under Reverend Georg Richter's supervision. Reverend Richter also set up the Government Central School in 1869 and served as its principal for several years. This school, now more than 150 years old, continues to impart quality education.

6

THE RAGE OF A RAJA

One of the notable edifices in Madikeri is the palace located within the fort, contoured to an irregular, hexagonal hillock. There are six bastions built at each angle of the hexagon. The fortress was originally built by Mudduraja sometime during the 1680s using mud. Hyder Ali and Tipu Sultan held sporadic sway over Coorg from 1780 to 1791. The latter fortified the battlement with stone ramparts.

Dodda Veerarajendra won back the Haleri dynasty's realm from Tipu Sultan and reigned from 1791 to 1809. He built a palace within the fort complex with the typical open courtyard at the centre. After the demise of Dodda Veerarajendra, his brother, Lingarajendra ascended the throne of Coorg in 1811. He reconstructed the palace in its current form by encompassing the earlier structure. According to an inscription on a metal plate in one of the rooms in the palace, the building was completed in two years and one month. The inscription concludes: 'The pious who praise Almighty God, by whose grace this magnificent palace was constructed, shall enjoy eternal happiness in this world and in the world to come.'[18]

The palace was designed by an Italian architect. Rumour

---

[18]Richter, Georg, *Manual of Coorg: A Gazetteer of the Natural Features of the Country and the Social and Political Condition of its Inhabitants*, B.R. Publishing Corp., Delhi, 1870.

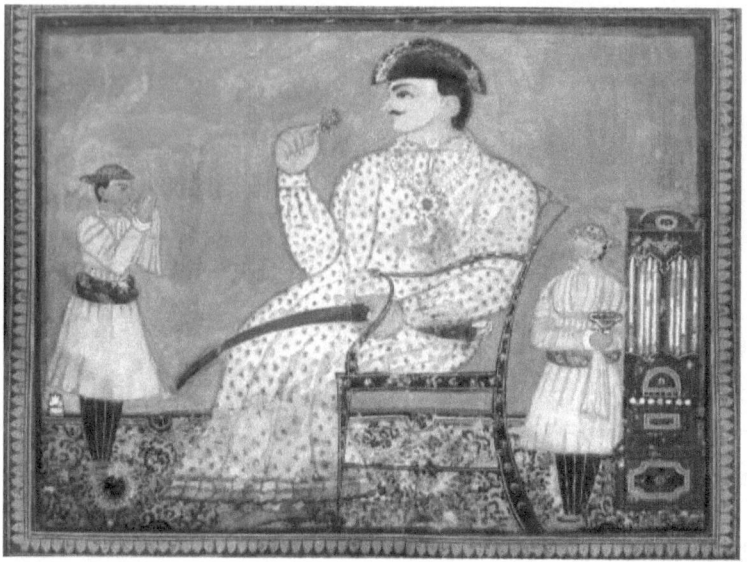

Figure 9: A painting of Lingarajendra in court, circa 1812.
Courtesy: Thathanda family

has it that once his task had been completed, Lingarajendra got the poor man bricked in a corner of the wall, lest he replicate the design elsewhere.

Lingarajendra was a crack shot, an able archer and could shoot a moving target while on horseback. His passion was hunting, and he spent a good part of his time in pursuit of this sport. British officers were his frequent guests. He organized spectacular hunts for them. As mentioned earlier, many, including General Welsh and Lieutenant Williamson, have left extensive records of their visits to Coorg and how Lingarajendra himself would ride an elephant as mahout and take his guests into the deepest parts of the dense forests. Selling elephant tusks, bison horns, antlers, tiger pelts and other trophies was part of his revenue, which he used to purchase thoroughbred horses from Arab traders in Kerala. Lingarajendra also boasted of a veritable zoo where he kept a menagerie of tigers, bears, leopards, panthers and so forth. One of the entertainments for his special European guests were the fights between a tiger and a bear.

Within the fort complex, there is a unique and intriguing attraction. Life-sized statues of two elephants made of mortar and painted black stand prominently in one corner of the fort. Here is their tale:

Lingarajendra was known to be generous to those close to him but had a nasty temper. Many suffered horrendous punishments whenever the Raja lost his temper. On one such occasion, Lingarajendra returned to his palace after a hunting expedition, which had lasted for several days. He was quite exhausted and was in a rather foul mood because the hunt had not been as successful as he had wished it to be. Most of his close associates kept a safe distance from the Raja. He retired to bed early and soon fell into a deep slumber.

Around midnight, two favourite elephants of the Raja housed in a shed nearby started trumpeting loudly, rudely awakening him. He shouted at his bodyguards to go and stop the ruckus immediately. The guards rushed outside but all their efforts failed to stop the two behemoths from their trumpeting. Lingarajendra tossed and turned, trying to get back to sleep, but the loud ruckus agitated him. In his rage, he picked up his powerful gun used to hunt elephants. He walked across to the shed and shot both the beasts and silenced them. Then, Lingarajendra went back to his chamber and tried to sleep.

It did not take him too long to realize the horrendous deed he had committed. He had shot two of his well-trained elephants. He spent the rest of the night weeping. The following day, a grief-stricken Lingarajendra, performed the last rites for the elephants. The Raja was most remorseful. He summoned

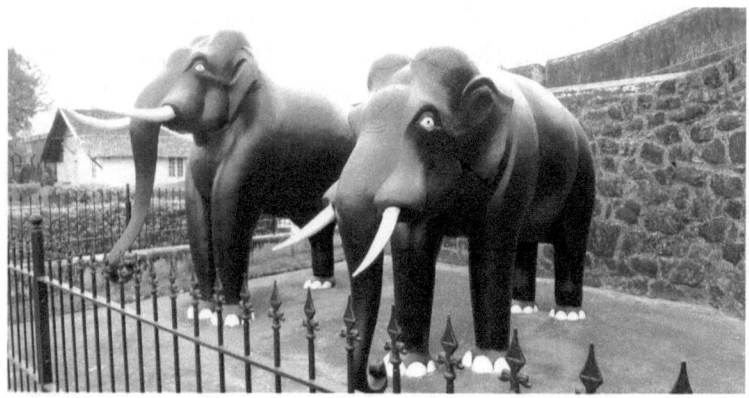

Figure 10: Elephant statues in Madikeri Fort.
Source: Author's collection

his master masons and commissioned them to immediately construct life-size statues of his pet elephants at a spot which was visible to him from his bedchamber. These two-centuries-old statues, mute spectators of many historical events, stand magnificent to this day.

7

ELEPHANT HUNT BY LINGARAJENDRA

Goddess Kaveri and Lord Paadi Igguthappa are the two revered deities of Coorg. If legends are to be believed, the Igguthappa temple, located atop a hill in a forested area in Kakkabe in the southern part of Coorg, has been in existence since 1153. Legend also has it that Igguthappa is one of the seven divine siblings, originally born in Kerala, who chose Coorg as his abode.

The temple became a prominent place of worship during Lingarajendra's reign. As per the oral history of the Parandanda family, whose members are the hereditary custodians of the temple, Lingarajendra came to the densely forested area surrounding the temple to hunt elephants in 1811. Lingarajendra's main source of income, besides taxes collected from his subjects, used to be the sale of cardamom and ivory. Every pod of cardamom grown and every tusk extracted from an elephant had to be surrendered to the Raja at a price fixed by him.

Lingarajendra camped at the nearby Nalknad Palace and instructed his Dewan, Apparanda Bopanna, to organize the hunt. Dewan Bopanna arranged for *machans* or platforms to be built on trees and had hunting dogs and drummers ready to herd the elephants. On the appointed day, Lingarajendra and Bopanna sat on a machan, armed with powerful guns that had been especially designed to shoot elephants. Despite the sound of the drums and dogs barking, not a single elephant was to be seen.

The Raja started getting restless and directed his ire at Bopanna. Worried about Lingarajendra's infamous, nasty temper, Dewan Bopanna, a devotee of Igguthappa, started silently praying for some divine intervention.

Suddenly, a huge pachyderm with mammoth tusks appeared silently from the nearby undergrowth. The elephant looked up at the machan where Lingarajendra and Bopanna were seated and started scratching itself against the tree trunk. The action of the elephant shook the large tree so violently that they were about to fall off from their perch. The Raja and his Dewan froze, too petrified to shoot the beast. This time around, Dewan Bopanna prayed loudly to Lord Igguthappa to save him and the Raja. A terrified Lingarajendra, too, joined Bopanna in prayer. Suddenly, the behemoth stopped and looked up again before gently sauntering away into the forest.

Lingarajendra, a Lingayat, was a worshipper of Shiva and had not visited the Igguthappa temple, which is dedicated to Vishnu. After the narrow escape, he asked Bopanna to immediately take him to the temple, located not too far away. It had been a modest shrine at the time. The head priest welcomed the Raja. In order to show his gratitude to the lord, the priest advised Lingarajendra to perform various poojas, including *tulabara* (donating grains equivalent to the weight of the devotee), to thank Igguthappa for saving his life.

After concluding the rituals, Lingarajendra asked the priest if there was anything the temple needed. The priest quickly requested a *punarnirmana* (renovation) of the temple. Lingarajendra readily agreed to this, and the temple was soon refurbished, with its approach road being improved. He also made grants of wetlands in the vicinity of the temple, the income from which continues to be used for its upkeep. When the reconstruction was completed, the Raja visited the temple again.

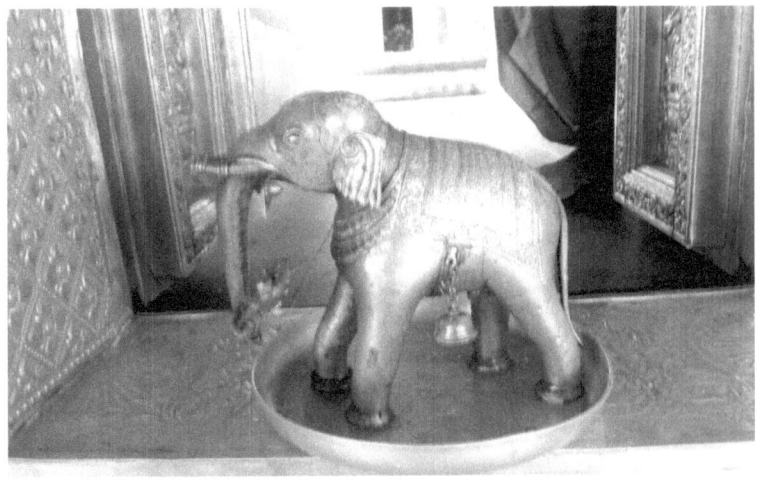

Figure 11: The silver elephant donated to Igguthappa temple by Lingarajendra, circa 1815.

Source: Author's collection

This time around, Lingarajendra brought a sack full of silver coins with him to the temple. He dipped both his hands in the sack and scooped out three large fistfuls of silver coins. Subsequently, he ordered Dewan Bopanna, who was present there with him, to get an idol of an elephant made from the coins. The best silversmiths from Mangalore were commissioned to craft this idol. The year in which the idol was dedicated to Igguthappa for favours granted to Lingarajendra is inscribed on the back of the idol in Halegannada (old Kannada). This exquisite silver elephant is still used every day in the poojas performed at the temple.

In 1835, a year after Lingarajendra's son Chikka Veerarajendra was deposed by the British, Dewan Apparanda Bopanna took it upon himself to renovate the temple again. The structure was reconstructed and fitted with tiles that replaced the earlier thatched roof. The temple, once again, went through punarnirmana in 2008. Descendants of Bopanna, along with other devotees, have gotten silver cladding made for the doors to the sanctum sanctorum.

8

SAGA OF THE SOMAYANDA FAMILY[19]

The Somayanda family, a large joint family from Coorg, owned, during the 1800s, a traditional, two-storeyed *ainmane*[20] in Hathur village, between Gonikoppal and Virajpet. They have been the hereditary chieftains of several villages in the area. Many Kodava families were awarded 'copper plate edicts' by the Haleri rajas, bestowing upon them the privilege of being chieftains. As was the practice, the family collected and paid taxes to the Raja and was ready to take up arms in case of any threat to the dominion. This practice continued for several decades and the Somayanda family lived in peace and prosperity within their sphere of influence.

According to the family history, narrated by the late Major Somayanda Appachanna, during the reign of Chikka Veerarajendra (circa 1825), the family fell out of favour with the erratic, juvenile Raja who was misguided by his wicked dewan: Kunta Basava. The Dewan instigated and convinced the Raja that the Somayanda family was plotting a rebellion against the latter's rule and came up with a diabolical plan to destroy the family. In a fit of anger, the Raja ordered Kuthi Nasha to be performed on the Somayanda family. This implied

---

[19]This chapter is based on the Somayanda family history as narrated by Major Appachanna.
[20]An ainmane is the ancestral house of a clan with roots in Kodagu.

that every member of the *okka*, or the extended family, would be eliminated.

However, a few weeks earlier, an event had taken place in the otherwise well-knit Somayanda family. Two brothers from the joint family had an acrimonious fight with the elders. The younger brother was named Madayya, but the name of the elder brother has gotten lost with the passage of time. In a meeting, the elders of the family decided to mete out exemplary punishment to the two brothers. The duo was excommunicated and ordered to leave the ainmane. This process was sealed with a ritual known as *Kare-Kithuva*, which means 'disownment'. As part of the ritual, the head of the family tears a piece of cloth in front of the *Devada Bolucha* (sacred lamp). Subsequently, Madayya and his brother left their village and took shelter in nearby Chembebellur village.

On that fateful day, the Somayanda family had been celebrating Puthari. There was a great deal of singing, dancing and gaiety. All the women-folk watched the goings-on from the first-floor balcony. Soon after, the ladies busied themselves with serving the feast, and the men were urged to have the last mug of toddy and sit down for lunch. Amid the raucous conversation, everyone enjoyed the meal. Just as they were about to get up after finishing the meal, a bullock cart laden with several vessels pulled up near the ainmane. Ominously, the cart was followed by a posse of armed Siddis.

The coachman got down and spoke very courteously to the *pattedar* (head) of the Somayanda family and told the latter that he had brought prasad (food offered to the deity during a pooja) that the Raja had specially sent for the family. It was customary for the Raja to send prasad to the village heads whenever a pooja was performed in the palace. However, here was a cartload of prasad in the form of payasa for the entire village. Before any questions could be asked, a few servants from the entourage unloaded the vessels and started serving the payasa to the people who were still sitting in front of the banana leaves they were using as plates.

It was considered an honour to receive prasad from the palace, and the children lost no time in lapping it up. Soon, the elders, too, tentatively started eating the payasa. The Siddis watched until everyone consumed it. Sometime later, the children started complaining of stomach ache and started collapsing one after the other. The pattedar and the elders soon realized what was happening. Men, women and children started writhing in pain and dropping dead. The entourage from the palace left only after ensuring that the Kuthi Nasha of the Somayanda family had been completed using the poisoned payasa.

According to Major Appachanna, Dewan Chepudira Ponnappa, who, in 1834, issued a public proclamation to ascertain if any member of the Somayanda family had survived the Kuthi Nasha. Ironically, the excommunicated Madayya and his brother were the only survivors from the Somayanda family. Madayya married and had a family, while his elder brother remained a bachelor. When Madayya's family was finally traced, Dewan Ponnappa used his influence to re-establish the Somayanda okka.

9

LORD WILLIAM BENTINCK'S VISIT TO THE OOTY CLUB AND THE DECLARATION OF WAR ON COORG

Courtesy our friends Pemmanda Jeppu and Jemy Ganapathy, we spent three wonderful days at the Ooty Club, a place steeped in colonial history. The trophies, silverware, honours list and photographs of the 'Masters of the Fox Hunt' there date back to the early 1840s.

During our stay, I got to read a well-documented book, which is otherwise kept under lock and key, from the Club library titled *Ootacamund: A History* written by Sir Frederick Price in 1908. I was particularly interested in the visit of Governor General Lord Dalhousie to Ooty in 1856, a few details of which I had gathered while writing about Princess Victoria Gowramma. However, what I stumbled upon was equally interesting. The book has a detailed account of Governor General William Bentinck's journey from Calcutta (now Kolkata) to Bangalore, Mysore and Ooty in 1834. One of the reasons for this extended stay in Ooty was to improve his not too robust health. He was familiar with the salubrious weather in Ooty, having served as governor of Madras Province from 1803–07. Although, this trip was primarily meant to coordinate military action against the 'problematic' Raja of

Coorg: Chikka Veerarajendra.[21]

The East India Company had been at loggerheads with the Raja since 1830. Governor General Bentinck, who was more concerned about reforming India than annexing new territories, had to finally deal with the Raja of Coorg, who had challenged the British by keeping one of their emissaries—Kullapally Karunakaran Menon—hostage.

Bentinck set out from Calcutta to Madras (now Chennai) on 3 February 1834 aboard the *Curacoa*. He reached Madras on 15 February 1834 and journeyed to Bangalore via Vellore. Travel those days was by horse carriages, bullock carts, palanquins and on horseback, with frequent camping en route.

Bentinck wanted a firsthand assessment of the situation in Coorg, and therefore, the Commander-in-Chief Sir Robert O'Callaghan was accompanying him. Strategies on military action against Coorg were finalized in consultations with Sir Robert while they were in Bangalore.

Bentinck stopped over in Mysore and stayed at the precursor to the Rajendra Vilas Palace atop Chamundi Hill, which was originally built by Arthur H. Cole, the British Resident at Mysore from 1811–27. Years later, it was acquired by the Wodiyars of Mysore and remodelled as their summer palace. The Governor General had extensive discussions with James Archibald Casamajor, the Resident at Mysore, who had been part of several unsuccessful meetings with the Raja in 1833 to defuse the hostilities.

Finally, Bentinck set out for Ooty. While camping at Gundlepet on 15 March 1834, he officially declared war on Coorg. Brigadier C.B. Lindsey was to command the operation, with an invading force of 6,000 men.[22] General James Stuart

---

[21]Price, Frederick, *Ootacamund: A History*, Government Press, 1908.

[22]Krishnayya, D.N., *Kodagina Ithihasa*, University of Mysore, 1974.

Fraser was appointed as the political agent of the Governor General. Coorg was surrounded from four fronts. Chikka Veerarajendra surrendered on 10 April 1834 and Coorg was annexed by the East India Company. Incidentally, Coorg was the only province to be added to the Company during Bentinck's tenure. He was criticized back home in England for failing to expand the empire.

Lord Bentinck's entourage reached Ooty on 22 March. The only suitable accommodation for the Governor General and his staff there was Sir William Rambold's Large House, a grand hotel built in 1832 by William Rambold, an influential British entrepreneur. Rambold had run into financial difficulties soon after building the hotel. Consequently, it was frequently rented out for extended lengths of time by senior officers of the East India Company. In 1842, the hotel became the Ootacamund Club or the Ooty Club.

On 25 June 1834, while Bentinck was sojourning in Ooty,

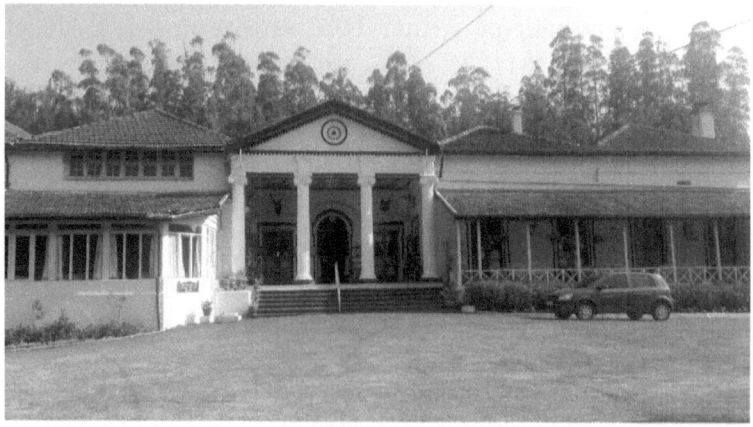

Figure 12: The Ooty Club in Nilgiris.
Source: Author's collection

Lord Thomas Babington Macaulay arrived at the hill station. Bentinck and Macaulay met each other for the first time at Rambold's Large House. Macaulay lived in the Rose Cottage nearby, where he drafted the Indian Penal Code. Governor General Bentinck stayed in Ooty till the end of September 1834.

Years later, Governor General Lord Dalhousie had a long sojourn in Ooty from 7 March 1855 to 29 October 1855 for health reasons. He suffered from acute gout and was due to retire soon. However, for some reason, he was not too comfortable in Ooty and shifted to a guest house in the nearby Kotagiri.

During Dalhousie's stay in the Nilgiris, one of his aide-de-camps (ADC) took permission to visit Coorg, where the ADC's brother was a coffee planter. Dalhousie was familiar with Coorg, having reluctantly given permission to the 'rascally raja of Coorg', as he derisively referred to Chikka Veerarajendra,[23] to travel to England along with his daughter Gowramma in 1852.

The ADC, on his return, narrated an amusing episode to his boss. News from the outside world took some time to reach Coorg because of its remoteness. Newspapers from England took anything from three to six months to reach Coorg. Very often, wild rumours circulated among the small but growing community of British planters and officers. One such rumour had been that the British and their allies had lost the Crimean War to the Russians, and that Queen Victoria and her family had fled to India.

However, Dalhousie, having gotten a temporary telegraph line installed in the Nilgiris, knew better. He had received the news that the British and their allies had, in fact, wrested the strategic port of Sevastopol in the Crimean Peninsula from the Russians.

---

[23] *Private Letters of Marquess of Dalhousie*, William Blackwood & Sons, 1910.

On his journey back to Calcutta, Dalhousie stopped over in Bangalore in early November 1855 and was the guest of Sir Mark Cubbon, the chief commissioner of Mysore and Coorg. Dalhousie narrated the 'Coorg rumour' to the British officers, much to their amusement. After inspecting the troops, he formally announced the victory of the British and their allies in Crimea.

10

REMEMBERING SIR MARK CUBBON

The people of Bangalore collectively utter the word 'Cubbon' a few thousand times every day thanks to the iconic Cubbon Park, named after Sir Mark Cubbon, located in the heart of the city. Sir Mark arrived in India as a 26-year-old cadet in 1801. Young Mark was commissioned in the then Madras Army. His maternal uncle, Colonel Mark Wilks, who had been in India for a while already, encouraged him to explore the greener pastures in the colony. Sir Mark fell in love with India and its people. He had great empathy for their culture and traditions. Having proven his mettle as an administrator, he was appointed the chief commissioner of Mysore and Coorg in 1834. He spent most of his career in Bangalore and was totally involved in his work.

In sharp contrast to the unpopular rule of the last Raja of Coorg, Sir Mark endeared himself to the people and extended all the help he could to improve their standard of living. He provided timely assistance in establishing schools and helped the German missionaries Reverends Hermann Mögling and Georg Richter in upgrading the standard of education in the region. The administration was streamlined and infrastructure improved in the province. He liked the people of Coorg for their progressive outlook. Respecting their loyalty and responsible use of firearms in their socio-religious customs, he exempted the community from the Disarming Act that was enacted after the 1857 uprising.

Many of his contributions to Coorg are remembered to this day.[24]

Sir Mark worked closely with the Wodeyars of Mysore to streamline the administration, simplify revenue collection and implement several important infrastructure projects in the princely state and the province of Coorg. By the time India became independent, Mysore was one of the most prosperous and developed regions in the country due to the foundation laid by Sir Mark. Likewise, Coorg too developed and was one of the provinces with high per capita income and literacy rate at the time the country got Independence.

Sir Mark remained a confirmed bachelor all his life. Having risen to the rank of lieutenant general, he retired in 1861, after spending 60 years in India. During his eventful career, he never visited his home in the Isle of Man in England. After his superannuation, he set sail for his hometown for the first time since his arrival in India. Sir Mark was 86 years old then and not in good health. Although his personal physician travelled with him, his condition deteriorated aboard the ship, and he died on 23 April 1861, upon reaching the newly opened Suez Canal in Egypt.

He was one of the few colonial officers who were genuinely fond of India. Though the British rule was essentially exploitative, the services of some of the officers, like Sir Mark, come under the euphemistic dictum of 'enlightened self-interest'. In other words, though the intention behind the actions of the British was the best interest of the East India Company, they led to collateral benefits for India. The colonizers also gave a moral twist to their occupation of India by terming it the 'white man's burden': a mission to civilize the people of the subcontinent.

Besides the iconic park named after him in Bangalore, the

---

[24]Venkatasubba Sastri, K.N., *The Administration of Mysore under Sir Mark Cubbon (1834-1861)*, George Allen and Unwin Ltd., London, 1932.

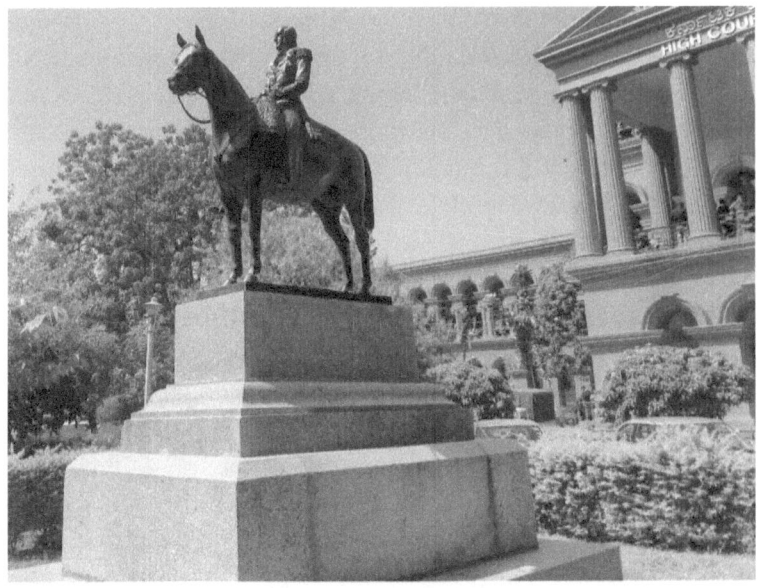

Figure 13: An equestrian statue of Sir Mark Cubbon in Bangalore.
Source: Author's collection

city also has an area called Cubbonpet and a road named Cubbon Road. A particularly controversial monument in memory of Sir Mark is the equestrian statue of the longest serving chief commissioner of Mysore and Coorg. The bronze statue with all four legs of the horse on the ground, which indicates that the rider has survived wars unharmed[25], was first installed in the Parade Grounds (currently known as Field Marshal Manekshaw Parade Grounds) in 1866. The statue was made by the famous artist, Baron Carlo Marochetti, who was Queen Victoria's favourite sculptor. Interestingly, Marochetti also sculpted the

---

[25]Kadylak, Jesseka, 'Washingtoniana: What's Up With Those Horse Statues?', Washingtonian, 2 October 2008, https://tinyurl.com/2sdrefs6. Accessed on 9 February 2023.

highly acclaimed marble busts of Princess Victoria Gowramma of Coorg and of Maharaja Duleep Singh of the Punjab in 1856.

Around the 1870s, the statue of Sir Mark was shifted to the front of the newly constructed Attara Katcheri (currently the High Court of Karnataka). Years after Independence, under pressure from advocates, the statue was moved to the back of the High Court buildings, facing Cubbon Park. The advocates found it inappropriate to hoist the tricolour while the statue of a colonial officer towered nearby. I located the statue behind the building and took a few photographs. Surprisingly, I found a fresh garland adorning the neck of Sir Mark. His good deeds have not been forgotten to this day.

In 2020, Mark Cubbon's equestrian statue was shifted, once again, close to the bandstand inside Cubbon Park. This truly is the rightful place for Sir Mark. Members of the Cubbon Park Walkers' Association (CPWA) are happy with this decision because they can now honour Sir Mark, whom they hold in high esteem, without any restrictions.

11

THE THIRTEEN WIVES OF CHIKKA VEERARAJENDRA OF COORG

On 24 April 1834, the 30-year-old Chikka Veerarajendra, the last raja of Coorg, was ingloriously dethroned by the British and exiled, first to Vellore and then to Benares. On the afternoon of that fateful day, his entourage—comprising his 13 wives, other women, cooks, Siddi bodyguards and servants—left Madikeri Fort through the elephant gate for the last time. The Raja rode out on his favourite elephant and later switched to a horse. The tearful women were carried in 70 palanquins followed by 50 bullock carts carrying their personal effects. The political agent of the British, General Stuart Fraser, sardonically ordered a 21-gun salute to the deposed Raja as his subjects watched the spectacle with mixed emotions. The Raja added to the tragicomedy by asking his palace band to play the joyful tune 'The British Grenadiers' in a desperate bid to please his detractors. Not all subjects were unhappy though. As the palanquin bearers struggled with their load, some snide remarks were heard. Captain Carpenter, who was appointed as the governor general's agent to keep an eye on the deposed ruler and his family, accompanied the entourage with his troops.[26]

---

[26]Krishnayya, D.N., *Kodagina Ithihasa*, University of Mysore, 1974.

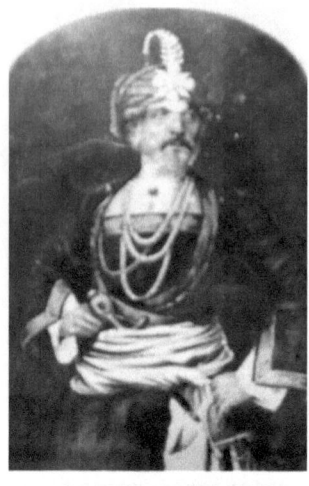

Figure 14: Painting of Chikka Veerarajendra, circa 1840.
Courtesy: Kongetira family

D.N. Krishnayya, in his book *Kodagina Ithihasa*[27], gives the names of 13 wives of Chikka Veerarajendra who accompanied him. Three of the queens were the *pattada ranis* or principal consorts: Gangamma, Devamma (Kunjalgeri Mukkatira) and Nanjamma. The 10 minor wives were: Rajeevamma, Kalamma, Gowramma-I, Kongetira Kaveramma, Parvathiamma, Gowramma-II, Subbamma, Janakamma, Subhadramma and Mudduveeramma. During their sojourn in Vellore, Nanjamma died. At the time of leaving his kingdom, the Raja also had a six-year-old son named Chithrashekara, born to Gowramma-II.

Alexei Soltykoff, a Russian artist, visited India in 1841 and 1844. He painted some of the ranis of Chikka Veerarajendra.[28] He sketched portraits of Gangamma, Subhadramma and Mudduveeramma during their stay at Benares. At the Nalknad Palace in south Coorg, one of the rooms has rather faded paintings on the walls of three of the Raja's wives. The paintings were most likely made by the court painters Gangojirao and his son Pirojirao.[29]

The British confiscated the Raja's wealth, and, for his

---

[27]Ibid.
[28]Soltykoff, Alexis, *Prince Alexei Saltykov's Journeys Across India: Dedicated to the 65th Anniversary of the Diplomatic Relations Between Russia and India*, Palace Editions, 2012.
[29]Krishnayya, D.N., *Kodagina Ithihasa*, University of Mysore, 1974.

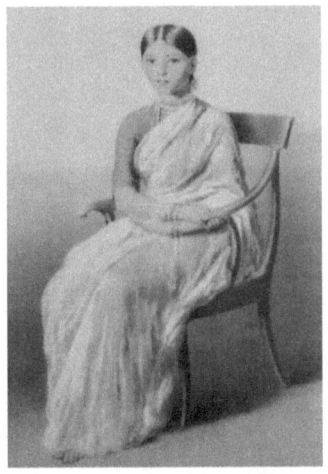
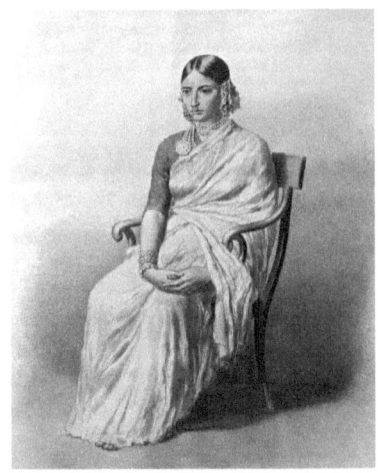

Figure 15: Painting of Rani Gangamma by the Russian artist Alexi Soltykoff.

Figure 16: Painting of Rani Mudduveeramma by Alexi Soltykoff.

personal expenses, permitted him to carry ₹10,000 (roughly equivalent to ₹1,200,000 in contemporary times), a fraction of what had been in his treasury. He was also to receive an annuity of ₹60,000.[30] The day before his banishment, Chikka Veerarajendra instructed his wives and other women to hide as much of their jewellery, gold and other valuables in their clothing and undergarments as possible. This was the reason the palanquin bearers struggled with the load. At the first camp at Harangi, quite a few of the weary bearers abandoned the camp. In desperation, the Raja and his wives buried some of the valuables in the privacy of their tents to lighten the burden and hoped to return one day to recover the treasure. They repeated this at

---

[30]Richter, Georg, *Manual of Coorg: A Gazetteer of the Natural Features of the Country and the Social and Political Condition of its Inhabitants*, B.R. Publishing Corp., Delhi, 1870.

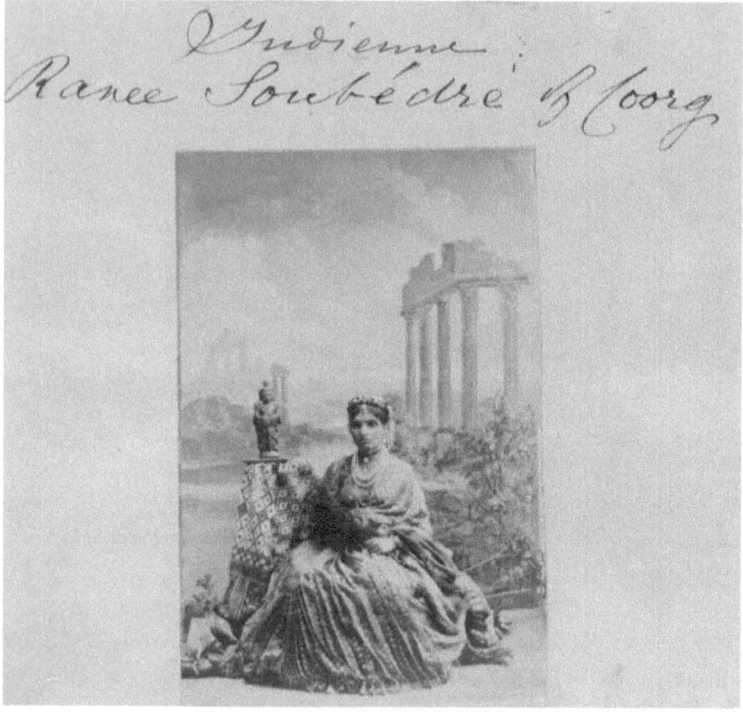

Figure 17: Painting of Rani Subadramma by Alexi Soltykoff.

various campsites on the way. Few of the Raja's supporters who were following him got wind of this. Days later, they returned to the sites and helped themselves to some of the treasure. Soon this news reached General Fraser who threatened to take stern action against the fortune hunters. Most of them grudgingly surrendered some of the valuables to the British for which they were rewarded. Despite this, the Raja and his wives were able to smuggle out a substantial portion of their treasure.

Chikka Veerarajendra and his 12 wives reached Benares in early 1837. They were under virtual house arrest in a large haveli, which the British disdainfully named 'Coorg Nest'. By 1852, the Raja had four daughters and seven sons. His favourite pattada rani Devammaji tragically died in childbirth in 1841. Her daughter, named Gowramma, acquired global fame as Princess Victoria Gowramma of Coorg, after Chikka Veerarajendra took her to London as an 11-year-old in 1852. Upon embracing Christianity, Queen Victoria added the prefix 'Victoria' to Gowramma's name after the former took the Indian princess under her wing as her goddaughter.

Chikka Veerarajendra took his youngest wife Mudduveeramma and a concubine named Siddaveeramma with him to England. They spent seven years with the Raja in London. The two women returned to Benares after Chikka Veerarajendra's demise in 1859.

Upon hearing of the death of their husband, two of the Raja's wives in Benares committed sati by overdosing on opium. Two more tried to starve themselves to death but the British authorities prevented them from doing so. Chikka Veerarajendra's mortal remains were shipped to India in 1861. He was buried in Benares in accordance with the Lingayat tradition.

12

DEWAN CHEPUDIRA PONNAPPA[31]

One of the four dewans in the court of Chikka Veerarajendra was one of my direct ancestors, Chepudira Ponnappa. The other three dewans were Apparanda Bopanna, Laxminarayana and Kunta Basavanna.

Dewan Ponnappa, my great great great grandfather, born in 1767, was a colourful personality. As a teenager, he attracted the attention of Chikka Veerarajendra's grandfather, Lingaraja (1774–80), when he accompanied the Raja on a hunting expedition. They were camping by the side of a stream and the Raja was in a relaxed mood. At a distance, a herd of buffaloes were grazing. A crow sat on the back of one of the buffaloes. Lingaraja asked if anyone could shoot the crow without hurting the buffalo. (The Coorg rajas used to commonly challenge their subordinates to do this). Young Ponnappa took him up on the challenge and impressed the Raja with his marksmanship. He was immediately inducted into the army and rose rapidly up the ranks. He was appointed as a commander of the army during the final years of Dodda Veerarajendra's reign. When Lingarajendra succeeded his brother, Ponnappa was elevated to the position of a dewan.

Ponnappa was also trusted with the additional responsibilities of collecting land revenue and enforcing law and order. For this,

---

[31] All the information in this chapter is based on the author's family oral history.

he had to be away from home for long periods of time. Ponnappa married Cheyyavva from the Kodandera family. By 1800, they had three sons and four daughters. His wife was a formidable lady who took on the responsibilities of looking after their vast paddy fields during her husband's absence.

Ponnappa built a large house in Kirgoor. It was one of the best-constructed buildings of its time. There is an interesting oral narrative about the carpenter who helped build the house. The same carpenter had worked extensively on the Raja's palace. After settling his dues, the Raja had given him a paltry bonus. The carpenter had supposedly commented later: 'What kind of a raja is this? His official, Ponnappa, tipped me double the amount of gold coins'. The Raja was furious when he heard this, but by then the carpenter had safely returned to Kerala.

During one of Ponnappa's extended revenue collection tours, he camped in a remote village for a week. He was the guest of the village headman who belonged to the Manjera family. The headman's beautiful young daughter, Somavva, was serving food to the important visitor; and the lass soon started making eyes at the handsome 30-year-old. Ponnappa was also smitten by the attractive damsel. He mustered all his courage to ask the headman for his daughter's hand in marriage. Somavva's father and the Manjera family members were elated at this offer from the powerful and prosperous Ponnappa, even though their daughter would be his second wife. The village elders insisted on the marriage taking place immediately, and Somavva gave her much feigned coy assent. Ponnappa extended his stay and the villagers enthusiastically started preparations for the wedding. There was excitement all round. The influential new son-in-law of the village was heartily felicitated.

A week later, it dawned upon Ponnappa that he now had the delicate task of facing his first wife with his new bride. As he approached his house in Kirgoor, an unsuspecting Cheyyavva came out to greet her husband who had been away for over a month. When Cheyyavva saw Ponnappa with a demure Somavva by his side, still in her bridal finery, she flew into a rage. She brandished an *odi kathi* (a short, heavy sword) and stood menacingly near the entrance and would not allow the 'newlyweds' to step inside the house. Ponnappa had no choice but to relent. He started constructing another house, identical to the one built earlier, to start a family with Somavva. He had four sons and three daughters with Somavva.

Dewans Ponnappa and Bopanna were disillusioned with the erratic and despotic rule of Chikka Veerarajendra. By 1830, Ponnappa was in his sixties and distancing himself from actively participating in the administration, though he continued as a

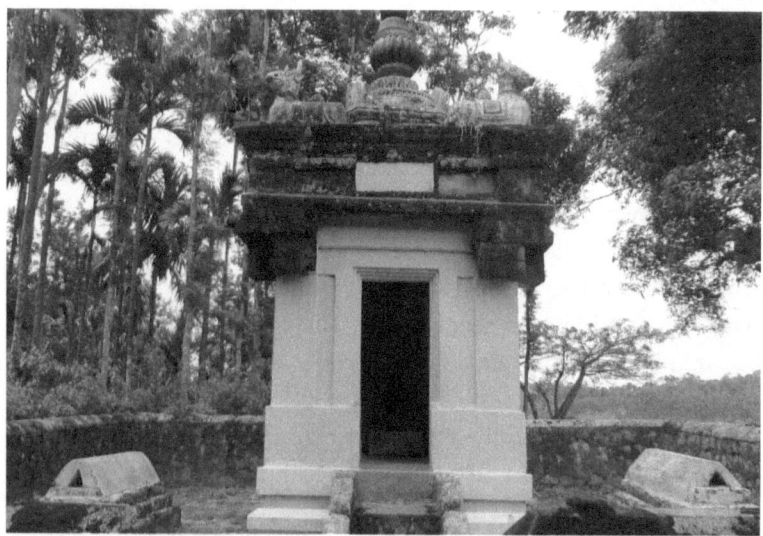

Figure 18: The tomb of Dewan Ponnappa.
Source: Author's collection

dewan. Chikka Veerarajendra listened more to the uncouth Dewan Kunta Basava, who had been his childhood companion and his father's kennel keeper. Dewan Kunta Basava was intensely disliked by the citizens, who added the prefix 'Kunta', which means cripple in Kannada, to his name because he had a limp.

As mentioned earlier, the young Raja went on a collision course with the British who were well-entrenched in the neighbouring

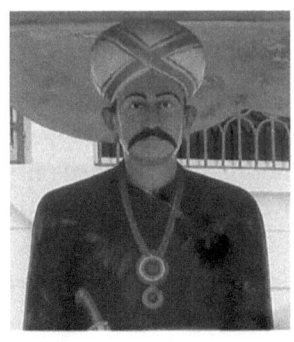

Figure 19: A statue of Ponnappa in Ponnampet.
Source: Author's collection

areas of Karnataka and Kerala. In 1833, Chikka Veerarajendra angered the British by taking Kullapally Karunakaran Menon, an emissary of the British East India Company, hostage. By early 1834, the British decided to attack Coorg and surrounded it from Mysore, Kodlipet, Kannur and Mangalore. The besieged Raja called Dewan Ponnappa for advice. Dewan Ponnappa's counsel was to immediately and unconditionally release Menon. He was forthright and advised the Raja that the British could not be countered militarily. This enraged Dewan Kunta Basava and he slapped the older Dewan. Ponnappa momentarily lost consciousness but soon recovered. Without uttering another word, he walked out of Madikeri Fort.

This was a defining moment in the history of Coorg. Dewan Bopanna and other Kodava elders were appalled, and they felt it would be better if the administration of Coorg were taken over by the British. They decided not to resist the impending British intervention. On 10 April 1834, the East India Company, led by their political agent, General James Fraser, marched into Madikeri Fort and announced the ouster of Chikka Veerarajendra. Coorg was annexed and the Raja was permanently exiled from his kingdom.[32] The British very diplomatically continued the services of the Dewans Ponnappa and Bopanna and many other Kodava officials.

Dewan Ponnappa lived to the ripe old age of 76. Before he died in 1843, his first wife, Cheyyavva, extracted a promise from him and her sons. Upon her demise, Cheyyavva wanted to be buried closer to Ponnappa's grave than her bête noire, Somavva. This wish was fulfilled by her sons. The graves of Ponnappa's two wives are located on either side of his tomb, with Cheyyavva's being closer by about a foot.

Madayya, one of Ponnappa's sons, was highly influential in the region. In 1866, he renamed a small hamlet known as Balelesanthe (a place famous for selling banana leaves, an important commodity in those days) as Ponnappanapete after his illustrious father. Over the years, the name was transformed to Ponnampet, which is is currently a flourishing town in Coorg. In 2020, Ponnampet was upgraded to a taluk. The Chepudira family members installed a statue of Dewan Ponnappa in Ponnampet when the clan hosted the Kodava Hockey Festival in the town in 2000.

In 1952, Dewan Ponnappa's great-great grandson, C.M. Poonacha was elected as the chief minister of Coorg. In 1957, Dewan Ponnappa's great-great-granddaughter's son, Kodandera S. Thimayya, took charge as the third chief of army staff of India. The numerous descendants of Dewan Ponnappa from his two wives are now spread all over the globe. I prepared a family tree of my clan[33] a few years ago, which has been recently digitized by my distant cousin Dr Chepudira Pete Ponnanna, who lives in Canada.

---

[32]Mögling, Herrmann, *Coorg Memoirs: An Account of Coorg and of the Coorg Mission*, Wesleyan Mission Press, 1855.

[33]Family Tree, https://tinyurl.com/mrxc49j6. Accessed on 9 February 2023.

13

THE THREE GERMANS IN COORG

In 1836, 25-year-old Reverend Hermann Mögling, a German missionary from the Basel Mission, arrived in Mangalore[34]. Christianity was already popular on the west coast of India. He laid the foundation for Mangalore becoming a centre for education by founding the Basel Evangelical Mission Seminary, which became a hub for not only learning religion but also Indian languages and culture. The institution exists till date in Mangalore with a new name: Karnataka Theological College. Mögling, a linguist, was fluent in English, Sanskrit and Persian, besides his native German. He started learning Kannada and soon became proficient in the language. The credit for starting the first Kannada-language newspaper—*Mangaluru Samachara*—also goes to him. The maiden issue of this newspaper was brought out on 1 July 1843. This eventful day is celebrated as 'Kannada Press Day'. Reverend Mögling went on to translate several Kannada classics to German and vice versa.

In 1852, Reverend Mögling was preparing to leave for Germany for medical treatment when he had an unexpected visitor from Coorg: Alamanda Somayya. He was a tall, impressive-looking man dressed as a sanyasi. After a brief discussion, he surprised the Reverend by requesting to be accepted into the Christian fold. Somayya went further and offered his land in

---

[34]Havanur, Shrinivas, 'Herr Kannada', *Sunday Herald*, 18 January 2004.

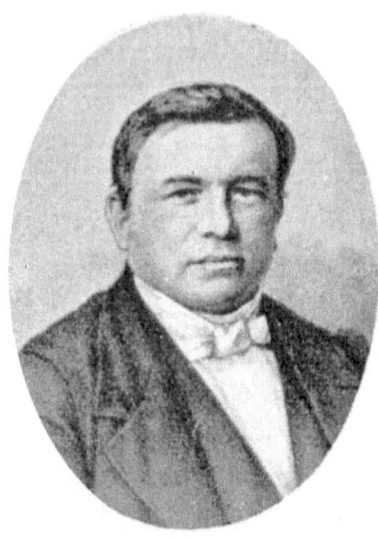

Figure 20: Reverend Hermann Mögling
Source: 'File:Hermann Friedrich Mögling.png', Wikimedia Commons, https://tinyurl.com/2p8fsrnv. Accessed on 22 February 2023.

Coorg to construct a church. The Reverend was immensely impressed with Somayya's resolve. Believing this to be a divine message, Mögling cancelled his trip. Accepting Somayya's offer, he lost no time in moving to Coorg with his wife and adopted spiritual son, Reverend Anandarao Kaundinya.

Alamanda Somayya was baptized by Reverend Mögling on 6 January 1853 in a makeshift church built on the latter's land in Armeri village and was christened Stephanas Somayya.[35] The Reverend built a house nearby and started his evangelical activities in Coorg. Soon, he sought assistance from the British government to start a school. Lieutenant Colonel Mark Cubbon was the chief commissioner of Mysore and Coorg at the time, and he encouraged Reverend Mögling to establish a Protestant church and school in Madikeri.

Another notable personality involved in the field of education and evangelical activities in Coorg was Reverend Georg Richter[36],

---

[35]Ibid.
[36]A recent book by Albercht Frenz titled *Georg Richter: His Work in Kodagu on the Basis of Official Reports* provides insights into Reverend Richter's journey in India, how he landed in Coorg and spent 38 years there, except for an 18-month furlough in Germany.

who also hailed from the Basel Mission in Germany. He was brought to Coorg by Reverend Mögling in April 1856 and was given charge of running the school that had been set up in Madikeri. Reverend Richter spent most of his life promoting education in Coorg and was the first principal of Central School in Madikeri, which was started in 1869. He later took charge as the inspector of schools. His book *Manual of Coorg: A Gazetteer of the Natural Features of the Country and the Social and Political Condition of its Inhabitants*, published in 1870, is a comprehensive record of the social, cultural, historical and geographical aspects of Coorg. Reverend Richter's wife, Armella, supported her husband and encouraged girls to take up education seriously. She also taught them needlework and other crafts.

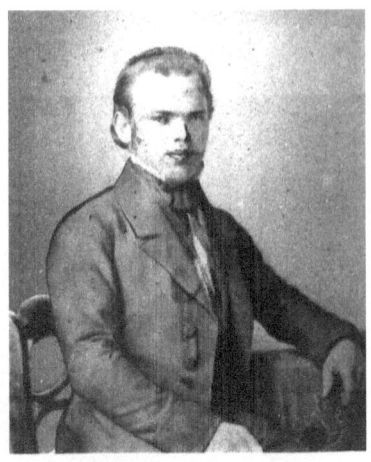

Figure 21: Reverend Georg Richter
Source: Frenz, Albrecht, Georg Richter (1829-1913): His Work in Kodagu on the Basis of Official Reports, Albrecht Frenz, Stuttgart, 2014.

The people of Coorg took to education most enthusiastically and encouraged their sons and daughters to get educated. The British government, through their policy of 'enlightened self-interest', supported education and introduced English along with Kannada. By the 1850s, there were several educated locals taking up jobs in the government, especially in the police, forest and revenue departments and later even in the armed forces. The British effectively used this strategy of enlightened self-interest to their advantage as they added new territories to their realm.

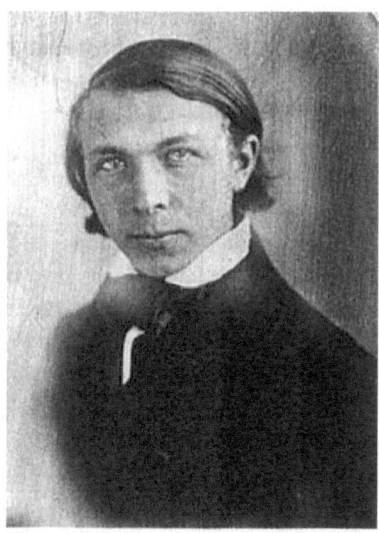

Figure 22: Reverend Ferdinand Kittel
Source: 'File:Kittel, Ferdinand (1832-1903).jpg', Wikimedia Commons, https://tinyurl.com/7pnvnet8. Accessed on 28 February 2023.

The British administration granted 97 acres of land in Siddapur to Reverend Mögling to establish a church and support a Christian settlement by starting a coffee estate. The work on this ambitious project most likely started in 1857.[37] Even though Reverend Mögling had his hands full with preaching the Gospel and opening the coffee plantation, he found time to author two books on Coorg.[38] The one in German, *Das Kurgland: Und die evangelische mission in Kurg*, details his evangelical work in Coorg. The other, written in English, titled *Coorg Memoirs: An Account of Coorg and of the Coorg Mission*, is one of the first in-depth studies of the history of Coorg.

Reverend Anandarao Kaundinya and Reverend Richter ably assisted Reverend Mögling, their mentor. The new settlement was named Anandapura or 'region of happiness'. Reverend Mögling found Coorg to be an ideal place to live and called it his second country. In 1860, Reverend Mögling left for Germany

---

[37]Rice, Benjamin Lewis, *Mysore and Coorg: A Gazetteer Compiled for the Government of India,* Mysore Government Press, 1878.
[38]'Hermann Friedrich Mogling', Missionaries of the World, 13 September 2012, https://tinyurl.com/25yx94n4. Accessed on 13 February 2023.

to be with his ailing wife. He was also in poor health. To his great disappointment, his illness did not permit him to return to Coorg. He died in 1881.

One of the major hurdles faced at the Anandapura settlement was malaria, which the Europeans referred to as the 'Coorg Fever'.[39] There were many deaths and, gradually, this scourge affected the project adversely. The Anandapura coffee estate was subsequently taken over by British planters who had shifted to Coorg from Sri Lanka. The coffee estate grew in extent and is now a part of Tata Coffee Limited. It still retains the name Anandapura Estate.

After Reverend Mögling's death, the work at Anandapura continued under the guidance of his disciple and fellow German missionary: Reverend Ferdinand Kittel. An Indologist and a polyglot, Reverend Kittel first came to India in 1853. In time, he became a renowned Kannada scholar.[40] He too translated some of Kannada classics to German and wrote several books and poems in Kannada. His most famous work is the first Kannada–English dictionary consisting of 70,000 words that he painstakingly compiled and published in 1894.[41] While in Coorg, he started perfecting his proficiency in Kannada. He continued Reverend Mögling's initiative in the field of education. Reverend Kittel also wrote a book on Kannada grammar. He was also a regular contributor to *Mangaluru Samachara*. His work took him to Mangalore and Dharwad as well. In recognition of his contribution to Kannada, an impressive statue of Reverend Kittel stands prominently on M.G. Road in Bangalore. Furthermore,

---

[39]Ibid.
[40]'Karnata F Kittel—Font Release Event', Sanchaya, 13 November 2022, https://tinyurl.com/yvu5xvhn. Accessed on 9 February 2023.
[41]Kittel, Ferdinand, *Kannada-English Dictionary*, Basel Mission Book & Tract Depository, Mangalore, 1894.

the Kittel Science College and the Kittel Arts College in Dharwar are named after him. There is also talk of starting a university in his name. This would be a fitting tribute to this great champion of Kannada.

These three Germans pioneered and promoted education in Coorg. Several of their colleagues spent brief spells in Coorg to further their evangelical work. However, their hope of making Kodavas embrace Christianity did not find favour beyond Alamanda 'Stephanas' Somayya and his family.

14

COORG-BORN FIRST WORLD WAR HERO[42]

The first coffee estate in Coorg, named Madikeri Estate, was started in 1854 by J. Fowler.[43] By 1906, coffee was being cultivated on nearly 33,000 acres of land in Coorg by the English and the local landlords. The profits were good, which attracted many British settlers to Coorg to take up coffee cultivation. However, planters had to face several ups and downs from time to time.

According to the family history provided by Gabriel and Christopher Irwin, grand-nephews of William Leefe Robinson, Horace Robinson and his wife, Elizabeth Leefe, were one of the British couples to arrive in Coorg in 1883. Horace was encouraged to take up coffee cultivation by his elder brother Dr Mark Robinson, who worked briefly in Madikeri as a surgeon major during the early 1880s. Horace purchased Kaimabetta

---

[42] I am thankful to Koothanda P. Uthappa, the former Executive Director of Tata Coffee Limited, for introducing me to Gabriel Irwin, grandson of Ruth and Jack Irwin. I thank Gabriel, his brother Christopher and K.P. Uthappa for extensively talking to me and providing the material for this essay. The information in this chapter has been sourced from the article 'Coorg Planting Families' written by Christopher Irwin, grand nephew of William Leefe Robinson, in 2004. This article was in private circulation among the former British planters in Coorg and their families.

[43] Rice, Benjamin Lewis, *Mysore and Coorg: A Gazetteer Compiled for the Government of India*, Mysore Government Press, 1878.

Estate near Pollibetta, and both husband and wife busied themselves in developing their new home and property.

Horace and Elizabeth actively participated in social activities and were members of the Bamboo Club, established in 1886 in Pollibetta. There were quite a few English families in Coorg by then. There were frequent get-togethers between members of clubs in Pollibetta, Madikeri and Belur. One of the highlights of such social activities used to be the annual Madikeri Week, which included tennis and horse racing. People used to travel to Madikeri for this event on horseback or in tongas, waggonettes, bullock coaches, horse-drawn dogcarts or humble bullock carts, known as *banddies*. This event has continued into the present and is observed annually as the Tennis Week in the Bamboo Club sans horse racing.

Horace and Elizabeth had three sons (Ernest, Harold and William) and four daughters (Katherine, Grace, Irene and Ruth). William Leefe Robinson (Billy), the youngest, was born in 1895. William and Harold completed their early

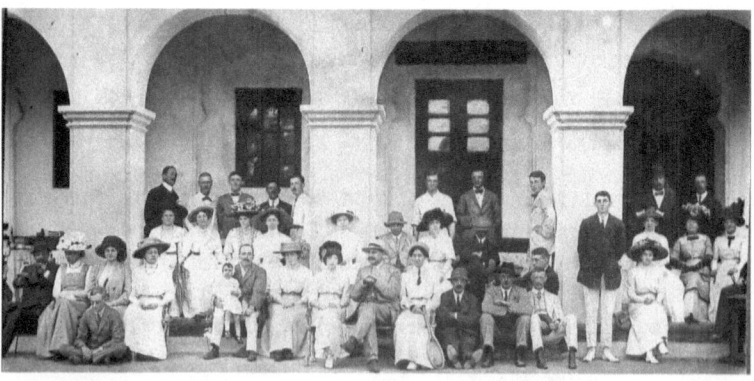

Figure 23: A group photo of British coffee planters at the annual sports get-together at Madikeri from 1912.

Courtesy: Gabriel and Christopher Irwin

schooling from Bishop Cottons in Bangalore. In 1909, both the boys were sent to boarding school in England.

The three sons pursued careers in the armed forces. Ernest went to Sandhurst and served in the Indian Army. Harold was attached to 103rd Grenadiers (now Maratta Light Infantry). Unfortunately, Harold died in war in 1916 during the disastrous siege of Kut in Iraq.

Billy joined the Royal Military Academy Sandhurst in 1914. A year later, he was transferred to the Royal Flying Corps. His squadron was assigned to artillery-ranging duties and reconnaissance over the battle area.

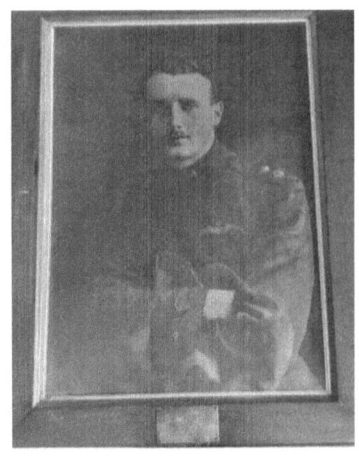

Figure 24: William Leefe Robinson
Courtesy: The Bamboo Club, Pollibetta, Coorg

During one of his sorties, Billy was hit in the arm by shrapnel when a shell burst close to his plane while he was observing a German advance. He later discovered that a half-penny, kept in his breast pocket, had been bent, presumably by deflecting a stray shard of shrapnel. After recovering from his injuries, he underwent special training in night flying.

Germans started the dreaded Zeppelin attacks on Britain in 1915. These raids normally took place at night. On the cloudy night of 2 September 1916, the Germans staged a major attack with 16 formidable SL11 Zeppelins.

Billy was first in the air at 11.08 p.m. He had enough fuel to last him three and a half hours and three drums of ammunition. At 2.05 a.m., Billy caught sight of an airship at 12,900 ft. He flew his diminutive aircraft—one twentieth of the size of the airship—closer to the Zeppelin. After two failed attempts, he poured the contents of his last drum of ammunition onto the back of the Zeppelin. It caught fire and its blazing wreck fell in slow motion to the ground in a spectacular ball of fire visible in a radius of 50 km.

The official history of the Worcestershire Regiment has a record of the public response to Robinson's feat, as per Gabriel and Christopher Irwin:

> For thousands of people it was without doubt one of the most memorable events of the entire war. It is difficult to imagine one man achieving anything more spectacular. The blazing wreckage of SL11 slowly fell to earth in a field in Cuffley, Hertfordshire. London was celebrating in boisterous fashion oblivious to the fact that other enemy airships were overhead. There was singing and dancing in the streets, small boys paraded up and down while their parents hugged one another or burst into patriotic song. Factory hooters and engine whistles added to the din...[44]

During the next couple of days, nearly 10,000 people visited the village of Cuffley to see the wreckage and collect pieces from the Zeppelin as souvenirs. One of the relatives of a Coorg planter picked up a shard of wood and a piece of rope from the debris. This was later presented to the Bamboo Club in Coorg (see figure 24). These memorabilia, along with a photograph of William Leefe Robinson, has been preserved at the Bamboo Club.

The following day, Lieutenant General Henderson, the Commander of the Royal Flying Corps, recommended that Billy

---

[44]This quote has been sourced from the article 'Coorg Planting Families' written by Christopher Irwin in 2004.

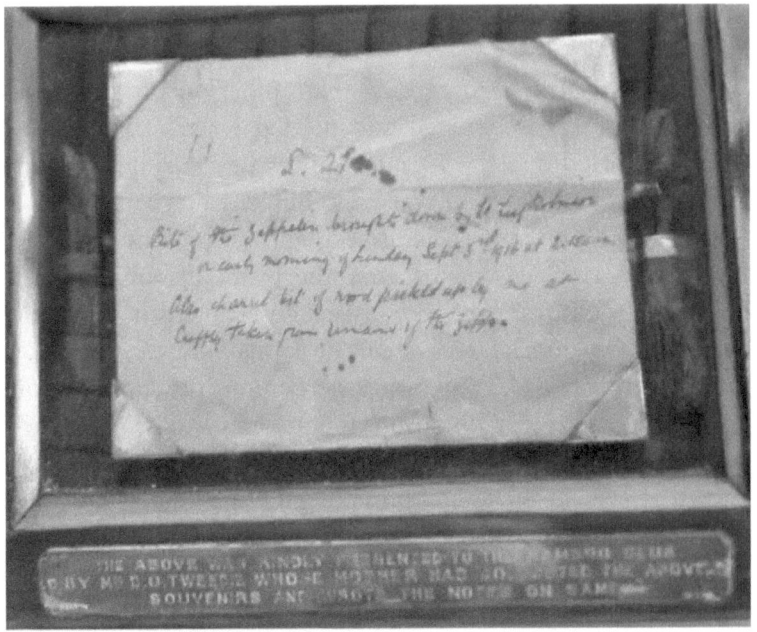

Figure 25: The letter with a piece of the Zeppelin.
Courtesy: The Bamboo Club, Pollibetta, Coorg

should be awarded the highest military honour, the Victoria Cross, 'for the most conspicuous gallantry displayed in this successful attack'.[45]

Billy, by then a well-known hero, continued to be an active member of the Royal Flying Corps. On 5 April 1917, he was apparently forced to land behind enemy lines in the Pas de Calais, Flanders. He was taken prisoner and was a considerable catch for the German authorities. During his time as a prisoner of war, Billy busied himself with sports, theatricals, developing a library and making repeated attempts to escape. The Germans

---

[45]Based on author's conversation with Gabriel and Christopher Irwin.

were increasingly harsh on him after every attempt. This took a toll on his health.

Following the armistice in November 1918, Billy was released. He was debilitated and needed a walking stick. He quickly fell victim to the 1918–19 influenza epidemic that took more lives than the World War itself. Billy died on 31 December 1918, aged 23, of cardiac failure brought on by influenza.

In July 1995, 100 years after the birth of William Leefe Robinson, the Royal Air Force invited descendants of his family to attend a memorial service at All Saints Church at Harrow Weald. Family friends from Coorg were among the congregation.

Ruth was the only Robinson sibling to remain in Coorg. She married John Williamson Irwin (1865–1944), who was popularly known as Jack, at the church in Pollibetta in October 1912. The wedding reception was held at the Bamboo Club next door. Jack owned Jumboor Estate located in north Coorg. The estate is now part of Tata Coffee Limited. The Kaimabetta Estate changed hands after Horace and Elizabeth returned to England and is currently owned by former Finance Minister P. Chidambaram and his family.

15

SUBEDAR CHEPUDIRA THIMAYYA

The portrait of the gentleman (see figure 26) in *Kupya-chele*[46], sporting a handlebar moustache, epitomizes the quintessential Kodava. This picture is frequently featured in quite a few brochures and write-ups on Coorg.

We, as a family, are proud of the gentleman in figure 26 who is our great grandfather: Subedar Chepudira Thimayya. He was an influential personality in Coorg during the late nineteenth and early twentieth centuries. I have heard a great deal about Subedar Thimayya from my parents and grandparents and his story is a part of my family history.

Thimayya was born in 1845 to Chepudira Madaiah who was one of the seven sons of Dewan Ponnappa. He grew up to be a handsome young man. Thimayya was one of the five sons of Madaiah. According to Reverend Georg Richter, Madaiah was one of the largest landowners in south Coorg during the latter half of nineteenth century. Being the grandson of Dewan Ponnappa was indeed a privilege. All the 22 grandsons of the Dewan got the advantage of education and later employment in the government as assistant commissioners, *subedars, parpathegars,* munsifs etc. Thimayya's cousin, Subayya, was the

---

[46]Kupya is a collarless, short-sleeved coat (wrap-around) that reaches below the knees and worn by Coorg men on formal occasions. It is held in place with a gold embroidered sash known as chele. A short ornamental knife, known as *peeche-kathi*, is tucked into the chele.

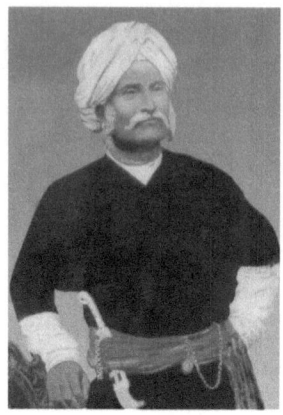

Figure 26: Subedhar Chepudira Thimayya
Source: Author's collection

first Kodava to become an assistant commissioner during the British rule. Incidentally, Chepudira Subayya was the maternal grandfather of General Kodandera S. Thimayya.

Subedar Thimayya wielded considerable influence due to his position in the revenue department. He and his cousin, Subayya, constantly competed with each other. With the appointment of Subayya as the assistant commissioner, he scored a point over my great grandfather.

Subedar Thimayya married Mukkatira (Kunjalgeri) Thangavva. The couple had 10 sons and one daughter. Subedar Thimayya gave the best education to his sons. My grandfather, Muthanna, was trained as a veterinary doctor at Chennai. Two of Subedar Thimayya's bright sons, Machayya and Aiyanna, were sent to England for education. Machayya became a barrister at law, and upon his return, set up a flourishing legal practice in Bellary. However, Subedar Thimayya was very disappointed and infuriated when Machayya married outside the community. Machayya was disowned by his father and deprived of inheritance. Barrister Machayya's granddaughter, Jayanti, married the well-known cricketer of yesteryears, the swashbuckling M.L. Jaisimha from Hyderabad. Unfortunately, Aiyanna, a student at a medical college in Brighton, died in a swimming accident. Another son, named Belliappa, died in college.

Subedar Thimayya's only daughter was the youngest of his brood. He was very fond of her and doted on her. However, tragedy struck one day while he was playing with the little girl by throwing her up in the air and catching her. Suddenly, the child slipped from his hands, landed on the hard ground and was critically injured. All efforts to save the child were futile. Thimayya was devastated and heartbroken.

Subedar Thimayya went about settling his remaining seven sons down in various parts of Coorg. As and when one of his sons was ready to be married, he would purchase a property for him and make sure the young couple were well provided for. When my grandfather, Chepudira Muthanna, came of age, Thimayya purchased more than 200 acres of land in an auction for a then princely sum of ₹6,010. I have the original deed of this purchase made in 1900. The property came with a large bungalow, which is over 120 years old now. That is where I spent my childhood along with my siblings and cousins.

Subedar Thimayya was actively involved in several public causes of the day. He built a school at Kakotuparambu, which is functioning to this day. He donated land for the Government Hospital and the Government School in Gonikoppal. He was one of the main promoters of the Victoria Club in Virajpet. He also planted an avenue of jackfruit trees along the Gonikoppal–Virajpet road and Virajpet–Madikeri Road. Some of these trees, which were there until a few years ago, have now been felled for road widening. Thimayya built a landmark house in Madikeri for himself and his large family. He had a room for each of his seven sons in this house, which he grandly named 'Crystal Palace'. This building is still standing and is occupied by some of the family members.

Another interesting story about Subedar Thimayya is about him being fined four annas (25 paise) by the British for an alleged violation of a rule. Thimayya vehemently defended himself. He spent more than ₹100 fighting this case, which was a substantial sum in those days, to prove that he was not in the wrong.

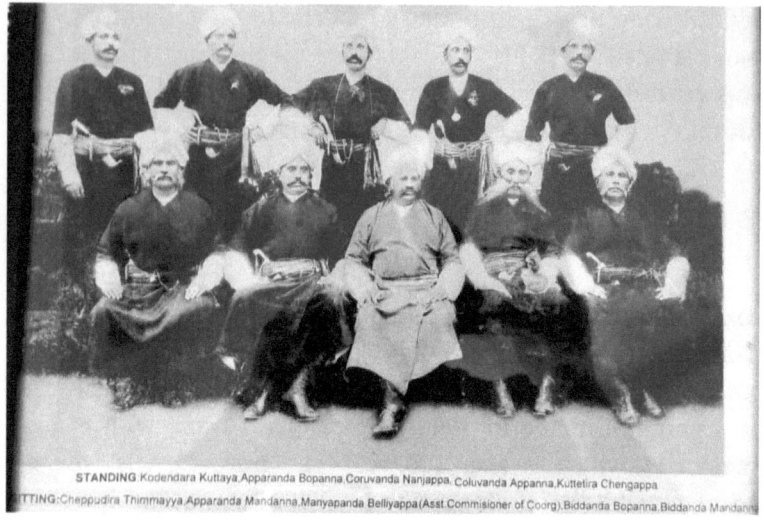

STANDING Kodendara Kuttaya,Apparanda Bopanna,Coruvanda Nanjappa, Coluvanda Appanna,Kuttetira Chengappa
ITTING:Cheppudira Thimmayya,Apparanda Mandanna,Manyapanda Belliyappa(Asst.Commisioner of Coorg),Biddanda Bopanna,Biddanda Mandann

Figure 27: *The delegation from Coorg, 1895.*
Source: Coorg Planters' Association Centenary Souvenir (1879-1979)

In 1895, Subedar Thimmayya was part of a 10-member delegation, headed by the then Assistant Commissioner of Coorg Manepanda Belliappa, to meet the Viceroy Lord Elgin II in Mysore.[47] They presented the Viceroy a list of development work required in Coorg. In a historic photograph (figure 26) of the delegation, where everyone is dressed in traditional *Kupya-chele*, Subedar Thimayya is seated first from the left. Curiously, one of the demands was for a railway line to Coorg. Fortunately, till date, railways have not made inroads into Coorg. Proposals for a railway line have been presented, but it is vehemently opposed by local environmentalists because of the massive damage it will cause to the pristine environment of this area.

---

[47]Excerpt of a memorandum presented to the Viceroy by the delegation in 1895 from the Coorg Planters' Association Centenary Souvenir, 1879–1979.

Thimayya was the pattedar of the Chepudira family in 1904. He was conferred the title 'Rao Bahadur' by the British. It is a happy coincidence that Subedar Thimayya's grandfather was Dewan Ponnappa and his grandson C.M. Poonacha was the chief minister of Coorg from 1952 to 1956. Subedar Thimayya passed away in 1907.

16

A CENTURY OLD CONVENT SCHOOL IN COORG

Educational institutions were first started in Coorg after it was taken over by the British in 1834.[48] The Kodavas took to education most enthusiastically. In 1909, St Joseph's Convent was founded by Catholic nuns in Madikeri. It was primarily a school for girls, but boys were allowed to study there till seventh standard. The school catered to both boarders and day scholars. This school offered quality education to the children of those locals who aspired to see their sons and daughters well-prepared to take advantage of the lucrative career opportunities under the colonial dispensation. This school saw several generations of students, especially women, pursue higher education and excel in diverse professional fields at a time when women were not very involved outside the traditional responsibilities of raising a family. I recently came across a remarkable group photograph (figure 28) from 1911 of the students of St Joseph's Convent with the European nuns who ran the school.

Figure 28 has members from the Codanda family, which became famous between the 1930s and 1950s. According to the family history, narrated by Codanda B. Poovaiah, one of

---

[48]Richter, Georg, *Manual of Coorg: A Gazetteer of the Natural Features of the Country and the Social and Political Condition of its Inhabitants*, B.R. Publishing Corp., Delhi, 1870.

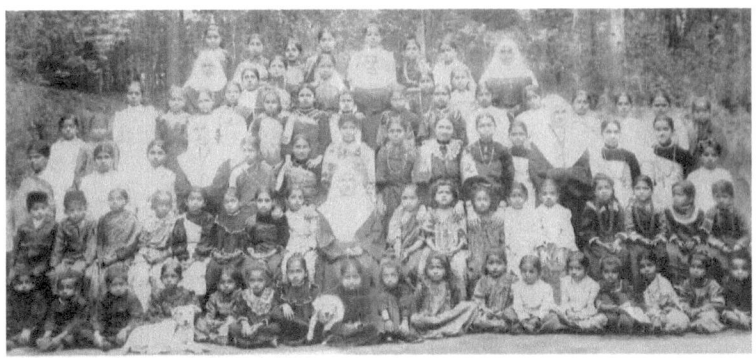

Figure 28: Students of St Joseph's Convent, Madikeri, 1911.
Source: 'St Joseph's Convent Composite High School Madikeri', https://tinyurl.com/bddp6jdx. Accessed on 22 February 2023.

the descendants of the family, the famous members of the Codanda family are the seven daughters and one son of the first lawyer from Coorg: Codanda D. Poovaiah. Six of his daughters continued their education outside Coorg. The sisters excelled in various fields and soon came to be known as the 'Poovaiah Sisters of Coorg'. One of them, Rohini, was the first woman from Coorg to acquire a degree. She later became the principal of Crosthwaite College, a well-known institution in Allahabad. She was familiar with the Nehru family and played a brief role in the education of the young Indira Gandhi. She was awarded the Padma Shri in 1973. Another sister, Ashlesha, was one of the first lady doctors from Coorg. Yet another sister, Swati, completed her nursing degree and later went on a scholarship to Columbia University in 1948 for further studies. The three younger sisters—Sita, Chitra and Lata—became renowned Kathak dancers and were much sought after not only for their performances all over India but also to choreograph dances in Hindi movies. All the sisters participated in the freedom movement. Chitra and Lata defied prohibitory orders during the Quit India movement, were arrested and jailed for two weeks. Sita earned a PhD in Arts from the University of Bombay (in ni University of Mumbai) and became the first Kodava lady to get a doctorate degree.

My father, C.M. Poonacha, knew the family well. The only brother of the Poovaiah sisters (my namesake right down to our initials) was the *boja-kara* (best man) at my father's wedding. I had the privilege of being invited to their home on Malabar Hill in Bombay in 1968. Except for Ashlesha, all the sisters remained unmarried.

Over the years, several girls who received their early education in this school went on to achieve great feats in various fields. Konganda Accamma, who passed out of this school in the 1920s, joined Lady Hardinge Medical College in New Delhi. She was one of the first Kodava women to earn an MBBS degree. She headed the Vanivilas Women and Children's Hospital in Bangalore for several years.

One of the most distinguished alumnae of this school was C.B. Muthamma, who was the first woman to qualify for the Indian Foreign Service (IFS) in 1949.[49] She also has the distinction of being the first lady ambassador from the IFS cadre. Muthamma had to face gender discrimination while in service. She fought against the government and took the matter to the Supreme court in 1979 for redressal.[50] The apex court passed a judgement in her favour, which paved the way for other women civil servants from being discriminated against. She authored a

---

[49]Sanchari Pal, 'The Untold Story of C.B. Muthamma, India's First Woman IFS Officer and Ambassador', The Better India, https://tinyurl.com/3feexeaw. Accessed on 9 February 2023.
[50]Ibid.

book titled *Slain by the System*[51] in 2003.

St Joseph's is now a co-education school and continues to be as vibrant as ever.

---

[51]Muthamma, C.B., *Slain by the System: India's Real Crisis: A Collection of Essays,* Viveka Foundation, 2003.

17

THE COMMISSIONER'S WIFE

After Coorg came under British rule in 1834, it was administered by a chief commissioner. William Pell Barton, an officer of the Indian Civil Service, was the British Resident at Mysore and the chief commissioner of Coorg from 1920–25.[52] In those days, the residence of the chief commissioner used to be within the premises of the Madikeri Fort, overlooking the main road where the Kodava Samaja building is now located. This edifice built on the ramparts of the fort is a prominent landmark in Madikeri.

William Pell Barton and his wife, Evelyn Agnes, divided their time between Mysore and Coorg. While in Coorg, they occupied the official residence of the chief commissioner. With the growing number of British coffee planters, the social life in Coorg was good, and the popular North Coorg Club was just a short distance away. With the salubrious weather reminding them of home, the couple enjoyed the peaceful environment of Coorg.

However, amid this near idyllic lifestyle, there was a recurring 'nuisance' that bothered Mrs Barton. After a few months, this irritation became unbearable for her. As for Mr Barton, his domestic bliss was in jeopardy. The cause for this

---

[52]'William Pell Barton', People Pill, https://tinyurl.com/frw43chb. Accessed on 22 February 2023.

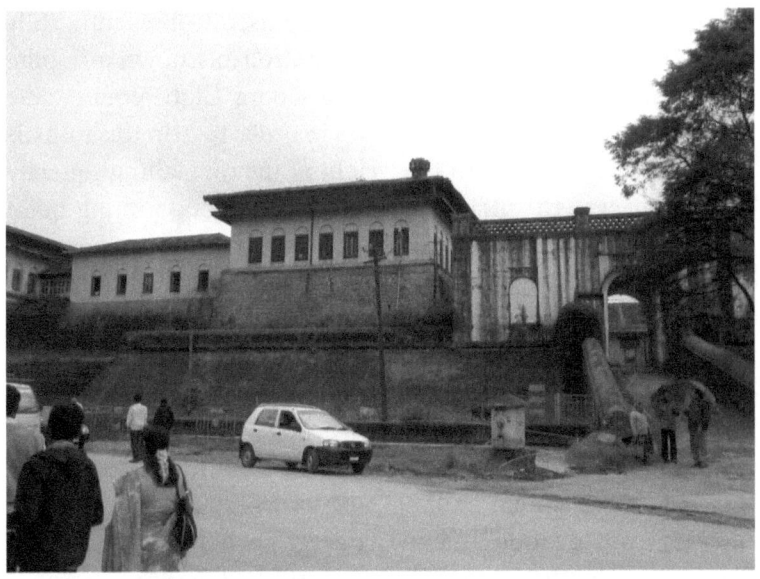

Figure 29: Madikeri Fort
Source: Author's collection

crisis was the umpteen noisy bullock carts that used to ply the main road outside their residence.

All the daily necessities for Madikeri, including groceries, vegetables, firewood etc., reached the town early in the mornings in bullock carts so that the household needs of the citizens were met at the beginning of the day. The winding roads in Madikeri were especially hard on the animals pulling the carts. These vintage bullock carts had a device known as *beeri* that was used as a brake. This was a simple contraption with two logs of wood fixed across the steel rim of the cart's large wooden wheels. The two logs were tied to a rope, which was tethered to the front of the cart and lay below the driver. When the driver stepped on the ropes, the logs pressed against the steel rim and slowed down the cart. The beeri was primarily used to prevent a fully laden bullock cart from moving uncontrollably down a sloping road. The steep descent after North Coorg Club required the driver to literally stand on the ropes in order to help the animals gently move forward with the weight of the cart falling squarely on their necks. This manoeuvre produced a loud grating noise as the logs pressed hard against the moving wheels.

Mrs Barton could not take this jarring racket disturbing her sleep early every morning. Her objections became so vehement that Mr Barton had no option but to ban bullock carts from plying on the main road under the Police Act. This action caused great inconvenience to the towns people, as their daily needs had to be carried on foot by hordes of labourers. This caused the cost of every item to shoot up.

However, no one had the courage to question the Chief Commissioner. But an eight standard student, N.K. Ganapayya, from the Government Central School was infuriated and took a bold decision. Ganapayya wrote a letter to the editor of *Sri Kanteerava*, which was published from Mangalore, about the arbitrary actions of the Chief Commissioner because of which an entire town was suffering. *Sri Kanteerava* published the letter, which created a flutter. Ganapayya became an instant hero at his school. At the same time, everyone in school and the residents of Madikeri were worried about what dreadful actions would be taken against the young Ganapayya.

As feared, the editor of *Sri Kanteerava* and Ganapayya were apprehended by the police and produced before the court at Madikeri Fort. My father and his friends bunked class that day to be in the courtroom to see what would happen to their friend. The magistrate levied a fine of ₹50 on the editor. Since Ganapayya was a juvenile, his punishment was to remain standing in the courtroom till the court adjourned. He was then let-off with a stern warning. Ganapayya's heroic deed spurred many youths from Coorg to join the freedom movement. Even my father, C.M. Poonacha, two years junior to Ganapayya in the same school, was full of admiration at the courage of his senior. It led to the first stirrings of nationalistic feelings in my father, who later became one of the leading freedom fighters of Coorg.

After this incident, the British administration built a separate bungalow for the Chief Commissioner, 'away from the plebeians', as it were.

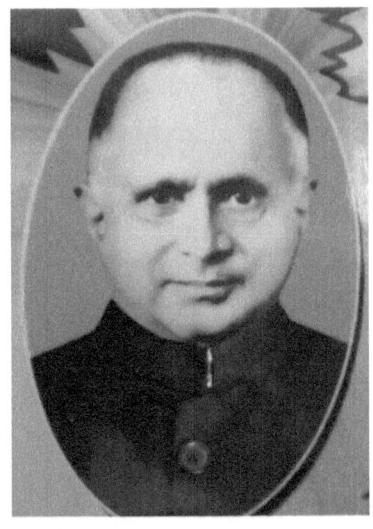

Figure 30: N.K. Ganapayya
Courtesy: Dr N.G. Ravindranath (son of Ganapayya)

This colonial dwelling in Madikeri, named 'Bauer Bungalow', is located deep inside a vast wooded area. It continued to be the residence of the chief commissioners of Coorg from 1947 to 1956. Renamed 'Sudarshan', it now serves as the government guesthouse.

My father and Ganapayya became lifelong friends after this episode. Ganapayya grew up to be an ardent champion of freedom, free enterprise and community service. He went on to establish a large coffee estate in Sakleshpur. He also joined hands with C. Rajagopalachari and was a pioneering member of the Swatantra Party. When Indira Gandhi declared Emergency in 1975, he was incensed. He shot off a series of letters to her, criticizing her undemocratic actions. As expected, the police arrested the then 70-year-old Ganapayya, who ended up spending two years in jail. Ganapayya was a true patriot and a generous philanthropist. He continued to passionately pursue all the social upliftment activities he was engaged in well into his octogenarian years.

PART II
THE VICTORIA GOWRAMMA PAPERS

18

QUEEN VICTORIA'S FAVOURITE GODDAUGHTER: PRINCESS VICTORIA GOWRAMMA OF COORG

Queen Victoria's long reign, popularly referred to as the Victorian Era, is marked by its prudish and conservative values. However, the Queen, at the height of Britain's unabashedly racist colonial power, had a surprisingly soft corner for her subjects from India. She was particularly fond of three Indians in her court. The first was Princess Victoria Gowramma of Coorg, who reached England in 1852 with her father, Chikka Veerarajendra, the last and ousted Raja of Coorg. Queen Victoria stood sponsor at the 11-year-old Gowramma's (spelt Gauromma in Victorian England) baptism and announced herself as godmother to the young princess from Coorg. She surprised her court when she generously asked Gowramma to add the prefix 'Victoria' to her name.[53] Queen Victoria presented an autographed Bible to the Indian princess on the day of her baptism. This Bible is currently in the possession of A. Franklin, an art collector in Bangalore, who very kindly allowed me to take photographs (see figure 31) of this rare artefact.

The next Indian royal to land in England in 1854 was the 16-year-old dethroned Maharaja Duleep Singh of Punjab.

---

[53]Dalhousie Login, Edith, *Lady Login's Recollections: Court Life and Camp Life 1820—1904*, Smith, Elder & Co., London, 1916.

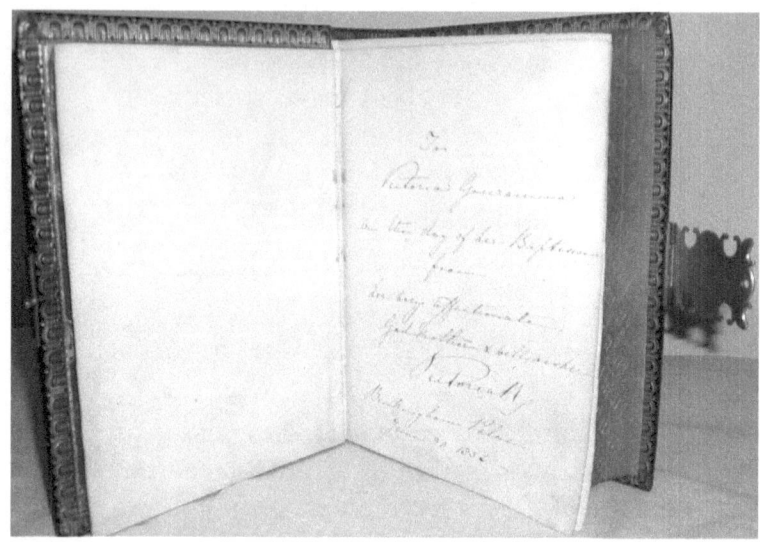

Figure 31: The Bible autographed and presented to Victoria Gowramma by Queen Victoria in 1852.

Courtesy: A. Franklin, who now owns the Bible

Maharaja Duleep, too, had embraced Christianity. Both the Queen and her Royal Consort Prince Albert were impressed by the handsome Maharaja. Princess Victoria Gowramma and Maharaja Duleep received Western education and were taught Christian values. They were regular invitees at various events at the numerous palaces of the Queen and even socialized with the royal children. The Queen and Prince Albert fervently hoped and tried their best to bring about a matrimonial alliance between the two royal Indian Christian converts. They envisioned this union to popularize Christianity in India.

The third Indian to attract the attention of Queen Victoria was Abdul Karim, who was sent by the East India Company from Agra to London in 1887 to serve the Queen during the Jubilee celebrations.[54] Over a period of time, Abdul Karim became a confidante of the Queen and wielded considerable influence over her personal life. He taught the Queen Urdu and cooked Indian curry for her.

Queen Victoria and Prince Albert established a private residence named Osborne House in the picturesque Isle of Wight. It was the Queen's favourite retreat, where she and her growing family could enjoy some privacy and be away from the constant public gaze. Princess Gowramma and Maharaja Duleep were frequent guests of the royal family at this idyllic seaside retreat, which Queen Victoria often referred to as the one of the prettiest places imaginable. The two Indian royals joined the Queen's children in learning gardening, growing vegetables and in familiarizing themselves with housekeeping.

Two important artefacts of Princess Gowramma are on display at Osborne House, and I was able to see them in their original glory. The first is an iconic painting of Gowramma by a renowned artist: Franz Xaver Winterhalter. Winterhalter was the Queen's favourite visual artist and has painted several portraits of the royal family that are on display at various palaces in the UK. This watercolour of Gowramma (see figure 32) holding a Bible was commissioned in 1854, two years after her baptism. Winterhalter also pointed Maharaja Duleep, and both the paintings of the Indian royals grace the Durbar Corridor in Osborne House. The Durbar Corridor has many paintings of Indian attendants of the queen, including that of Abdul Karim. One of the star attractions of this corridor is the Durbar Room which was added in 1891. This impressive room has many elements of Hindu, Jain and Mughal architecture.

The second artefact is an equally stunning piece of art. It is a

---

[54]Basu, Shrabani, *Victoria & Abdul: The True Story of the Queen's Closest Confidant*, The History Press, 2010.

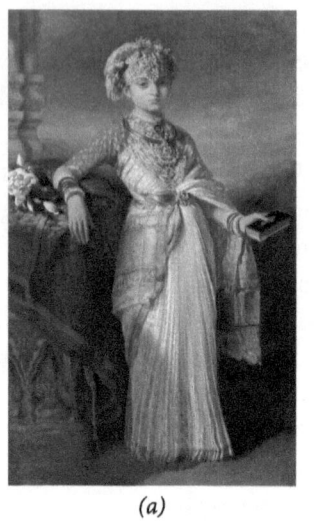 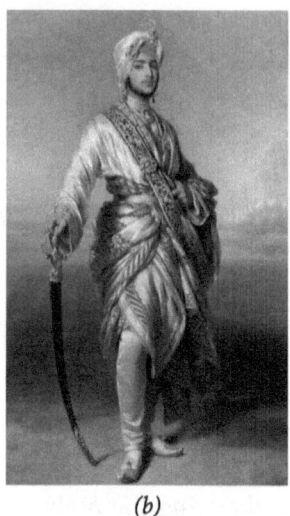

(a) (b)

Figure 32 (a-b): Paintings of Princess Victoria Gowramma and Maharaja Duleep Singh by Franz Xaver Winterhalter, 1854.

Courtesy: The Royal Collections® 2023, His Majesty King Charles III

marble bust of Victoria Gowramma sculpted by Queen Victoria's favourite sculptor, Baron Carlo Marochetti, in 1856.[55] This marble bust was further enhanced by painting it to bring out the oriental complexion and features of Gowramma. It is on display along with a marble bust of Maharaja Duleep, also sculpted by Marochetti. In order to ensure that her Indian favourites were properly respected, Queen Victoria bestowed upon Princess Gowramma and Maharaja Duleep the unprecedented status equivalent to that of European prince, and princesses. Likewise, Abdul Karim was given the title 'The Munshi'. Towards her later years, the Queen depended on Abdul Karim to a great degree, much to the displeasure of her son and Prince of Wales, Edward (later King Edward VII).

---

[55] *The Times*, 16 April 1856.

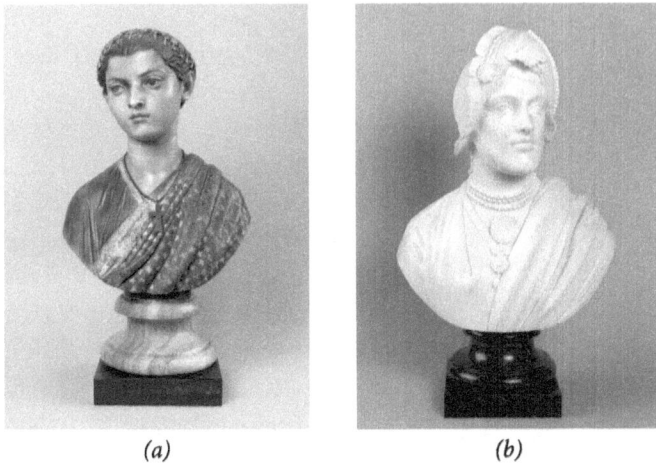

Figure 33 (a-b): Marble busts of Princess Victoria Gowramma and Maharaja Duleep Singh by Baron Carlo Marochetti 1856.

Courtesy: The Royal Collections® 2023, His Majesty King Charles III.

Princess Gowramma was particularly close to Princess Alice, the third child of Queen Victoria. They met and exchanged letters frequently. Later, Princess Alice married the German Prince Louis of Hesse. Princess Alice had a rather unhappy marriage and a sad death in 1878 at the age of 35. However, the direct descendants of Alice's first daughter, Victoria, are Lord Louis Mountbatten (great grandson), who was the viceroy of India at the time of India's independence, and Prince Philip (great great grandson), the royal consort of Queen Elizabeth II. That makes King Charles III of the UK a direct descendant of Princess Alice.

Had Princess Victoria Gowramma lived to a ripe old age, she would have witnessed many historic events. Furthermore, there is also speculation about what would have become of Maharaja Duleep's marriage to her if it had happened, as per the Queen's wishes.

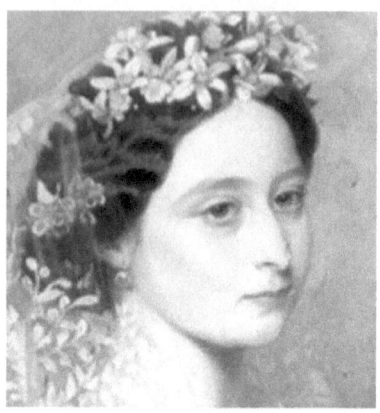

Figure 34: Painting of Princess Alice, daughter of Queen Victoria, by Franz Xaver Winterhalter, circa 1860.

Source: 'The Captivating Life of Princess Alice of the United Kingdom', Salon Privé, 13 September 2022, https://tinyurl.com/bdeay8j3. Accessed on 23 February 2023.

Sadly, Princess Gowramma's marriage to Colonel John Campbell soured after a couple of years. She contracted tuberculosis and died at the age of 23 on 30 March 1864, survived by her husband and three-year-old daughter, Edith Victoria.[56] She was buried in Brompton Cemetery in London. I visited the cemetery in 2010 to locate the final resting place of the Princess, only a couple of days after launching my book on her life—*Victoria Gowramma: The Lost Princess of Coorg*. The process of unearthing facts about Princess Gowramma and her father, Chikka Veerarajendra, the last Raja of Coorg, and then reconstructing their lives was like putting together a jigsaw puzzle after finding all the pieces. The Princess was the favourite daughter of the Raja of Coorg. Chikka Veerarajendra and Princess Gowramma were the first Indian royals to sail to England in 1852.

Brompton Cemetery, located in Southwest London, covers an area of about 40 acres. This burial ground, established in 1836, is now used as a park and is popular with cyclists and joggers. The cemetery is located not far from Stamford Bridge, home to Chelsea Football Club. The office of the sprawling

---

[56]Dalhousie Login, Edith, *Lady Login's Recollections: Court Life and Camp Life 1820—1904*, Smith Elder & Co., London, 1916.

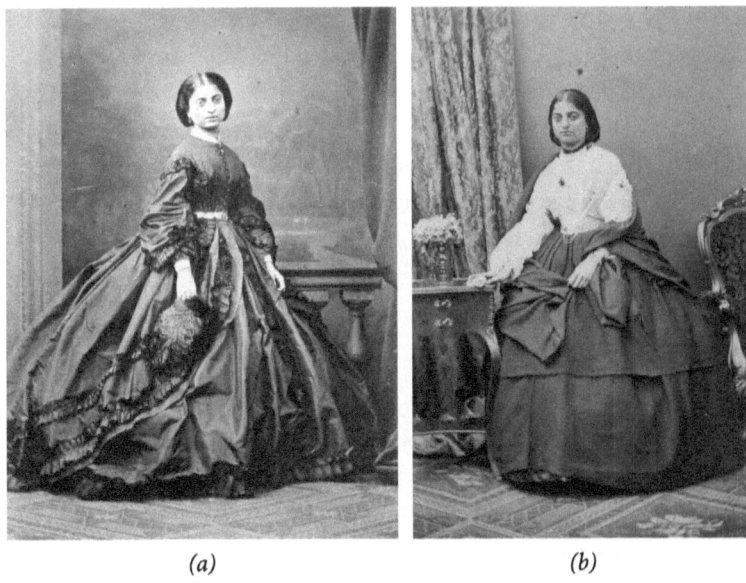

Figure 35 (a-b): Victoria Gowramma, circa 1860.
Courtesy: Anne Phillips

cemetery has painstakingly recorded the names of the people buried there since its inception and has a data bank that is regularly updated. I was shown a map of the area where the grave I was looking for was situated. It took me more than an hour to locate the tombstone of Gowramma. The cross on the headstone was broken and covered with thick undergrowth.

I stood there trying to picture that day, 4 April 1864, when the horse-drawn hearse carrying the body of the Princess would have arrived, followed by her husband Colonel Campbell and their three-year-old daughter Edith. Also present would have been Lady Lena Login, the long-time guardian and later sister-in-law of the Coorg Princess. It would have been a particularly painful experience for Colonel Campbell, as the grave where his second wife was to be buried already had the mortal remains of his second son, Colin, from his first wife. The boy had died in a freak accident in 1856. Interestingly, Colin was born in 1842 in Bellary, Karnataka, while Colonel Campbell was serving in the 38th Madras Native Infantry.[57]

This burial spot is where my story of Princess Victoria Gowramma ends, having started with her birth in 1841 in Benares. The epitaph on her tombstone, drafted by Queen Victoria, is still legible:

> Sacred to the memory of Princess Victoria Gowramma, daughter of the ex-Raja of Coorg, the beloved wife of Colonel John Campbell, born in India 4 July 1841. She was brought up early in life to England: baptized into the Christian faith under immediate care and protection of Queen Victoria, who stood sponsor to her, and took deep interest in her through life. She died 30 March 1864.
>
> 'Other sheep I have, which are not of this fold.' (John X, 16)

---

[57]Ibid.

19

THE ART AND CREATIVE JOURNEY OF VICTORIA GOWRAMMA

Over the last 12 years, my book, *Victoria Gowramma: The Lost Princess of Coorg*, published in December 2009, has generated a great deal of interest in creative and academic circles. Quite naturally, the story of Victoria Gowramma attracted considerable attention in the UK, as the Princess came under the patronage of Queen Victoria and spent 12 years of her life in England, until her death in 1864. The story has inspired lectures, discussions, dance dramas, musical renderings and paintings by notable musicians and artists.

The main catalyst behind the creative and academic activities in the UK is Dr Nima Poovaya-Smith. She was conferred the Order of the British Empire (OBE) in 2016 and was appointed Deputy Lieutenant (DL) of West Yorkshire in 2019.

Having studied the life of Maharaja Duleep Singh in great detail and delivered several lectures on the history of the Punjab, Dr Poovaya-Smith was fascinated with the interconnections between the lives of Victoria Gowramma and Maharaja Duleep. The saga of the two Christian Indian royals and the fact that Queen Victoria had taken them under her wing, with Gowramma being her goddaughter, was relatively unknown in the UK. The staid Queen Victoria even surprised her court by adding the prefix 'Victoria' to Gowramma's name: a rare honour at the time for a dethroned member of Indian royalty.

After *Victoria Gowramma: The Lost Princess of Coorg* was published, many articles about Victoria Gowramma have been published in periodicals and references about her made in books.[58] Dr Poovaya-Smith's husband, Paul Smith, a sociologist, has summarized some of the observations and spin-offs from my book *Victoria Gowramma: The Lost Princess of Coorg*:

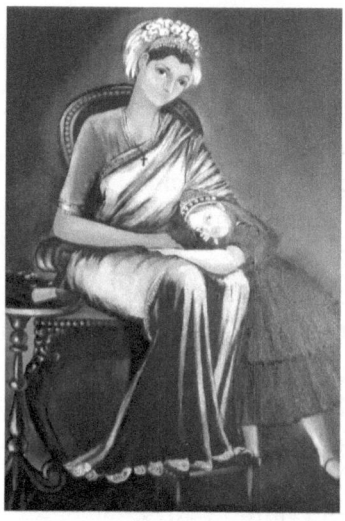

Figure 36: *A conceptual painting of Victoria Gowramma and her daughter, Edith Victoria, by Jayashree Pathak, commissioned by author.*
Source: Author's collection

Victoria Gowramma is a story that captures the imagination. A princess whose life was unusual by any reckoning, befriended by the most powerful Empress in the world—Queen Victoria—and then there is the pathos of her early death. The missing jewels and absconding husband further add to the drama. It has resulted in a mini dance drama, for instance, choreographed and performed by Rashmi Sudhir with fusion music compositions by David Wilson and Inder 'Goldfinger' Matharu. It was first performed in Harewood House in 2012 (fittingly the Earl of Harewood is a great

---

[58]Two scholarly books on Queen Victoria have my book listed in their bibliography. They are: Wilson, A.N., *Victoria: A Life*, Atlantic Books, 2014; Taylor, Miles, *The English Maharani: Queen Victoria and India*, Penguin Random House India, 2018.

great great grandson of Queen Victoria). Seated in the audience were the distinguished historian and writer Charles Allen and the internationally acclaimed artist Sutapa Biswas. The latter, in particular, was extremely moved by Victoria Gowramma's story. This mini dance drama was also performed in 2014 in the iconic Leeds Library—one of the oldest subscription libraries in the country.

In 2014, the late Jayashree Pathak produced two paintings of Victoria Gowramma—again as a direct result of the book.

Christella Litras and Rob Green have set two poems inspired by the book into evocative songs—'My name is Victoria Gowramma' and 'I'm the Son of the Lion of the Punjab'. They performed it at Nima's mother Ammanichanda Muthie Poovaya's memorial service on 25 January 2020. Even more recently, a detailed analysis of the Winterhalter's paintings of Victoria Gowramma and Duleep Singh, commissioned by Queen Victoria herself, was the subject of a talk at the distinguished luncheon club at Devonshire Hall, Leeds. Without Belliappa's book, the interest in the two paintings would not have been triggered...[59]

---

[59] Written by Paul Smith for this essay. To access some of the material mentioned here, see: 'Victoria Gowrama: The Lost Princess', David Wilson Music, https://tinyurl.com/ypdynhpc. Accessed on 10 February 2023.

20

HISTORICAL CONNECTIONS

I have made a series of serendipitous discoveries since I started researching and reconstructing the story of Princess Victoria Gowramma of Coorg. As I wrote, I stumbled, quite fortuitously, upon several hitherto unknown details of the prolonged sojourn of Chikka Veerarajendra and his daughter in Victorian England from 1852 to 1864. Princess Gowramma had the unique privilege of being Queen Victoria's goddaughter. She was baptized, as an 11-year-old, in the presence of the Queen, who lent her own name 'Victoria' to the Indian princess.

I have reconstructed the life of Victoria Gowramma in my book *Victoria Gowramma: The Lost Princess of Coorg*. Queen Victoria's desire that her goddaughter should marry another Christian Indian royal—Maharaja Duleep Singh of the Punjab—did not materialize. Gowramma

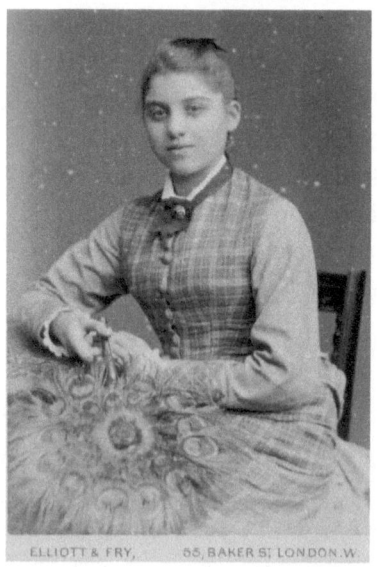

Figure 37: *Victoria Gowramma's daughter, Edith Victoria, circa 1876.*
Courtesy: Anne Phillips

finally married Lieutenant Colonel John Campbell, a widower 30 years her senior. They had a daughter named Edith Victoria. After Gowramma's death in 1864, Queen Victoria invited young Edith to Buckingham Palace a few times and announced an annuity of £250 for her. The Queen also commissioned a miniature painting of Edith. Henry Victor Yardley, Edith's only son immigrated to Australia. Unfortunately, he died in a motorbike accident in 1936.[60] I concluded that there were no further descendants of Gowramma.

During the launch of my book at the Nehru Centre in London in 2010, I adventitiously met Anne Phillips, a direct descendant of Colonel Campbell from his first wife Margaret Matthew. As stated earlier, Colonel Campbell had served as an officer in the 38th Madras Native Infantry in India.

I was elated when Anne told me that Victoria Gowramma's grandson, Yardley, had married Ethel May Field in 1910 and they had three children: one son and two daughters. Anne also gave me some rare photographs of Gowramma and Edith, from her private collection. Anne's late mother had recollections of having met Edith and had preserved the photographs and other memorabilia. Anne now possesses a beautiful bracelet along with a handwritten letter from Queen Victoria, presented to Lady Lena Login (sister of Colonel Campbell) for looking after her goddaughter Princess Victoria Gowramma who had a troubled but eventful life in England.

My wife and I visited Anne's home in London. Anne had visited us in Coorg in 2015. We collaborated to track the descendants of Victoria Gowramma in Australia. Using the meticulously documented Australian Registry of Births, Marriages, and Deaths, we were able to gather information

---

[60]Krishnayya, D.N., *Kodagina Ithihasa*, University of Mysore, 1974.

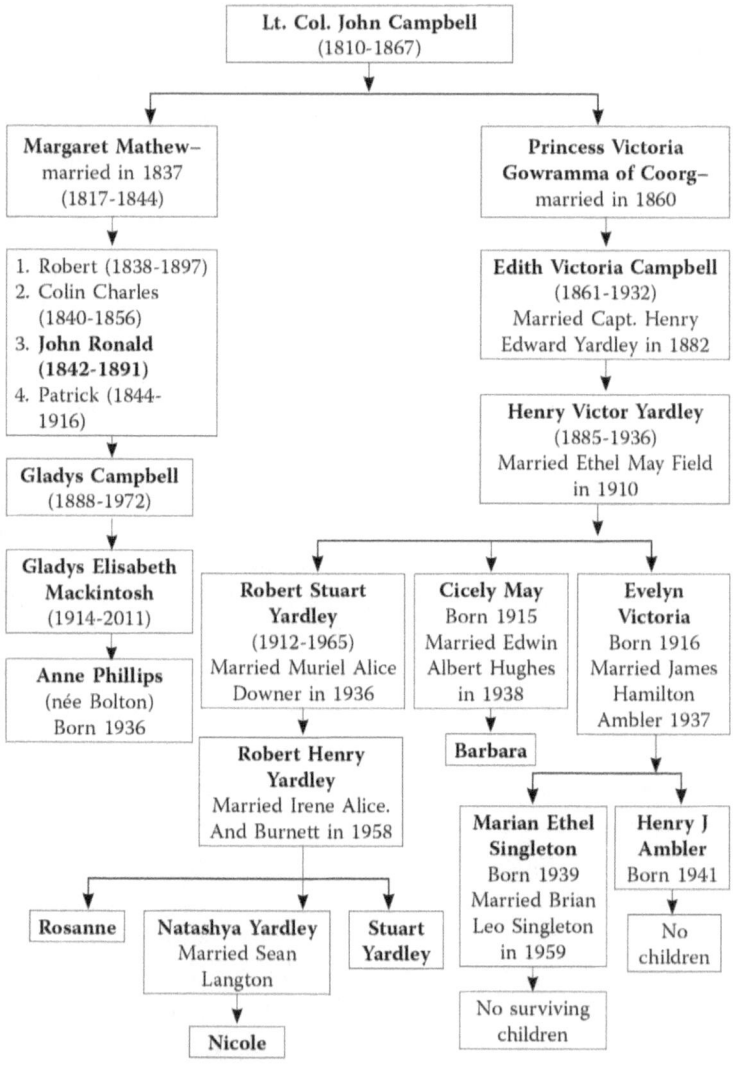

Figure 38: A family tree of Victoria Gowramma.
Source: Jointly compiled by Anne Phillips and the author

available online to draw the family tree of Gowramma's descendants (see figure 38). However, we could not get in touch with the family.

Serendipity happened again when, to my delight, Robert Yardley, a great great grandson of Victoria Gowramma, read my book and left a message for me on one of the blogs. Yardley's family is settled in New South Wales in Australia. We have been exchanging notes ever since.

Yardley's daughter, Natashya Yardley, got in touch with me in 2016 and informed me of her visit to Coorg with her husband Sean Langton. Natashya is Gowramma's great great great granddaughter. It was indeed exciting to meet a direct descendant of Princess Victoria Gowramma.

Natashya sent me a rare photograph of her great grandfather (and grandson of Gowramma), Henry Victor 'Rajendra' Yardley,

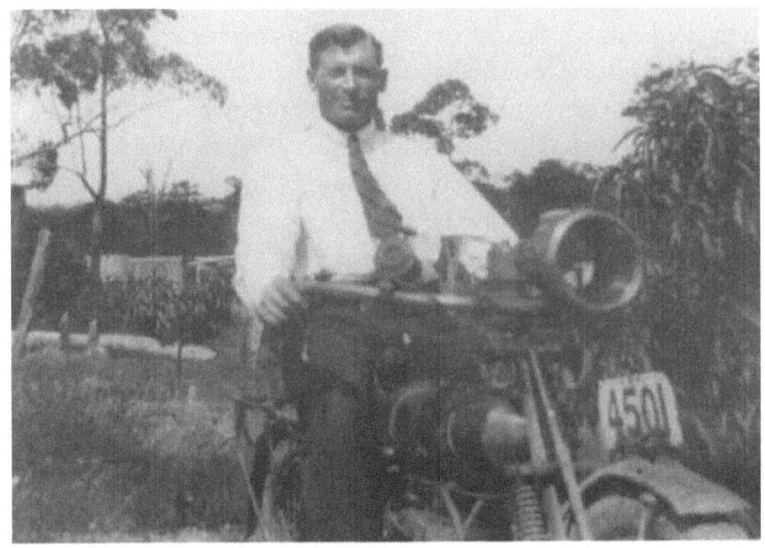

Figure 39: Henry Victor 'Rajendra' Yardley on his motorbike.
Courtesy: Yardley family

sitting on his motorbike. It was a revelation that 'Rajendra' was part of his name. Natashya has a half-sister, a brother, and a teenaged daughter named Nicole. Thus, Victoria Gowramma's lineage continues.

◆

My books, *Nuggets from Coorg History* and *Victoria Gowramma: The Lost Princess of Coorg*, evoked responses from some of the descendants of the historical personalities who figure in the books. I was pleasantly surprised by the unexpected responses that came from India, UK, Australia and Nepal. Interactions with these descendants enabled me to update my books with additional information, portraits and details.

The first one to get in touch with me was Dr Praveen Sirdesai, a direct descendant of Chikka Veerarajendra (1802–59). Dr Sirdesai, a well-known ENT surgeon in Secunderabad, was intrigued about his ancestors after reading my book *Nuggets from Coorg History*. Around that time, I was completing my book on Victoria Gowramma. After interacting with Dr Sirdesai, I was able to include more details about Chikka Veerarajendra's family left behind in Benares, including the ten other siblings of Gowramma. Dr Sirdesai visited Coorg along with his mother, wife and two daughters. He showed me photographs of some of the artefacts, such as silver bowls, swords etc. that belonged to Chikka Veerarajendra.

In 2011, I was invited by Dr Nima Poovaya-Smith OBE, DL, founder of Alchemy Anew, a cultural organization based in Leeds, UK, to participate in the Ilkley Literature Festival. There, I got to meet David Lascelles, the eighth Earl of Harewood. He is a great great great grandson of Queen Victoria, a nephew and godson of Queen Elizabeth II. He was fascinated by the fact that Queen Victoria had an Indian goddaughter. Lascelles is a devout follower of Buddha's teachings and identifies as a Buddhist. He also frequently visits India. At the time of his birth, he was thirteenth in line to the British throne.

I was also pleasantly surprised to receive a message from Nigel Cole from Wales, UK. He is the great great grandson of Robert Andrews Cole, who served as the superintendent of Coorg during the mid-1860s. Cole wrote the iconic book *An Elementary Grammar of the Coorg Language* in 1867. He also penned a book titled *A Manual of Coorg Civil Law*. Cole's books provide splendid insight into life in Coorg during the mid-1860s. In 2017, Murry Cole (cousin of Nigel Cole) visited Coorg with his wife, Jeannie, to trace the footsteps of his ancestor. They came to my place, and we exchanged notes on his ancestor.

Yet another person who got in touch with me was Subodh Shumsher Rana from Nepal. He is a scion of the Rana family, although not a direct descendant of Prime Minister Jung Bahadur Rana, who married Chikka Veerarajendra's other daughter, Gangamma, in 1852 (for details, see the following essay). We have had several interactions to trace the details of Princess Gangamma's life, known as Ganga Maharani after her marriage to Jung Bahadur Rana, the de facto ruler of Nepal at the time.

Through my ancestor Dewan Chepudira Ponnappa, I feel connected to all these historical figures and find it quite amazing that I was able to personally interact with their direct descendants.

21

GANGAMMA: THE OTHER FORGOTTEN PRINCESS OF COORG

In 1841, two wives of the exiled Raja of Coorg, Chikka Veerarajendra, added two daughters—Gowramma and Gangamma—to his brood of children. Gowramma, as we know, became famous as Queen Victoria's goddaughter.

British officials in India at the time, who had seen the two young princesses, have invariably extolled Gangamma's beauty. One of the earliest references to her is one by Lord Dalhousie, who met both the sisters in Benares. Of the two, he found Gangamma to be one of the prettiest girls in India.

Jung Bahadur Rana, the all-powerful prime minister of Nepal, visited Chikka Veerarajendra in Benares and instantly fell for the 11-year-old Gangamma. She was betrothed to him in 1852, just before Chikka

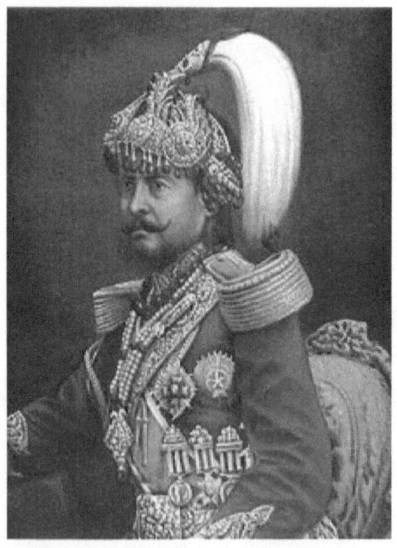

Figure 40: Jung Bahadur Rana of Nepal.
Source: 'File:Jang Bahadur Ranaji.jpg', Wikimedia Commons, https://tinyurl.com/msjpcmbb. Accessed on 23 February 2023.

Veerarajendra and Gowramma journeyed to England. Lord Dalhousie made the following racist comments in 1852 on this alliance and the two daughters of Chikka Veerarajendra in general:

> ...While marrying off one daughter [Gangamma] to Jung Bahadur, ruler of Nepal, the raja [Chikka Veerarajendra] had turned the other [Gowramma] to a Christian...The little heathen sister [Gangamma] whom Jung Bahadur took away with him to Nepal was really very pretty. The orthodox one [Gowramma] is nearly not so good looking...[61]

Dr Henry Ambrose Oldfield, who treated Gangamma in Kathmandu in 1854, narrates this incident:

> In August 1854, Jang asked me to prescribe for one of his wives, daughter of the ex-Raja of Coorg, who was very ill. I declined doing so, unless I saw the patient. He then allowed me to see her. Her apartments are low, narrow, passage rooms, and she was lying on a mattress-bed on the floor, with a slave-girl using a hand-punkah over her. Her hair was unconfined, and loose over her shoulders. On the second visit I opened a large abscess on her right side, much to Jang's delight and the astonishment of his own two native doctors, who were present. On her being a little faint, I told them to give her a little water; while she drank it, I had to stand up in the sill of an open window, looking into the Court, so that my feet might not touch the mattress, or any part of the furniture directly or indirectly connected with her bed, although two minutes before there

---

[61] *Private Letters of Marquess of Dalhousie*, William Blackwood & Sons, London, 1910.

was no objection to my feeling her pulse, examining and lancing her side—a regular case of swallowing the camel and straining at the gnat![62]

Margaret Oldfield, wife of Dr Oldfield, gives an excellent account of Gangamma and life in Jung Bahadur's zenana, in this description of a royal wedding between Jung Bahadur's daughter and the Crown Prince of Nepal in 1857. She not only describes Princess Gangamma as the best-looking wife of Jung Bahadur but also mentions that she was an accomplished piano player.

> About 5 o'clock in the afternoon of 25 June 1857, a very handsome English-built close carriage (with a large gilt sun on it by way of a coat of arms) came to the Residency for Mrs. Byers and me...
>
> Jung Bahadur Rana asked us if we would allow him to introduce his wives to us, for, as there was no gentleman with us, he had no objection to their being seen. We, of course, were only too happy, and he went and brought out 4 of them. He led them up one by one, and introduced them to each of us separately, making them shake hands with us, and telling us what King's daughter each was. His favourite (who was also much the best looking) is the Coorg Rajah's daughter [Gangamma], whose sister [Gowramma] has become a Christian and is living in England. He then told the Maharanee, or principal wife, to lead Mrs. Byers by the hand, and the Coorg one to lead me to the Pianos. Monsieur Chavdon, who teaches them music then made his appearance, and these two Ranees began to play some polkas and waltzes for us, sometimes both pianos together, and sometimes separately.

---

[62]Oldfield, Henry Ambrose, *Sketches from Nipal*, Vol I, W.H. Allen & Co., London, 1880.

Jung placed us on chairs between his wives, so that while they were playing, we had a good look at their dress. The skirts (with no crinolines under) were a kind of brown net, so completely covered with gilt lace flowers that you could only see a *thread* or two of net, their bodies were tight velvet, of a dark red or purple colour, covered with gold lace, and they had a kind of thin gauze veil with gilt sprays on them, thrown about them in a native way. Their head-dresses were most costly, the hair was drawn tightly off the face, and hung down their backs in one thick, long plait. The Coorg Ranee wore a most lovely tiara of diamonds and emeralds, in the form of a large bunch of flowers, very like those belonging to the Queen of Spain in the Exhibition of 1851, but much more splendid. They all wore necklaces and bracelets of most beautiful diamonds, emeralds and pearls and well as their rings worn one on each finger *outside* a pair of white thread gloves, so when they played, each took off 10 superb rings... Jung himself was very pleasingly dressed... Jung then took us round the rooms, and showed us all his pictures of himself, his wives and brothers.[63]

Colonel Ramsey, the British Resident in Nepal, in a letter to his friend Sir John Login in 1860, expressed surprise after hearing news about Lady Lena Login's brother, Lieutenant Colonel John Campbell, having married Princess Victoria Gowramma in London.

...Pray offer my best regards to Lady Login. That is surely not a brother of hers [Lieutenant Colonel John Campbell] who married the Princess Gowramma of Coorg the other

---

[63]Ibid

day! Her sister [Princess Gangamma] who married Jung Bahadur some years ago, is now a very fine-looking young woman, and seems happy enough...[64]

I am thankful to my Facebook friend Subodh Shumsher Rana for some of the details of 'Ganga Maharani' (as Gangamma was known in Nepal). She was clearly one of Jung Bahadur's favourite wives. Unfortunately, there are no paintings or photographs of Gangamma, whose good looks have been mentioned by many who met her. I am sure more information and images of Gangamma remain unexplored in some archive or the other, waiting to be unearthed. There are no available records of Gangamma's descendants either.

---

[64]Ibid.

22

REDISCOVERING PRINCESS VICTORIA GOWRAMMA

My interest in Princess Victoria Gowramma was kindled after reading the Jnanpith Award-winning author Masti Venkatesha Iyengar's book *Chikka Veerarajendra*[65], first published in 1956. Though a work of historical fiction, the book has some tantalizing insights into the life and character of Chikka Veerarajendra, the last Raja of Coorg, and his daughter, Gowramma. (It was a matter of great joy for me when, in 2011, the granddaughter of Masti Venkatesha Iyengar, Dr V. Vasanthasree, requested me to write a brief note about Chikka Veerarajendra and Victoria Gowramma's life in Victorian England for the 10th edition of her grandfather's book).

Initially, I collected information about Gowramma, though not in detail, from Georg Richter's *Manual of Coorg* and D.N. Krishnayya's *Kodagina Ithihasa*. I also found the most insightful details on Gowramma's life in England from the book *Queen Victoria's Maharaja*[66] by Michael Alexander and Sushila Anand.

Since around 2000, I was hunting for three books written by people who had interacted closely with Veerarajendra,

---

[65]Iyengar Srinivasa, Masti Venkatesha, *Chikka Veerarajendra*, Masti Venkatesha Iyengar Jeevana Karyalaya Trust, 2011.
[66]Alexander, Michael and Sushila Anand, *Queen Victoria's Maharajah: Duleep Singh, 1838-93*, Phoenix Press, 1980.

Gowramma and Maharaja Duleep Singh. They were: *Private Letters of Marquess of Dalhousie, Lady Login's Recollections* and *Coorg & Its Rajahs*. Until 2008, I could not find these books in the libraries I visited in India. In 2008, while casually surfing the internet, I was absolutely amazed to find online versions of these three books, on a website called 'Internet Archive'[67], that were available for free download. The next major source of authentic information about Princess Gowramma, Maharaja Duleep and Chikka Veerarajendra was the archive of *The Times*, London.

Armed with these documents, I was able to reconstruct the life of Princess Gowramma right from her birth in 1841 to her demise in 1864. My book, *Victoria Gowramma: The Lost Princess of Coorg,* covers the parallel narrative of Maharaja Duleep's life along with that of Princess Gowramma. It was destiny that their lives should converge in the court of Queen Victoria. I added an epilogue in the new version of my book, with further details of Victoria Gowramma and her descendants. I am most grateful to Anne Phillips, the great great granddaughter of Lieutenant Colonel John Campbell, for her help and cooperation in this effort.

Collecting all this information and collating it to reconstruct the extraordinary life of Princess Gowramma of Coorg was a wonderful experience for me. The love and affection she received from Queen Victoria and her family was extraordinary. The Queen was uncharacteristically forgiving of some of Princess Gowramma's indiscretions. The importance the Queen gave to her goddaughter can be gauged from the press coverage I found in the archives of *The Times*, after subscribing to the newspaper. I have reproduced some of the important news clippings and

---

[67]Internet Archive, https://tinyurl.com/bdz5s776. Accessed on 10 February 2023.

court circulars pertaining to Princess Gowramma, Maharaja Duleep and Chikka Veerarajendra below.

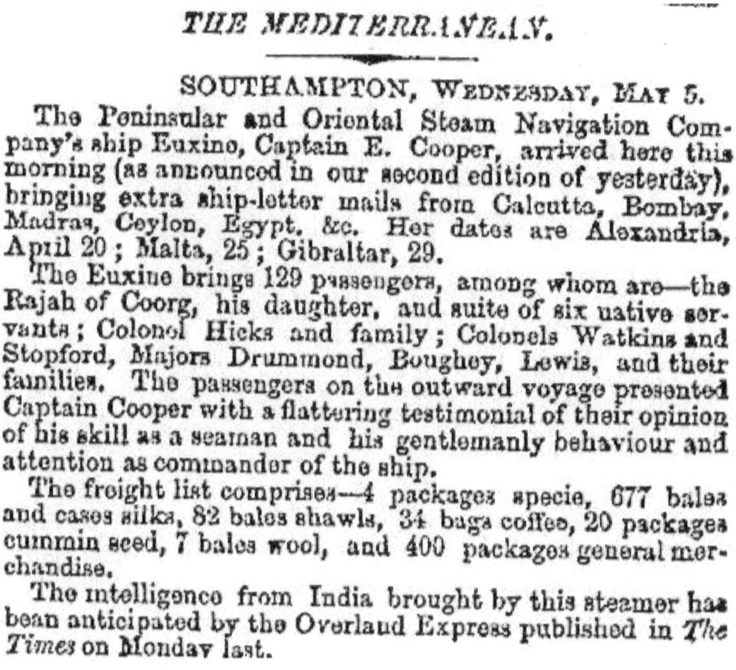

THE MEDITERRANEAN.

SOUTHAMPTON, WEDNESDAY, MAY 5.

The Peninsular and Oriental Steam Navigation Company's ship Euxine, Captain E. Cooper, arrived here this morning (as announced in our second edition of yesterday), bringing extra ship-letter mails from Calcutta, Bombay, Madras, Ceylon, Egypt, &c. Her dates are Alexandria, April 20; Malta, 25; Gibraltar, 29.

The Euxine brings 129 passengers, among whom are—the Rajah of Coorg, his daughter, and suite of six native servants; Colonel Hicks and family; Colonels Watkins and Stopford, Majors Drummond, Boughey, Lewis, and their families. The passengers on the outward voyage presented Captain Cooper with a flattering testimonial of their opinion of his skill as a seaman and his gentlemanly behaviour and attention as commander of the ship.

The freight list comprises—4 packages specie, 677 bales and cases silks, 82 bales shawls, 34 bags coffee, 20 packages cummin seed, 7 bales wool, and 400 packages general merchandise.

The intelligence from India brought by this steamer has been anticipated by the Overland Express published in *The Times* on Monday last.

Figure 41: An article describing the arrival of Veerarajendra and his daughter, Gowramma, at Southampton Port.

Source: 'The Mediterranean', *The Times*, 5 May 1852.

◆

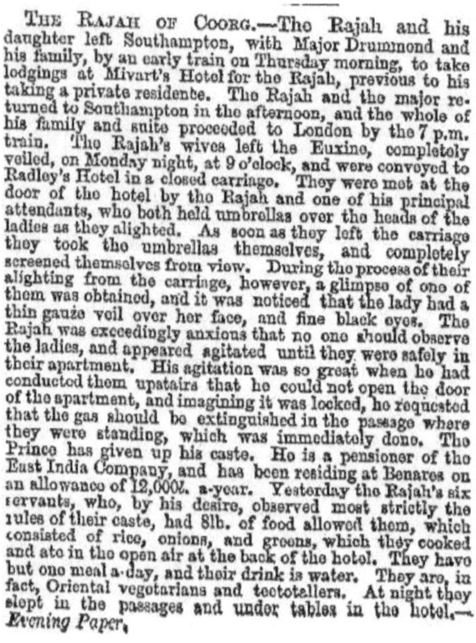

> THE RAJAH OF COORG.—The Rajah and his daughter left Southampton, with Major Drummond and his family, by an early train on Thursday morning, to take lodgings at Mivart's Hotel for the Rajah, previous to his taking a private residence. The Rajah and the major returned to Southampton in the afternoon, and the whole of his family and suite proceeded to London by the 7 p.m. train. The Rajah's wives left the Euxine, completely veiled, on Monday night, at 9 o'clock, and were conveyed to Radley's Hotel in a closed carriage. They were met at the door of the hotel by the Rajah and one of his principal attendants, who both held umbrellas over the heads of the ladies as they alighted. As soon as they left the carriage they took the umbrellas themselves, and completely screened themselves from view. During the process of their alighting from the carriage, however, a glimpse of one of them was obtained, and it was noticed that the lady had a thin gauze veil over her face, and fine black eyes. The Rajah was exceedingly anxious that no one should observe the ladies, and appeared agitated until they were safely in their apartment. His agitation was so great when he had conducted them upstairs that he could not open the door of the apartment, and imagining it was locked, he requested that the gas should be extinguished in the passage where they were standing, which was immediately done. The Prince has given up his caste. He is a pensioner of the East India Company, and has been residing at Benares on an allowance of 12,000l. a-year. Yesterday the Rajah's six servants, who, by his desire, observed most strictly the rules of their caste, had 8lb. of food allowed them, which consisted of rice, onions, and greens, which they cooked and ate in the open air at the back of the hotel. They have but one meal a-day, and their drink is water. They are, in fact, Oriental vegetarians and teetotallers. At night they slept in the passages and under tables in the hotel.—*Evening Paper.*

Figure 42: An article describing Veerarajendra and his family moving to Mivart's Hotel (renamed Claridge's Hotel) in London.

Source: 'The Rajah of Coorg', *The Times*, 6 May 1852.

◆

Rajah of Coorg accompanied by his daughter and an attendant, was presented to the Queen at an audience yesterday at Buckingham Palace by the Right Hon. J.C. Harries, President of the Board of Control for the Affairs of India.

> —Excerpt from an article describing Veerarajendra and Gowramma's meeting with the Queen.[68]

◆

---

[68]'Court Circular', *The Times*, 18 May 1852.

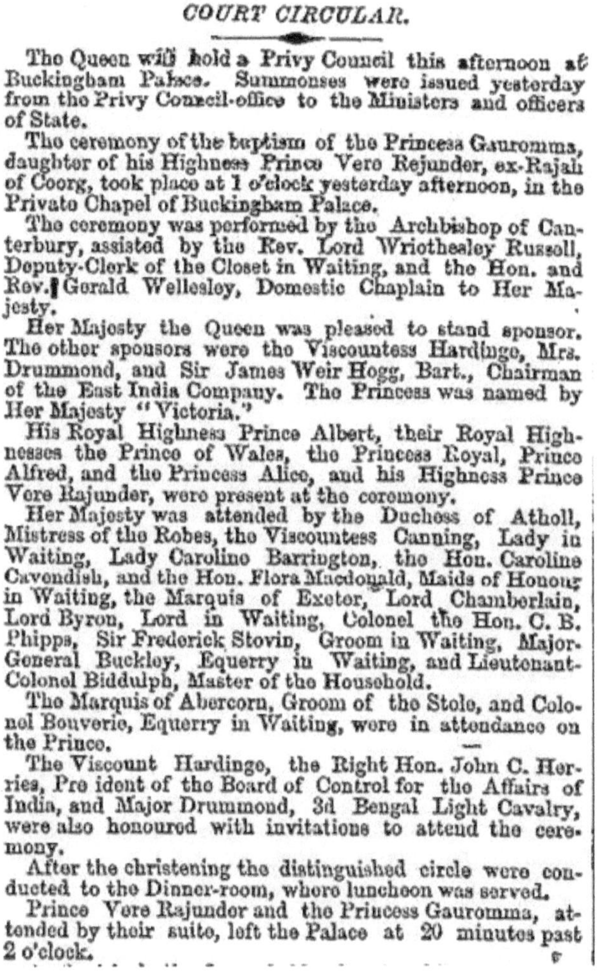

COURT CIRCULAR.

The Queen will hold a Privy Council this afternoon at Buckingham Palace. Summonses were issued yesterday from the Privy Council-office to the Ministers and officers of State.

The ceremony of the baptism of the Princess Gauromma, daughter of his Highness Prince Vero Rejunder, ex-Rajah of Coorg, took place at 1 o'clock yesterday afternoon, in the Private Chapel of Buckingham Palace.

The ceremony was performed by the Archbishop of Canterbury, assisted by the Rev. Lord Wriothesley Russell, Deputy-Clerk of the Closet in Waiting, and the Hon. and Rev. Gerald Wellesley, Domestic Chaplain to Her Majesty.

Her Majesty the Queen was pleased to stand sponsor. The other sponsors were the Viscountess Hardinge, Mrs. Drummond, and Sir James Weir Hogg, Bart., Chairman of the East India Company. The Princess was named by Her Majesty "Victoria."

His Royal Highness Prince Albert, their Royal Highnesses the Prince of Wales, the Princess Royal, Prince Alfred, and the Princess Alice, and his Highness Prince Vere Rajunder, were present at the ceremony.

Her Majesty was attended by the Duchess of Atholl, Mistress of the Robes, the Viscountess Canning, Lady in Waiting, Lady Caroline Barrington, the Hon. Caroline Cavendish, and the Hon. Flora Macdonald, Maids of Honour in Waiting, the Marquis of Exeter, Lord Chamberlain, Lord Byron, Lord in Waiting, Colonel the Hon. C. B. Phipps, Sir Frederick Stovin, Groom in Waiting, Major-General Buckley, Equerry in Waiting, and Lieutenant-Colonel Biddulph, Master of the Household.

The Marquis of Abercorn, Groom of the Stole, and Colonel Bouverie, Equerry in Waiting, were in attendance on the Prince.

The Viscount Hardinge, the Right Hon. John C. Herries, President of the Board of Control for the Affairs of India, and Major Drummond, 3d Bengal Light Cavalry, were also honoured with invitations to attend the ceremony.

After the christening the distinguished circle were conducted to the Dinner-room, where luncheon was served.

Prince Vere Rajunder and the Princess Gauromma, attended by their suite, left the Palace at 20 minutes past 2 o'clock.

Figure 43: An article describing Gowramma's baptism at the Buckingham Palace, London.

Source: 'Court Circular', *The Times*, 30 June 1852.

◆

The Rajah of Coorg and the son and grandson of the Great Tippo Saib were there, wearing dresses of truly Oriental magnificence.

—Excerpt from an article describing Her Majesty's Birthday.[69]

♦

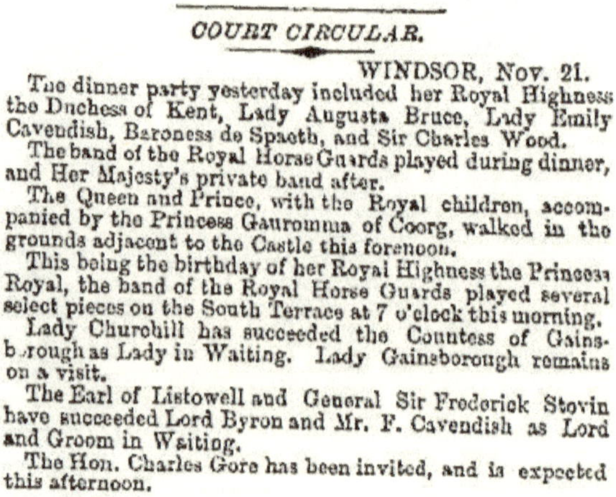

COURT CIRCULAR.

WINDSOR, Nov. 21.

The dinner party yesterday included her Royal Highness the Duchess of Kent, Lady Augusta Bruce, Lady Emily Cavendish, Baroness de Spaeth, and Sir Charles Wood.

The band of the Royal Horse Guards played during dinner, and Her Majesty's private band after.

The Queen and Prince, with the Royal children, accompanied by the Princess Gauromma of Coorg, walked in the grounds adjacent to the Castle this forenoon.

This being the birthday of her Royal Highness the Princess Royal, the band of the Royal Horse Guards played several select pieces on the South Terrace at 7 o'clock this morning.

Lady Churchill has succeeded the Countess of Gainsborough as Lady in Waiting. Lady Gainsborough remains on a visit.

The Earl of Listowell and General Sir Frederick Stovin have succeeded Lord Byron and Mr. F. Cavendish as Lord and Groom in Waiting.

The Hon. Charles Gore has been invited, and is expected this afternoon.

Figure 44: An article describing Victoria Gowramma at a dinner party with Queen Victoria and her children at Windsor Castle.

Source: 'Court Circular', *The Times*, 21 November 1854.

♦

The following visitors arrived in the afternoon—Princes Victoria Gauromma of Coorg and Mrs Drummond, General Count Alphonso Del La Marmora...

---

[69] *The Times*, 22 May 1854.

A dramatic performance took place at the Castle in the evening. Shakespeare's play, in five acts of the Merchant of Venice was selected...

About 8 o' clock Her Majesty the Queen and his Royal Highness the Prince entered St George's Hall accompanied by the Royal Highnesses the Prince of Wales, the Princess Royal, Prince Alfred, the Princess Alice, and other members of the Royal Family, the Royal Highness the Duchess of Kent, His Royal Highness the Duke of Cambridge, the Princess Victoria Gauromma of Coorg, the Alphonso Del La Marmora...

—Excerpt from an article describing Victoria Gowramma's visit to the Windsor Castle for a staging of Shakespeare's The Merchant of Venice.[70]

♦

The Princess Gauromma of Coorg visited Her Majesty and the Royal Princesses at Buckingham Palace...

—Excerpt from an article describing Victoria Gowramma's visit to the Buckingham Palace, London.[71]

♦

Court of Chancery, Lincoln's Inn, (Before the Lords Justices of Appeal)

Veer Rajundur Wadeer (Ex-Rajah of Coorg) vs the East India Company

The arguments in this appeal from an order of the Master of the Rolls, directing the production of documents admitted by

---

[70]'Court Circular', *The Times*, 25 January 1856.
[71]Ibid.

the answer of the Company to be in their possession relating to the matters in dispute in the cause, were resumed. The suit relates to a claim by the ex-Rajah of Coorg, as a creditor on the Company upon two promissory notes.

Mr Wigram, Mr Lloyd, and Mr Melville are for the East India Company, in support of the appeal; Mr Roundell Palmer and Mr A.J. Lewis are for the respondent, the plaintiff, sustaining the order of the Master of the Rolls.

The case is not yet concluded.

—Excerpt from an article about the court hearing of Veerarajendra's suit against the East India Company.[72]

◆

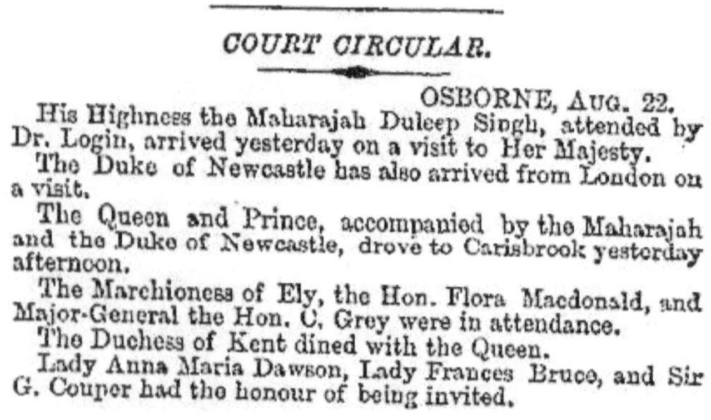

COURT CIRCULAR.

OSBORNE, AUG. 22.

His Highness the Maharajah Duleep Singh, attended by Dr. Login, arrived yesterday on a visit to Her Majesty.

The Duke of Newcastle has also arrived from London on a visit.

The Queen and Prince, accompanied by the Maharajah and the Duke of Newcastle, drove to Carisbrook yesterday afternoon.

The Marchioness of Ely, the Hon. Flora Macdonald, and Major-General the Hon. C. Grey were in attendance.

The Duchess of Kent dined with the Queen.

Lady Anna Maria Dawson, Lady Frances Bruce, and Sir G. Couper had the honour of being invited.

Figure 45: An article describing the arrival of Maharaja Duleep Singh in London. He soon became a favourite of the Queen and Prince Albert.

Source: 'Court Circular', *The Times*, 22 August 1854.

◆

---

[72]'Law Report', *The Times*, 14 March 1856.

The Princess Gauromma of Coorg visited the Royal Princesses at Buckingham Palace.
 The Queen had a dinner party in the evening...

> —Excerpt from an article describing Victoria Gowramma's visit to the Buckingham Palace, London.[73]

◆

We turn with greater interest to a marble bust of the Princess of Coorg in which the Baron has carried to a point much further than has yet been attempted the use of colour in sculpture. Not content to touch a few ornaments with colour, the artist has boldly painted the face, the hair, the dress to the life, using water colour of course, so that through this transparent medium the rich effect of the marble may not be lost [...] it must be pronounced eminently successful, and hereafter it will have strange historical interest in the Royal Collections. Perhaps part of the success is owing to the dark complexion of the Princess; but complexion has nothing to do with the eye, and we can conceive nothing finer than the eye as represented in this bust...

> —Excerpt from an article describing a painted marble bust of Victoria Gowramma by Baron Marochetti being displayed at the Crystal Palace Art Exhibition.[74]

◆

The Princess Gauromma of Coorg (attended by Mrs

---
[73]'Court Circular', *The Times*, 7 April 1856.
[74]*The Times*, 16 April 1856.

Drummond)...called during the day to learn the state of Her Majesty's health.

—Excerpt from an article describing Victoria Gowramma's visit to the Queen at the Buckingham Palace to see the newborn Princess Beatrice, the ninth child of the Queen.[75]

◆

The Rajah of Coorg...called during the day to learn the state of Her Majesty's health.

—Excerpt from an article describing Veerarajendra's visit to the Queen at the Buckingham Palace to see the infant Princess Beatrice.[76]

◆

Her Majesty gave a juvenile ball last evening. Invitations were issued to a party of 276 [...]

The Royal family were conducted to the White Drawing room where the Queen received her illustrious guests [...]

His Serene Highness Prince Edward of Saxe-Weimar and the Countess of Dornburg and the Princess Gauromma of Coorg were present [...]

Directly after the entrance of the Queen and Prince, and the Royal family into the Throne Saloon, the juveniles were formed into sets for dancing and the ball commenced [...]

—Excerpt from an article describing Victoria Gowramma being invited to a Royal Juvenile Ball at the Buckingham Palace.[77]

---

[75]'Court Circular', *The Times*, 16 April 1857.
[76]'Court Circular', *The Times*, 17 April 1857.
[77]'Court Circular', *The Times*, 26 April 1856.

◆

The Queen gave last evening a State Ball, to which a party of 1,900 were invited...

The following had the honour of receiving invitations [...] Maharajah Dhuleep Singh [...] the Princess Gauromma...

—Excerpt from an article describing Her Majesty's State Ball.[78]

◆

On the 24th inst., His Highness the Rajah of Coorg, at his residence at No. 20, Clifton Villas, Warwick-road, Maida-hill west.

—Excerpt of an article announcing the death of Chikka Veerarajendra.[79]

◆

On the 17th inst., at St George's Church, Hanover-square, the Princess Victoria Gauromma, daughter of the late Ex-Rajah of Coorg, to Lieut. Colonel John Campbell, of Her Majesty's Indian Army.

—Excerpt from an article announcing the marriage of Victoria Gowramma.[80]

◆

---

[78] *The Times*, 9 June 1859.
[79] *The Times*, 24 August 1859.
[80] *The Times*, 17 July 1860.

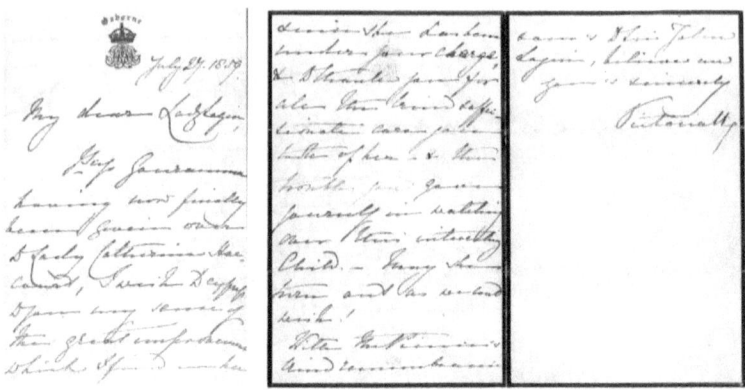

Figure 46: Queen Victoria's letter to Lady Login, dated 24 July 1859, in appreciation of her being Gowramma's guardian.

Courtesy: Anne Phillips

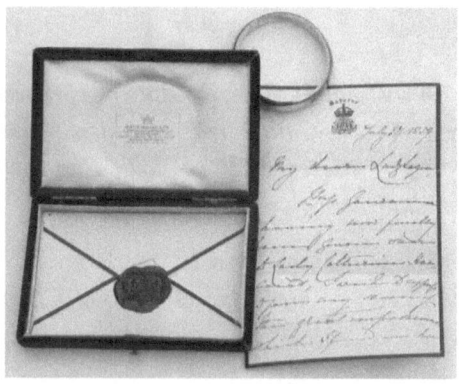

Figure 47: Queen Victoria's gifts to Lady Login in 1859, in appreciation of her being Gowramma's guardian.

Courtesy: Anne Phillips

PART III
FREEDOM, INDEPENDENCE AND MERGER

23

THE FREEDOM MOVEMENT IN COORG[81]

After the annexation of Coorg by the British in 1834, the people in the province experienced peace and stability for the first time in its turbulent history, albeit under an alien rule. The British improved the economy of the region with better infrastructure, establishment of educational institutions and introduction of coffee cultivation. There was all-round progress and the common man enjoyed much more freedom compared to what had existed during the rule of the rajas. For nearly 75 years after the takeover, the British administered Coorg without any resistance from the local populace.

In 1909, an organization named 'Jamindars' Society' was founded by Rao Bahadur Codanda Madaiah and Biddanda Ganapathy to advise the British Government on issues relevant to the people of Coorg.[82] In 1912, this society was renamed Jamindars' Sangha. Soon, the membership of this society swelled, and it became an influential voice of the people.

In 1921, the idea to start a newspaper in Coorg took seed. Most of the leading members of Jamindars' Sangha pooled

---

[81]This essay is based on information from two books: Ganapathy, B.D., *Swathantra Horata: Kodagina Kathe*, Kodagu Press, 1965; Ramachandrachar, D.B., *Avakashada Allegala Mele*, Sunanda Prakasana, 1990. Even though many people from Coorg have participated in the freedom movement, I could not include all their names.

[82]Ganapathy, B.D., *Swathantra Horata: Kodagina Kathe*, Kodagu Press, 1965.

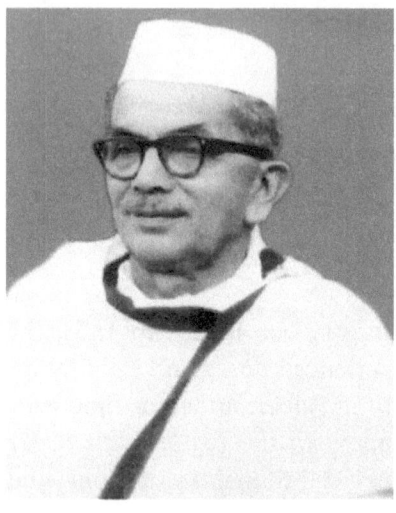

Figure 48: Pandyanda Belliappa
Courtesy: Vijay Belliappa

their resources to start the Kannada newspaper *Kodagu*.[83] Well-known Gandhian, Pandyanda Belliappa (popularly known as Kodagu Gandhi), who was one of the prominent individuals in the freedom struggle in Coorg, was its first editor. *Kodagu* soon became popular and substantially boosted the increasing awareness among people of their rights. The growing national movement to free the country from colonial rule was effectively represented through this publication.

Sensing the rapid build-up of the freedom movement in India, the British tried to placate the locals by involving them in the administration in an advisory capacity. The first Legislative Assembly in Coorg, with 24 members, was formed in 1924, headed by Chief Commissioner William Pell Barton[84].

Ketolira Chengappa was the district magistrate. Palecanda Medappa and Pandyanda Belliappa were members. Years later, Medappa, as the sub-judge, awarded prison terms to several freedom fighters, including Belliappa and my father Chepudira M. Poonacha. Medappa became the Chief Justice of Mysore in 1948.

---

[83]Ibid.

[84]'William Pell Barton', People Pill, https://tinyurl.com/2p9btu9b. Accessed on 11 February 2023.

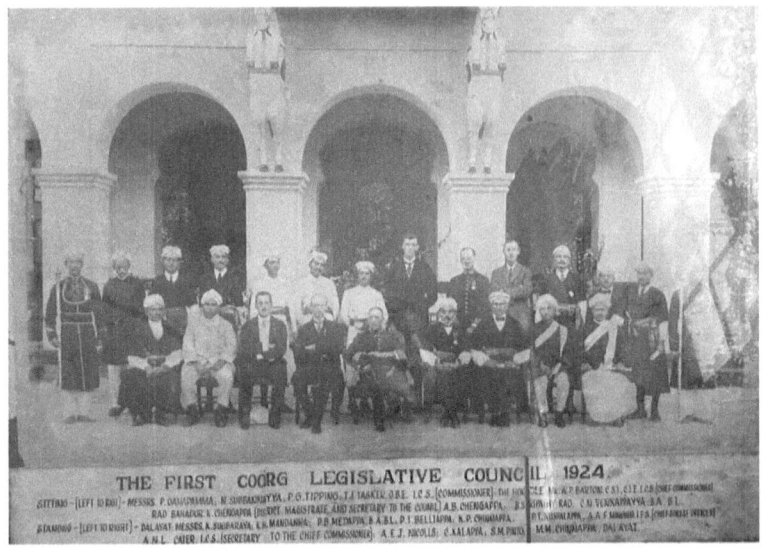

Figure 49: Members of the Legislative Assembly of Coorg. Pictured here (sitting fifth from left) are the Chief Commissioner Barton and Ketolira M. Chengappa. In the row behind them (starting third from the left) are Palecanda B. Medappa and Pandyanda Belliappa.

Courtesy: Kollimada Ajit Aiyappa

Jamindars' Sangha laid the foundation for the Indian National Congress to take roots in Coorg[85]. The Congress session presided over by Mahatma Gandhi at Belgaum in 1924 was attended by 35 members from Coorg. Inspired by this meeting, the Kodagu Zilla Congress Committee was formed on 4 January 1925, with Paruvangada Kushalappa, a popular leader, as the president. C.N. Venkappaiah was named the honorary secretary and M.M. Siddique the treasurer. In February 1925, a Khadi Bhandar was opened in Virajpet. People enthusiastically took to spinning cotton using *charkhas* supplied by the Congress.

---

[85]Ganapathy, B.D., *Swathantra Horata: Kodagina Kathe*, Kodagu Press, 1965.

Jamindars' Sangha, the *Kodagu* newspaper and the Congress together spread the message of self-rule among the people of Coorg.

Sadly, Paruvangada Kushalappa died suddenly in 1928, at the age of 38, on his way back from a Congress session at Calcutta, where he had been one of the delegates from Coorg. In his memory, a large open area was named Kushalpura in Ponnampet (next to present day Kodava Samaja). Ajjikuttira S. Chinnappa and Mallegada Chengappa were the first to hoist the national flag at this venue on 26 May 1929.[86]

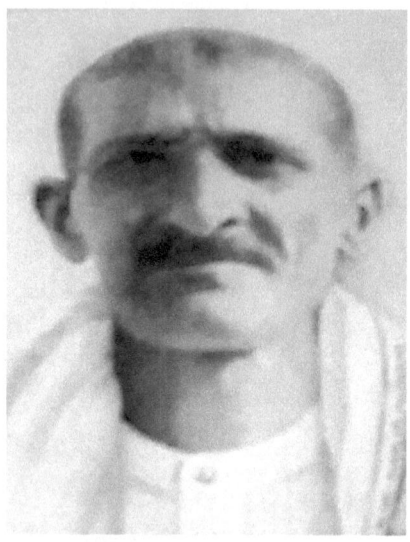

Figure 50: Kollimada Carumbaiah
Courtesy: Kollimada Ajit Aiyappa

On 26 January 1930, 'Poorna Swaraj' was declared by the Congress. At a public meeting in Gonikoppal, C.N. Venkappaiah, Kotera P. Chinnappa, Kollimada Carumbaiah (see figure 50) and Machimanda Muthanna spoke. Many senior leaders from Karnataka Congress such as Alur Venkata Rao, Ranganath Diwakar and Kamaladevi Chattopadhyay started visiting Coorg to motivate local leaders. Littérateurs like D.R. Bendre, K.V. Puttappa, Masti Venkatesha Iyengar and D.V. Gundappa also frequently visited Coorg to motivate people to fight for freedom.

Bhajans and *Harikathas* were organized in villages to spread

---

[86]Ibid.

Indian culture and heritage. The well-known exponent of Harikatha—Belur Keshavdas—visited Coorg, and his rendering of stories from the epics enthralled people and made them feel patriotic. The British government was rattled by these activities. For the first time, Section 144 was imposed in Coorg, and Keshavdas was barred from conducting Harikathas.

Imported goods were boycotted and protest rallies were held against the sale of alcohol. In 1930, under the leadership of Pandyanda Belliappa, the government was given an ultimatum to shut down the liquor shops in Coorg. When this was not heeded, on 10 June 1930, a large number of activists picketed peacefully in front of liquor shops at Ponnampet. Soon, similar protests were staged in other towns and villages. Liquor sales dropped, affecting the government's revenue.

Around this time, the women in Coorg decided to enter the freedom struggle and support their male counterparts. Among the women to take the initiative were Kotera Accavva and Pandyanda Seetha Belliappa and many women followed. On 30 May 1930, an impressive rally was held by the women in Madikeri. It included two of the well-known Codanda Sisters of Coorg—Chitra and Lata. The sisters gave up their education and became *satyagrahis*. It was during this time that 18-year-old Kavery, daughter of Kolera Cariappa, asked her father for permission to take part in the proposed picketing at Hudikeri on 15 September 1930. She was heartbroken when her father refused. Kavery, filled with intense patriotism, could not bear the disappointment. The following day, she died by suicide by jumping in a lake nearby.

While protest rallies against liquor sales and the rejection of imported goods intensified, the Swadeshi movement was receiving widespread support. On 20 September 1930, satyagrahis were arrested for the first time in Coorg. Prominent among the freedom fighters who courted arrest were Pandyanda Belliappa,

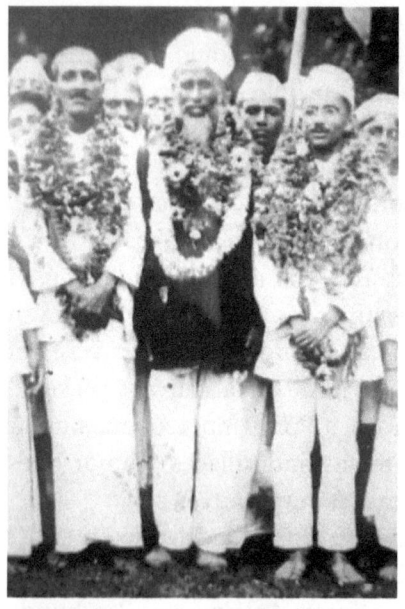

Figure 51: The freedom fighters Kollimada Carumbaiah, Abdul Gafoor Khan and Pandyanda Belliappa after being released from their prison sentence in 1930. Courtesy: Kollimada Ajit Aiyappa

Kollimada Carumbaiah, H.R. Krishnaiah, Iynanda Cariappa, Cheriyappanda Kushalappa and Abdul Gaffoor Khan. In addition, the newspaper *Kodagu* was brought under press ordinance because of which publication had to be stopped till a caution deposit of ₹1,000 (a large sum in those days) was paid to the government. All these measures spurred the citizens to protest the British rule with renewed vigour. Kollimada Carumbaiah, Abdul Gaffoor Khan, Pandyanda Belliappa (figure 51), and other leaders were given a hero's welcome upon their release from Kannur jail after serving their prison term.

An increasing number of young men and women were inspired to join the struggle in response to calls by Mahatma Gandhi and the local leaders. One of those who discontinued their studies to join the freedom movement was my father, 22-year-old C.M. Poonacha from Gonikoppal. It is said that though the population of Coorg at the time was around 200,000, the percentage of freedom fighters from the province was the highest in the country.

Some of the young satyagrahis took more proactive steps

to register their determination to end foreign rule. On 17 December 1930, three brave young men, Mallengada Chengappa, B.G. Ganapaiah and Mandepanda Cariappa, walked into Madikeri Fort, boldly removed the Union Jack and hoisted the Indian national flag. They happily courted arrest for their patriotic act.

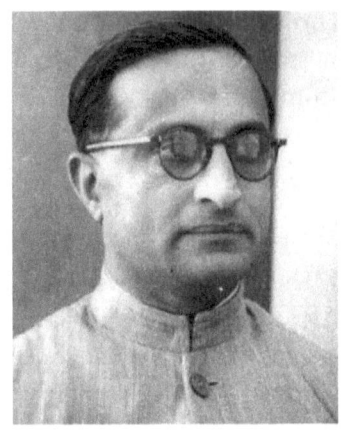

Figure 52: C.M. Poonacha
Source: Author's collection

On 7 January 1932, Section 144 was imposed across Coorg. Holding rallies was banned for a month. Defying this ban, on 10 January 1932, a huge public meeting was held at Gonikoppal. Pandyanda Belliappa and Ajjikuttira Chinnappa addressed the satyagrahis. Many leaders were arrested and had to serve sentences ranging from six to nine months in Kannur prison. On 27 January 1932, women satyagrahis: Pandyanda Seetha Belliappa, Baliyatanda Muddavva and Mukkatira Bojamma were arrested for distributing pamphlets to the public. Pandyanda Seetha Belliappa bravely carried her two young daughters aged six months and two years, respectively, as she walked into the jail. Notices were issued to many leaders, including Pandyanda Belliappa, Kollimada Carumbaiah, Iynanda Cariappa, Cheriappanda Kushalappa, Ajjikuttira Chinnappa, C.M. Poonacha, and Abdul Gaffoor Khan, banning them from picketing or making public speeches.

My father participated enthusiastically in the freedom movement. Seeing his commitment and flair for writing, the senior leaders gave him the task of composing, cyclostyling and distributing the underground publication—*Veerabharati*—to spread the message of independence. He did this clandestinely from his estate near Gonikoppal. The police extensively searched the area to locate the source of *Veerabharati*. When the cyclostyling machine was finally discovered, Poonacha was sentenced to nine months of rigorous imprisonment in Kannur.

In 1934, leaders of the Satyagraha movement requested Mahatma Gandhi to visit Coorg. He toured Coorg from 21 to 23 February and was impressed by the intensity of the freedom struggle in this picturesque hilly region. His visit to Coorg gave a huge fillip to the movement. Many women volunteered to donate their jewellery to the Mahatma to be used for the freedom of the country and the betterment of the downtrodden.

During his visit, Mahatma Gandhi stayed at the Ramakrishna Sevashrama in Ponnampet, where Swami Shambavanandaji (who belonged to the Thelapanda family) was the president. The Mahatma was enthusiastically greeted wherever he toured in Coorg. Gundukutti Manjunathayya, one of the leading coffee planters in Coorg and a freedom fighter, personally drove the Mahatma during his tour. The latter stopped over at Manjunathayya's residence at Sunticoppa, where a large number of his admirers had gathered. In figure 53, Mahatma Gandhi can be seen addressing a gathering from the balcony of Gundukutti Manjunathayya's house. It was here that the well-known feminist and author Kodagina Gowramma donated all her jewellery to the Mahatma.

With the Second World War breaking out in 1939, there was a lull in the Satyagraha movement all over the nation. Mahatma Gandhi, however, continued the call for independence on the principle of non-violence. His philosophy of *ahimsa* was spontaneously accepted by the satyagrahis in Coorg as well. Satyagraha Samithis were founded across Coorg. On 11 May

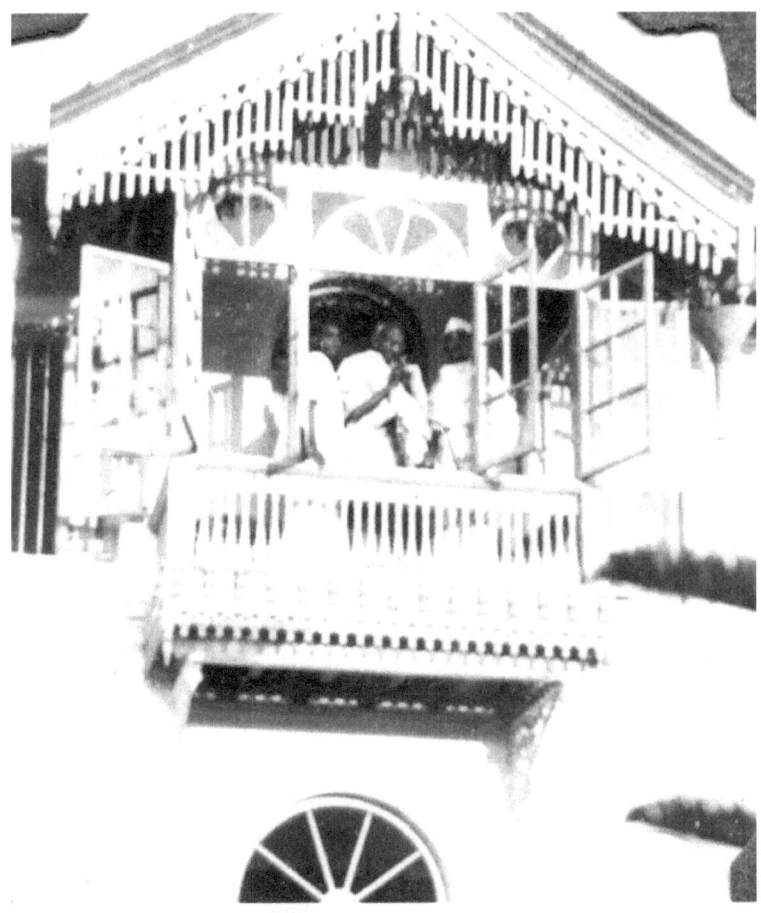

Figure 53: Mahatma Gandhi at Manjunathayya's house during his visit to Coorg in 1936.

Courtesy: Bose and Swathi Mandanna

1940, the first Satyagraha training centre was started in Virajpet.

On 8 August 1942, Mahatma Gandhi gave the movement the historic call: 'Quit India'. This had an electrifying effect on the nation. Freedom fighters in Coorg enthusiastically responded to Gandhi's call. Many leaders in Coorg, such as Pandyanda Belliappa, Kollera Karumbaiah, Chekkera Monnaiah, Kollimada Carumbaiah, Ajjikuttira Chinnappa, Kakamada Nanaiah, Chekkera Machaiah, Cheriappanda Kushalappa and others, were arrested. Poonacha was in Bombay to participate in the All India Congress Committee meeting held at Gowalia Tank Maidan (later named August Kranti Maidan), where Mahatma Gandhi made his famous 'Quit India' speech. Poonacha was arrested on 14 August 1942, upon returning to Coorg. Several students actively participated in the Quit India movement, including prominent student leaders like Ajjikuttira Appanna, Paruvangada Uthappa, Malachira Muthanna (who later became the director of the Indian Institute of Technology, Kanpur), Codanda Devaiah, Manepanda Chinnappa and Karthamada Subayya.

The long-cherished dream for freedom was finally realized on 15 August 1947. Houses were decorated all over Coorg and lamps were lit to usher in freedom at midnight. The then Chief Commissioner, Ketolira Chengappa, lowered the Union Jack and hoisted the Indian national flag at Madikeri Fort. Students took out celebratory processions in Madikeri and other towns. Senior leaders Pandyanda Belliappa and Kollimada Carumbaiah addressed the rejoicing crowds. Poonacha was in the Central Hall of the Parliament in Delhi as a member of the Constituent Assembly of India when Jawaharlal Nehru made his momentous 'Tryst with Destiny' speech.

24

C.M. POONACHA'S ROLE IN THE FREEDOM MOVEMENT[87]

As a student, my father C.M. Poonacha's ambition was to be a doctor. He was good at his studies, and in the SSLC board examination (circa 1928), he fared well, qualifing for the Imperial Scholarship worth ₹15.

As a 19-year-old, Poonacha enrolled in St Aloysius College in Mangalore for his intermediate course. While his goal to be a doctor was steadfast, the infectious fervour of the freedom movement deeply influenced him. In 1930, Mahatma Gandhi inspired and urged students to come out in large numbers to show their solidarity with the freedom fighters. Young Poonacha spontaneously joined a group of students and participated in a street demonstration. The principal of the institution was upset. Word spread that serious action was being contemplated against those who had hurt the reputation of the college.

That night, Poonacha made a radical, life-changing decision. The desire to rid the country of colonial rule replaced his ambition to be a doctor. He decided to give up his studies and resolved to join the struggle to free the nation of the foreign yoke. The following day, with a heavy heart, early in the morning,

---

[87]This is a personal history of my father as narrated by him and recorded in the following book about him: Ramachandrachar, D.B., *Avakashada Allegala Mele*, Sunanda Prakasana, 1990.

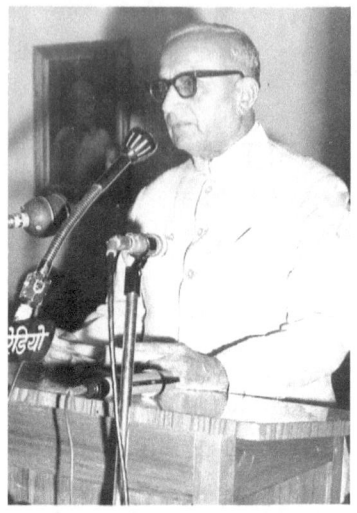

Figure 54: C.M. Poonacha
Source: Author's collection

he walked out of St Aloysius College forever. Before leaving, he stood in front of the gates of his alma mater and bowed deeply. He bid farewell to all the dreams he and his parents had had for his future. His parents were shocked to see him back home and were appalled at the drastic decision their son had taken.

Some of his young friends and contemporaries had already been active in the freedom movement in Coorg. He enthusiastically participated in various activities with Ajjikuttira Chinnappa, Mallengada Chengappa, Chekkera Monnaiah, Cheriappanda Kushalappa, Kakkamada Nanaiah, Kuppanda Muddappa and Chekkera Machaiah. One of the senior members of the Congress, Kollimada Carumbaiah, noticed the youngster's eagerness and started giving him tasks, particularly spreading awareness among Dalits about the ill-effects of alcohol consumption. Poonacha was soon given full charge of a Dalit colony in Kaikeri village, which was close to his home. When Mahatma Gandhi visited Coorg in 1934, Poonacha showed him around the colony. The Mahatma was impressed by the efforts in Coorg to improve the overall conditions of Dalits.

After the Salt March, the freedom movement gained further momentum across the country. In early 1933, Poonacha, along with a few of his friends, took a group of Dalits to Madikeri and led them in a protest march, violating government orders.

He was arrested and brought before the sub-judge, Palecanda Medappa, at Madikeri. Justice Medappa was a close relative of the family summoned Chepudira Muthanna, Poonacha's worried father, to his chambers. The judge instructed Muthanna to advise Poonacha to stop participating in unlawful activities. A stern Justice Medappa granted bail on the condition that Poonacha appear before him 10 days later and plead 'guilty'. He assured the young rebel that only then would he be let off with a warning.

During the next 10 days, a stoic Poonacha was repeatedly and vehemently instructed by his parents and relatives to renounce the freedom movement. He was ordered to plead guilty to avoid being jailed. On the day of the hearing at Madikeri, Poonacha was brought before the judge and his 'crime' was read out. Justice Medappa's piercing stared over his reading glasses and asked, 'Poonacha, do you plead guilty to the charges levelled against you?'

Poonacha took a while before responding in a clear and unambiguous tone, 'I am not guilty.'

A visibly upset Justice Medappa brought the gavel down and thundered, 'The offender is sentenced to four months imprisonment.'

Along with Poonacha, his friends Iynanda Cariappa and Jammada Medappa received a similar punishment and were sent to the Central Jail at Kannur. There, the youngsters from Coorg had the opportunity to meet Kamal Nath Tiwari, a charismatic revolutionary and one of the associates of Bhagat Singh, who was later hanged for killing a young British policeman. Tiwari spoke at length about the atrocities of the British against Indians, including the horrendous Jallianwala Bagh massacre of 1919. This further consolidated Poonacha and his friends' resolve to continue fighting for freedom.

After enduring the substandard prison food for a month, Poonacha protested. Seen as a troublemaker, he was promptly transferred to Vellore jail. Poonacha found himself in the company of several stalwarts of the freedom movement there—C. Rajagopalachari, Kumaraswami Kamaraj Nadar, E.M.S. Namboodripad, Tanguturi Prakasam, S. Satyamurthy and L.S. Prabhu. Listening to these scholarly leaders was a boon to several young freedom fighters like Poonacha. This was a rare opportunity to learn from the intellectuals and nationalists of the time.

On the day Poonacha was to be freed after having completed his prison term, L.S. Prabhu wanted him to smuggle out a detailed report that he had compiled about the indifferent way in which the freedom fighters were being treated in the cells, the appalling conditions, lack of medical care and the deteriorating health of some of the elder inmates. Prabhu pinned the report on Poonacha's shawl and draped himself in it as he came to see his cellmate off. After a thorough check by the guards, Poonacha was about to step out of the prison gate. Just then, Prabhu shouted, 'Poonacha, you have forgotten your shawl.' He then threw the shawl towards Poonacha in front of the unsuspecting guards. A few days later, one of the national newspapers carried the full report by Prabhu, much to the chagrin of the jailers.

Upon returning to Coorg, Poonacha plunged into the activities of the Congress. In 1932–33, he was appointed secretary of Kodagu Congress Samithi. As mentioned earlier, around this period, the party purchased a portable cyclostyling (printing) machine and Poonacha was tasked with writing, typing, cyclostyling and distributing a mouthpiece of the party. Initially, the underground publication was assertively named *Sarpastra* (slayer of enemies). Poonacha hid the machine deep in his coffee estate. Once a week, he would secretly print about

100 copies of the newsletter containing fiery articles against the British. He would fasten the bundle onto his bicycle and set out to Virajpet around 4.00 a.m. At Virajpet, his lawyer friend Ramamurthy school-going brother, Mariappa, would collect the bundle from Poonacha and hide the copies in the desks of students. These students would then distribute the *Sarpastra* to people in their respective villages and neighbourhoods—an excellent example of how local networks of all ages were utilized simply and effectively in the movement. *Sarpastra* soon became a popular newsletter, eagerly awaited by the people. It not only kept the freedom movement alive in Coorg but also prompted many to join the struggle. After six months, the newsletter was renamed *Veerabharati*.

The police could not trace the origin of the publication. They suspected Pandyanda Belliappa, the editor of *Kodagu*, and raided his office and home. The homes of Bairettira Chengappa, Jammada Madappa, Machimanda Nanjunda, Iynanda Cariappa, Mandepanda Somaiah and Chepudira Poonacha were also raided. The printing machine could not be located and *Veerabharati* continued to be printed and distributed like clockwork. This covert activity continued undetected for nearly two years.

One day, Poonacha, after working late into the night to get copies of *Veerabharati* ready, set out for Virajpet in the early hours of the morning. As usual, the bundle was strapped to his bicycle. By the time he reached Ammathi, the sun was rising over the horizon. As he raced down the slope after Ammathi towards Virajpet, the bundle came undone, and the 100-odd copies were strewn across the road. As Poonacha got on all fours, hurriedly collecting the newsletter, he felt a presence next to him. When he looked up, he saw a uniformed policeman with a baton in hand. Poonacha flinched, anticipating the baton to come down on him with brutal force. Instead, the policeman knelt next to him and joined him in retrieving copies of the newsletter. It was Constable Ganapathy, who looked at the young man and said, 'So Poonacha, you are behind *Sarpastra*. I am just getting back from the night beat. Now, hurry up and disappear from here before anyone else sees you. I have not seen you.' Relieved, Poonacha peddled his cycle furiously towards Virajpet.

Poonacha continued this covert task for another month or so—leading a charmed life on the outside. Under pressure from the British administration, the local police were frantically looking for the 'culprits' behind the publication. Considering this, the Congress leaders thought it would be prudent to shift the machine to another location. So, it was packed in a gunny bag and Mandepanda Cariappa was given the job of transporting it by bus to Virajpet. As luck would have it, the police were conducting spot checks on the bus and wanted to inspect the contents of Cariappa's gunny bag. The cat was literally out of the bag. The bag also contained some incriminating clues that revealed Poonacha's involvement. He was arrested and the munsiff at Virajpet sentenced him to nine months rigorous imprisonment at Kannur jail. After this revelation, the police started referring to Poonacha as *Sarpastra* Poonacha.

A British officer was in charge of Kannur jail. Recently posted from Bellary, he had a reputation for nastiness and sadism. He had confronted Poonacha's uncle, Barrister Chepudira Machayya, at Bellary, and since discovering their relationship, he had held a vendetta against Poonacha. The most backbreaking tasks in the jail were reserved for Poonacha. After a couple of days, Poonacha refused to obey the jailer point-blank. About 60 other detainees joined in the protest and tried to impress upon the warden that they were not criminals but political prisoners.

The enraged warden inflicted painful punishments, known as the 'standing handcuff', on the protesters. At 6.00 a.m., after a breakfast of gruel, the protesters were handcuffed and their legs were bound. They were then made to stand with their hands stretched above their heads. After a short break for lunch, the gruelling punishment was resumed until 5.00 p.m. Others from Coorg who were also subjected to this punishment, along with Poonacha, were Chekkera Monnaiah, Poojarira Ramappa and Mallengada Chengappa. When one of them collapsed, a doctor was called in. The doctor warned the warden that if the punishment was continued, the detainees were at risk of heart attacks and that the jailer would be in serious trouble. The brutal punishment was stopped after 15 days. The warden had failed to break the spirit of the freedom fighters.

The jailer did not give up on his determination to demoralize the detainees. He subjected them to another punishment known as the '24-hour lock up', which involved locking up about a dozen freedom fighters in a small, poorly lit room for 24 hours. They were let out only for their meals. Far from being despondent, the prisoners used this time to learn each other's languages. Poonacha learnt to read and write Malayalam. Even after 15 days of this inhumane treatment, the enraged jailer realized that Poonacha, Monnaiah and Ramappa were sniggering at him. Subsequently, they were thrown into solitary confinement for 15 days. This was a truly traumatic experience for Poonacha. His unlit cell was next to prisoners who were on death row. The condemned prisoners would be informed of their execution a few days earlier. Their agonized agitation as the dark day approached was heart-rending. Poonacha could barely sleep under these horrific conditions.

This is how Poonacha spent nine months—without tasting anything sweet, without soap for bathing and with just two pairs of prison clothes to wear. Like thousands of young freedom fighters across the country who experienced similar hardship, it toughened Poonacha both mentally and physically. After this, he was ready to face any challenge that life threw at him.

Upon returning to Coorg, he continued to work for the Congress. His aging parents now wanted him to devote more time to developing their property. Having shed all qualms about physical work, he worked alongside the labourers. In a couple of years, he started cultivating coffee and oranges on their uncultivated lands.

Sometime in 1935, two of the senior Congress leaders, Kollimada Carumbaiah and Jammada Madappa, met Poonacha's parents and requested them to allow their son, who had good writing skills, to work as the sub-editor of *Kodagu* under Belliappa. This meant that Poonacha had to spend more time in Madikeri. He occupied a room in 'Crystal Palace' built by his grandfather, Subedar Thimayya, and received a monthly salary of ₹30.

In 1938, Pandit Jawaharlal Nehru was visiting Mangalore. Poonacha was deputed to meet Nehru and invite him to Coorg. As a 28-year-old, he was excited at the prospect of meeting one of the most prominent leaders in the freedom movement. He sought Kamaladevi Chattopadhyay's help for an interview with Nehru. Kamaladevi, a pioneer in her own right, used to frequently visit Coorg and Poonacha knew her well. She was in charge of Nehru's programmes in Mangalore. Finally, a window of opportunity was arranged for Poonacha to sit with Nehru while he travelled by car. However, Nehru expressed his inability to make the trip to Coorg. Nonetheless, Poonacha went on to have many meetings with Nehru.

Around this time, Poonacha was selected as a member of the Karnataka Pradesh Congress Committee. In 1938, elections were announced for the 24-member Coorg Advisory Board. Congress leaders in Coorg were in a dilemma about whether they should be a part of this board, since it would only function in an advisory capacity to the British Chief Commissioner as it had since 1924.[88] To clarify this doubt Belliappa and Poonacha were deputed to seek counsel from Mahatma Gandhi at Vardha. The day of the meeting coincided with the day the Mahatma observed strict silence—*maun vrat*. However, the great man patiently listened to them. He then wrote on a piece of paper, 'Adopt any peaceful means that will enable you to serve the people.'

Upon returning to Coorg, Congress leaders decided to participate in the elections for the Coorg Advisory Board. Poonacha wanted to contest from Ponnampet in South Coorg, where he was popular. Despite making this request a number of times, the seniors in the party instructed him to stand for the seat from Madikeri. Poonacha lost the election. He was deeply disappointed. This was the beginning of rivalry within the Congress in Coorg.

Poonacha resigned from the position of sub-editor of *Kodagu* in 1939 and the noted writer B.D. Ganapathy took his place. In response to Mahatma Gandhi's call, Poonacha continued in the freedom movement as a sworn satyagrahi. In 1941, he participated in a demonstration in Madikeri against British policies, especially against involving Indian soldiers in the war. He was arrested along with other satyagrahis like Pandyanda Belliappa, Biddanda Cariappa, Korana Devaiah and Kollimada Carumbaiah. They were sentenced to four months of detention at Tiruchirappalli. This detention was different from earlier imprisonments—Satyagrahis were treated as political prisoners and were classified as Class 'A' and Class 'B' detainees. All the detainees from Coorg fell under the latter category. Within the

---

[88]Ramachandrachar, D.B., *Avakashada Allegala Mele*, Sunanda Prakasana, 1990.

detention camp, satyagrahis were free to move about and wear their own clothes. They were provided better food and reading materials. Most importantly, they were allowed to have group discussions and educational discourses.

For young satyagrahis like Poonacha, these detentions provided an opportunity to further their stalled education. There were several well-known intellectuals among the political prisoners, including stalwarts like C. Rajagopalachari, K. Santhanam, N.G. Ranga, V.V. Giri, Bezawada Gopala Reddy, Kumaraswami Kamaraj Nadar, Neelam Sanjiva Reddy, U. Srinivas Mallya, A.B. Shetty and R. Venkataraman. The highlight of every evening was C. Rajagopalachari's evening talk. He spoke eloquently on a variety of subjects, including Indian epics, Shakespeare and history. Rajagopalachari succeeded Louis Lord Mountbatten as the first Indian viceroy of India. V.V. Giri, who became the president of India years later, took classes on constitutional law. R. Venkataraman, who also became the president of India, delivered lectures on economics. They had group discussions and debates. Poonacha became good friends with Neelam Sanjiva Reddy, another future president of India. Poonacha used the detention to learn to speak, read and write Hindi and cleared the Rastrabasha examination. During one of his jail terms, Acharya Vinoba Bhave was in the same detention camp. Bhave delivered discourses on the Gita and the Upanishads. My father used to tell us that though he did not have a formal university degree, he got an equivalent or even a superior education from the intellectual giants of the time while he was in prison as a freedom fighter.

Upon returning from Tiruchirappalli jail, Poonacha's worried parents insisted that he marry and settle down. In May 1941, he married Gangamma from the Biddanda family. Subsequently, he started spending more time improving his agricultural property.

There was a brief lull in the freedom movement because of the Second World War.

In August 1942, as a member of the All India Congress Committee (AICC), he travelled to Bombay, where Mahatma Gandhi was to preside over the meeting at Gowalia Tank Maidan. On 8 August 1942, Mahatma Gandhi issued a momentous ultimatum to the British: Quit India. This terse call captured the national mood perfectly. It became a rallying cry that reverberated throughout the country. This historic venue is now known as the August Kranti Maidan. The entire country rose in unison to this clarion call from the Mahatma. In response, the British started arresting leaders of the Congress all over the country.

Most of the leaders of the Congress, including Belliappa, were arrested in Coorg. The police were also searching for Poonacha, but he was still away in Bombay. As a relatively junior member of the AICC, he could not be identified and arrested by the police in Bombay. At this time, some of the senior leaders of the party from Karnataka needed to send sensitive documents from Bombay to the Karnataka Congress Headquarters in Dharwad. Since they were sure to be arrested by the following morning, they identified Poonacha as the ideal person to covertly transport these documents.

Poonacha readily agreed to take on this task. He boarded the train to Dharwad, for a two-day, extremely uncomfortable journey, travelling third class. He had to avoid attracting the attention of the police. By the time the train pulled into Dharwad station, it was 2.00 a.m. Poonacha carried his precious cargo and walked towards the Karnataka Congress headquarters. It was 3.00 a.m. by the time he reached the office. He was totally exhausted and all he wanted was to sleep under the portico of the office. As he approached, he was dismayed to find the building brightly lit and swarming with police. They were pulling out documents from cupboards and checking the premises.

Poonacha beat a hasty retreat to avoid being apprehended. He remembered Srinivasrao Kaujalagi, an ardent Gandhian who was in charge of the Dharwad Khadi Bhandar, and decided to seek shelter with him. By the time he trudged up to Kaujalagi's house, it was about 4.00 a.m. He tentatively knocked on the door. The Kaujalagi family were sure that it was the police. They were relieved to see Poonacha and welcomed him in their home. By then, Poonacha was tired to the bone, sleep-deprived and ravenously hungry. Under the affectionate care of the elderly Kaujalagi couple, it took three days for Poonacha to recover from the fatigue of the arduous task. Having successfully accomplished the task entrusted to him, he set out homewards. That's when his lawyer friend, Ramamurthy, delivered the devastating news that his first-born child had passed away.

Back home, his wife and parents' grief was exacerbated by their worry about Poonacha, from whom they had heard no news ever since his trip to Bombay. The Coorg Police were waiting to arrest '*Sarpastra* Poonacha'. To avoid arrest, Ramamurthy arranged a car to collect Poonacha at the forest check post near Anechowkur, one of the entry points to Coorg. They drove straight to Palangala, where his wife was staying with her parents. By then, the police had got wind of Poonacha heading to his in-law's place and were there to 'greet' him. Sub-inspector A.S. Kalappa was ready to arrest Poonacha. Being familiar with the law enforcers, Poonacha requested Sub-inspector Kalappa to give him time until the following day to surrender on his own. The kind and understanding Sub-inspector Kalappa agreed. The following day, Poonacha was arrested under the Defence of India Act. He was first taken to Kannur jail and then transferred to Vellore jail, where he was sentenced to 20 months of detention.

After completing the prison term, Poonacha returned to Coorg and busied himself with the impending 24-member Coorg District Board election that was to happen in 1946. This time, he contested from Ponnampet and won. Poonacha was elected to the post of president of the district board against Belliappa, with an impressive majority. As part of this position, Poonacha was elected as a member of the Constituent Assembly of India.

Finally, after years of struggle, the British announced their departure and India's independence. As a member of the Constituent Assembly, Poonacha was deputed to New Delhi to participate in the momentous occasion of the formal transfer of power held in the Central Hall of Parliament on 15 August 1947. It was a dream come true for the people of India and for those who participated in the freedom struggle.

Poonacha went on to occupy many important positions at the state and national levels. However, for Poonacha, being present for Mahatma Gandhi's historic Quit India ultimatum, his presence at the Central Hall of Parliament on 15 August 1947 to usher in India's independence and the signing of the Constitution of India on 26 November 1949 were the most treasured moments.

When Mahatma Gandhi was tragically assassinated on 30 January 1948, Poonacha was in New Delhi as a member of the Parliamentary Committee on Defence Planning. The members of the committee

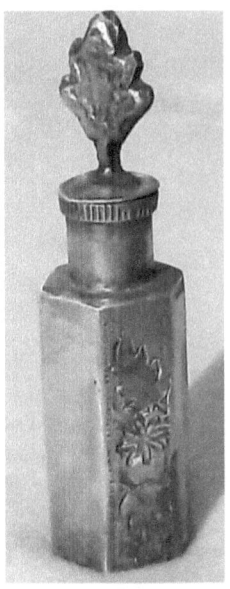

Figure 55: An ampule containing the ashes of Mahatma Gandhi.
Source: Author's collection

were in a meeting with the then Minister for Defence Sardar Baldev Singh. Stunned at the news, everyone dropped whatever they were doing and rushed to the streets. A grief-stricken Poonacha attended the massive funeral. Members of the Constituent Assembly were offered an ampule containing the Mahatma's ashes. Poonacha kept the ampule on his prayer table and paid his respects to the great man every day.

25

THE CONSTITUTION OF INDIA

By 1945, the British declared their intent to quit India. Subsequently, senior Indian leaders put in motion the process of taking over the administration of the country. The Constituent Assembly elected Jawaharlal Nehru as the prime minister of the Provisional Government of India on 2 September 1946. Lord Louis Mountbatten was appointed as the viceroy. The primary task of the Provisional Government was to enable a smooth transfer of power from British India to independent India. In addition, the central government had the important task of drafting a constitution for the newly formed nation. As the president of Coorg District Board, C.M. Poonacha was nominated to represent Coorg in the Constituent Assembly.

The first session of the Constituent Assembly was held on 9 December 1946.[89] The august body took three years to draft the historic document enshrining the guiding principles of this country. Initially, there were 389 members in the Constituent Assembly, of which 292 were representatives of the states, 93 represented the princely states and four were from the chief commissioner provinces of Delhi, Ajmer-Merwara, Coorg and British Baluchistan. This number came down to 299 after Partition in 1947. Members who had been active in the freedom

---

[89]'Constituent Assembly Debates on 9 December, 1945', *Indian Kanoon*, https://tinyurl.com/mryads2n. Accessed on 23 February 2023.

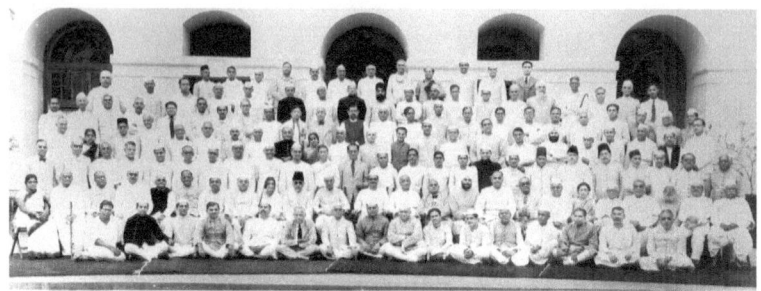

Figure 56: Members of the Constituent Assembly (Legislative) on 6 April 1949. C.M. Poonacha, my father, is standing first from the right in the fourth row.
Source: Author's collection

movement were inducted through indirect elections from the central and provincial assemblies to represent a broad cross section of the country. On 29 August 1947, the Constituent Assembly appointed a Drafting Committee with Dr B.R. Ambedkar as the chairman. My father, C.M. Poonacha, at 36 years of age, was one of the youngest members of the Constituent Assembly.

One of the earliest decisions taken by the members was to avoid the Constitution being written only by technical experts or the elite bureaucracy.[90] (Pakistan took this route, and their Constitution has been rewritten three times). The Indian Constitution was drafted through a combination of 'democratic-consensual' and 'elite-bureaucratic' approaches. This has resulted in a resilient and all-inclusive document that has withstood the test of time for seven decades. Subsequently, it has also undergone several amendments to suit the ever-dynamic needs of the people and the country.

---

[90]Misra, Salil, 'Making of the Indian Constitution', Lokayat, 1 December 2018, https://tinyurl.com/ycxju3wt. Accessed on 12 February 2023.

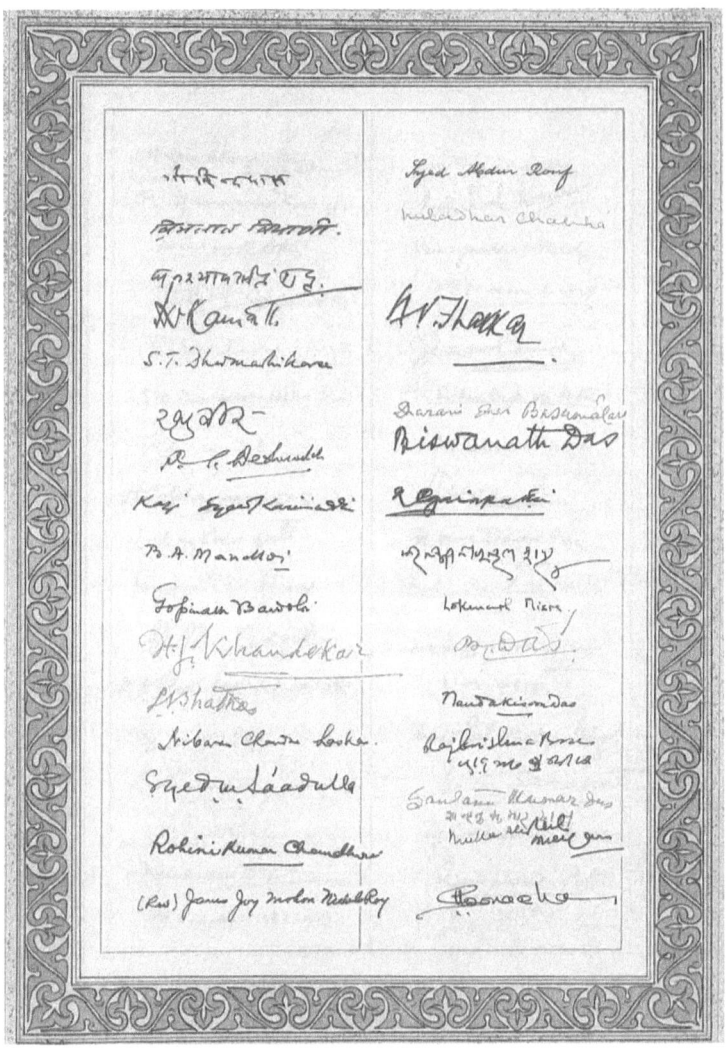

Figure 57: C.M. Poonacha's signature (last in the right column) on the original copy of the Constitution of India.

Source: 'File:Constitution of India (calligraphic) 463.jpg', Wikimedia Commons, https://tinyurl.com/mvyfm4ka. Accessed on 24 February 2023.

Another unique feature of the process behind drafting the Constitution was that every resolution was unanimously passed after extensive consultations and debates. Thus, every clause in the Constitution was discussed until all the members of committees and sub-committees agreed without dissent. None of the resolutions were put to vote to avoid the 'tyranny of the majority'.

The final draft of the Constitution of India was signed and adopted on 26 November 1949. C.M. Poonacha was one of the 299 signatories on this esteemed document (see the last signature in figure 57). The Constitution of India was brought into force on 26 January 1950, when India was declared a 'sovereign republic'. This date was chosen to coincide with the 'Poorna Swaraj', declared on 26 January 1930. Affixing his signature on the Constitution of India was one of the defining moments in the life of Poonacha. He is the only signatory of the Constitution of India from Coorg.

On a lighter note, I have a personal memory from the time when the Constitution of India was being drafted. I was around four years old at the time and, on a couple of occasions during the process, my father had taken us to Delhi. One particular incident during our stay there is etched in my mind.

All the members from different parts of India had been accommodated in a complex named Constitution House on Janpath Road. Connaught Place was nearby and we used to take leisurely walks there in the evenings when in my father was free. We would stop to have an ice candy, and it used to be the highlight of the day. On one of these strolls, we passed by a toy shop. The brightly lit shop with all the wondrous toys attracted me like a moth to a flame. I forced my parents, who were trying to divert my attention, to enter the shop. Once inside, my eyes lingered on a tricycle. It was unique, since it had a horse head in front of the handle. I caressed it, turned to my father and gingerly asked if I could have it. He looked at the price tag, shook his head and tried to beat a hasty retreat. I resisted. Soon, I was howling and attracting the attention of other shoppers.

The owner of the toyshop, a massively built sardarji, sauntered across to ask my parents if they needed any help. By then, I was hysterical and kept bellowing, '*Nakk ikka bondu* (I want it now).'

The kind sardarji offered to let me take the tricycle and told my father, who didn't have the cash at that time that he could pay the following day. My father was put in a tight spot and finally relented. I happily rode the brand-new tricycle all the way back to the Constitution House. I used to be a brat on the tricycle, ringing the bell and riding it on the long verandahs of the Constitution House, much to the amusement of the authors of our Constitution.

26

STATES REORGANIZATION AND MERGER OF COORG WITH KARNATAKA

Coorg had existed as a separate entity ever since the Haleri rajas brought it under their control by the mid-1600. Prior to the seventeenth century, Coorg had been ruled by feuding warlords known as Nayakas or Palegars. When the British East India Company dethroned the last Raja of Coorg, they retained it as a province administered under a chief commissioner, which continued till India's Independence in 1947. Coorg continued to be a chief commissioner's province until 1952, when an elected government took over its administration after it was categorized as a Part 'C' state.

In the first general elections held in 1952 for the 24 seats in the Legislative Assembly, 15 seats were won by the Congress Party, headed by C.M. Poonacha and nine seats by the Coorg Separatist Party, steered by Pandyanda Belliappa. Poonacha was elected the chief minister with Kuttur Mallappa as the home minister. Lieutenant Colonel Daya Singh Bedi (a direct descendant of Guru

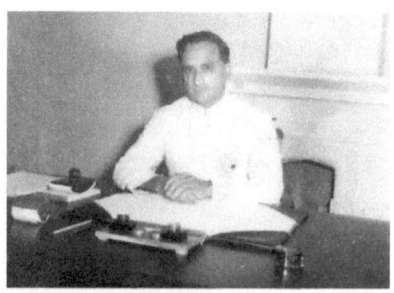

Figure 58: C.M. Poonacha as the elected chief minister of Coorg in 1952.
Source: Author's collection

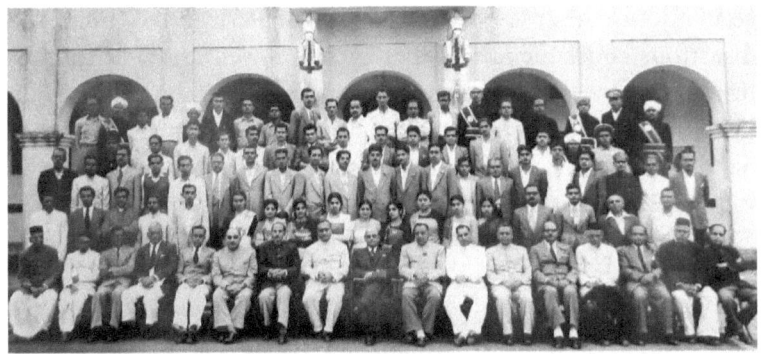

Figure 59: The officials of the Coorg Government with T.G.N. Ayyar, the new Chief Commissioner (1955-1956), circa 1955
Source: Author's collection

Nanak) was appointed by the central government as the chief commissioner of Coorg.

The compact ministry ran an efficient administration and was close to the people. Corruption, nepotism, incompetence and any form of discrimination were promptly addressed. The budget provided by the central government was utilized judiciously. Coorg, earlier praised as 'Ram Rajya' by Sardar Vallabhbhai Patel, earned the sobriquet 'The Tiny Model State of India'.

The chief minister, the home minister and other officials were easily accessible to the people. The premises of the Madikeri Fort continued to be used as the secretariat of the newly elected government of the state.

Outside Coorg, the country's political landscape was witnessing great many changes. The Constituent Assembly of India, formed in 1946, had elected Pandit Jawaharlal Nehru as the interim prime minister. Many issues needed to be addressed besides framing the Constitution of the nation. The most contentious matter to be resolved was the Partition of India. The disastrous consequences of that event are well-known. Another prickly issue was the accession of princely states into the Indian Union. The credit goes to Sardar Vallabhbhai Patel for tactfully handling this problem and for goading 565 princely states of varying sizes to sign the Instrument of Accession in 1947.

The administrative division of India under the British was unwieldy due, in part, to the diverse languages of the regions. The British ruled India as a colonial power. After Independence, the country had to be governed based on democratic principles. As a temporary provision, in the original Constitution of India that was adopted in 1950, the states in India were classified as Part 'A', Part 'B', Part 'C' and Part 'D'.

Part 'A' states comprised of the large British-administered provinces. There were nine of them, namely: Assam, Bihar, Bombay, East Punjab, Madhya Pradesh, Madras, Orissa, Uttar Pradesh and West Bengal.

Part 'B' states were the 565 former princely states that were clubbed together to form nine more states—Hyderabad, Jammu and Kashmir, Madhya Bharat, Mysore, Patiala and East Punjab States Union (PEPSU), Rajasthan, Saurashtra, Travancore–Cochin and Vindhya Pradesh.

There were 10 provinces categorized as Part 'C' states that had been directly under the British administration, including some of the princely states. They were Ajmer-Merwara, Coorg, Cooch Behar, Bhopal, Bilaspur, Delhi, Himachal Pradesh, Kutch, Manipur and Tripura.

Andaman and Nicobar Islands was categorized as a Part 'D' state.

An important task for the newly independent nation was to reorganize the states to facilitate unified, effective and efficient administration. In 1948, a commission was formed

States Reorganization and Merger of Coorg with Karnataka 159

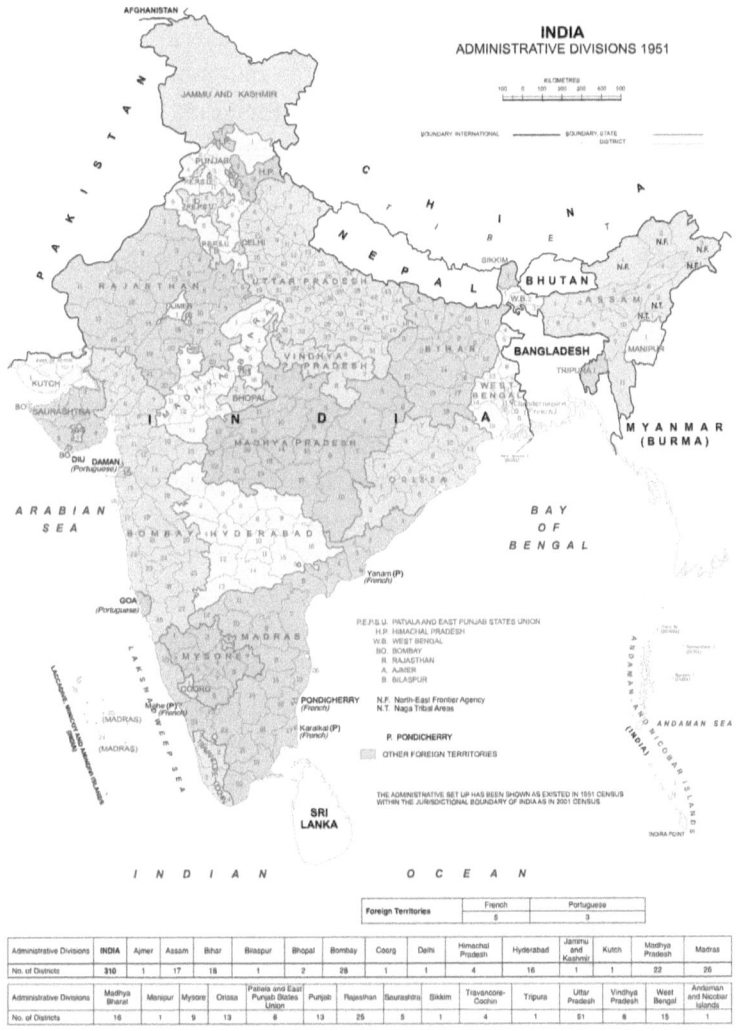

Figure 60: Map of the administrative divisions of India, 1951. Map not to scale.
Source: 'File:India Administrative Divisions 1951.svg', Wikimedia Commons, https://tinyurl.com/bdhsv59x. Accessed on 23 February 2023.

under S.K. Dhar, a judge of the Allahabad Court, to study the merits of reorganising Indian states based on language. However, the commission preferred the reorganization of states based on administrative convenience, including historical and geographical considerations, rather than on linguistic lines, even though the popular sentiment in the country was in favour of linguistically divided states.

In December 1948, a high power committee, with Jawaharlal Nehru, Vallabhbhai Patel and Pattabhi Sitaramayya (known as the JVP Committee) as its members, was formed to study the issue. The JVP Committee too did not favour reorganization on linguistic basis because they feared that it would lead to parochialism and linguistic chauvinism, which could bring about a situation similar to the Partition. Many alternative suggestions were floated. Maintaing the status quo was one of them. Some of the leaders felt splitting the country into about six large zones would be a better idea. On the other hand, C. Rajagopalachari opined that having compact states would be more desirable. He cited the example of Coorg, which was administered efficiently, was close to the people and was corruption-free.

But the popular mood was different. The demand for linguistic states came from every corner of the nation. A movement for forming a Kannada-speaking state has been active since the 1920s, under the Ekikarana Movement led by, Aluru Venkata Rao.[91] A prolonged agitation had been underway for a Telegu-speaking state, named Andhra Pradesh, to be carved out of the massive Madras Province, which extended from the Bay of Bengal to the Arabian Sea and stretched right down to the Indian Ocean. Besides Tamil, people in the Madras Province

---

[91]Salagare, Mallappa B., 'The Historical Movements in the Unification of Karnataka', Research Gate, January 2017, https://tinyurl.com/2p8hz6wt. Accessed on 12 February 2023.

spoke Telugu, Kannada and Malayalam. In 1953, Potti Sriramulu, who spearheaded the agitation for the Telugu-speaking Andhra state died while he was on a hunger strike. This event further ignited the issue, and the government had to bow to the wishes of the majority. It was realized that people were passionate about their languages, which could be an effective unifying factor across religion and caste.

On 22 December 1953, Prime Minister Nehru moved a motion in Parliament to appoint a commission, known as the States Reorganisation Commission (SRC), headed by retired judge Fazal Ali. After two years of extensive work, visiting every region in the country, the SRC submitted its report in 1955. Subsequently, on 31 August 1956, the Parliament passed the States Reorganisation Act. The Act came into force on 1 November 1956, after the abolition of Part 'A', Part 'B', Part 'C' and Part 'D' states by the Seventh Amendment to the Constitution of India. Thus, 14 states and six union territories were formed.

The new states were Andhra Pradesh, Assam, Bihar, Bombay, Jammu and Kashmir, Kerala, Madhya Pradesh, Madras, Mysore (Karnataka), Orissa, Punjab, Rajasthan, Uttar Pradesh and West Bengal. The six union territories were Andaman and Nicobar Islands, Delhi, Himachal Pradesh, Laccadive, Minicoy and Amindivi Islands (renamed Lakshadweep in 1973), Manipur and Tripura.

The overarching reason behind the reorganization of Indian states was language. Financial independence, efficient administration, religion, unique culture or emotional attachments were not the deciding considerations in the massive exercise undertaken by the SRC. All princely (Part 'B' states), except for Jammu and Kashmir, were rearranged and amalgamated to form larger states based on the languages spoken there. Out of the Part 'C' states, Himachal Pradesh, Manipur and

Tripura were made union territories. These provinces had quite an extensive area, their populations were sufficiently large and, more importantly, they shared sensitive international borders with neighbouring countries. Years later, they were made full-fledged states. After the States Reorganisations Act in 1956, the Gujarati-speaking section in the massive Bombay State agitated for a separate state, and the states of Gujarat and Maharashtra came into being in 1960. Nagaland was formed in 1963. Likewise, there was a prolonged demand by Punjabis for a separate Sikh state. In 1966, Punjab and Haryana were carved out of the original Punjab.

In accordance with the SRC report, Coorg was to merge with the new Vishal Mysore State (later renamed Karnataka). This was because Kannada was known to almost every citizen in Coorg and it had also been used in the administration and as a medium of instruction in schools ever since the British takeover in 1834. The size of Coorg is 4,102 sq. km, and its population, in 1956, was around 230,000. Understandably, not many in Coorg were in favour of the merger with Karnataka. Coorg, as a Part 'C' state, had made a name for itself as one of the best administered provinces in India. As mentioned earlier, national leaders, including Sardar Vallabhbhai Patel, had appreciated the Coorg Government for making the state a 'Tiny Model State' in India, to be emulated by other states.

Prior to the first general elections held in 1952, veteran Congressman Pandyanda Belliappa resigned from the party and formed the Separatist Party (also known as the Takkadi Party), primarily opposing the proposed merger of Coorg with Karnataka. The new party won nine out of 24 seats in the Coorg Legislative Assembly.

In a last-ditch effort, the Coorg Legislative Assembly submitted a memorandum to the visiting team of the SRC in

1954, requesting that Coorg should continue to be a separate state or made a union territory. It became a highly sensitive issue and Poonacha was caught between the pressures from the central government to accept the merger and demands from a section of the locals who wished for Coorg to continue as a separate state. In his own words, Poonacha had to suffer a *dharma sankata* (moral dilemma) during this period. The small area (see figure 62), the low population and the fact that Kannada was the dominant language spoken and written in the region, left no choice for Coorg to remain as a separate entity. It met all the criteria set by the SRC to be part of a Kannada-speaking state.

Finally, bowing to the recommendations of the Parliament-mandated SRC, Chief Minister Poonacha and the Congress had to support the inevitable merger.[92] Leaders from the Centre were firm about implementing the states reorganization in accordance with the SRC's report. Prime Minister Nehru wrote a cryptic note on 3 November 1951 to Pandyanda Belliappa, the leader of the Separatist Party, emphasizing that, ultimately, the Parliament will decide the issue of merger and reorganization. In fact, some people misinterpreted that Nehru had promised a referendum and that the people of Coorg had a choice. No referendum was held in any part of India. The Indian Parliament accepted the SRC report, and it was to be ratified by the respective elected legislative assemblies in the country to democratically formalize the process. What many people in Coorg fail to understand is that even if the Coorg Legislative Assembly had rejected the SRC's recommendations, the merger would have still happened with the Parliament overruling the Legislative Assembly. Nehru's missive to Belliappa is clear on that point.[93]

---

[92]Ramachandrachar, D.B., *Avakashada Allegala Mele*, Sunanda Prakasana, 1990.
[93]Ibid.

3rd November,

Dear Beliapa,

I have today received a letter signed by you and a number of others offering your resignations from the membership of the Indian National Congress. The letter is without date. I presume that you brought this letter with you when you came to Delhi somedays ago. That is to say that you had this letter with you when you saw me some time ago, you had in fact come with these resignations in your pocket when you came to Delhi.

I have repeatedly explained to you our position in regard to Coorg. The question of merger of Coorg does not arise at present and the coming elections will have nothing to do with it. Only recently Parliament passed Legislation governing various states in India including Coorg. This itself meant that no merger was intended in the near future and indeed for some time to come. Otherwise there was no point in having this legislation giving certain powers to an elected Assembly in Coorg.

Since this is so, this talk of running the elections on the merger issue seems to me completely beside the point and most inopportune and unwise. The new Coorg Assembly will certainly have the right to express its views about any matter, but even an expression of views on merger issue would be without much weight if this issue has been by force of circumstances postponed and not made an issue in the elections. In any event, it is not Coorg Assembly that will decide this matter but Parliament which will have to take into consideration not only the views of the people of Coorg but many other important factors.

However, if you insist on persuing the course that you indicated in your letter, you are perfectly welcome to do so. The Congress will naturally now adopt its candidates from other people. Even so we shall not concern ourselves with the merger issue.

Since you have offered your resignations from the membership of the national Congress, was shall in future deal with you as non-members. Resignations from the primary membership ought to be sent to the local committee concerned. We keep no record here of primary members.

Shri P. Beliapa,
Lal Bahdur,
Gen. Secry.
4-11-51.

Yours Sincerely,

Sd/ J. Nehru.

PTO

Figure 61: Letter from Prime Minister Nehru to Pandyanda Belliappa, dated 4 November 1951.

Source: Author's collection.

On 6 December 1955, the Coorg Legislative Assembly convened a special session to pass a resolution about the merger in accordance with the SRC report. There was spirited debate both for and against the motion moved by the Chief Minister Poonacha. All 24 members were given time to voice their opinions. Finally, when the motion was put to vote, it was carried with a majority in favour of merger. Out of the nine members of the Separatist Party, six, including Belliappa, voted in favour of the merger. Out of the remaining three members, A.C. Thimiah expressed his displeasure but accepted the merger as an inevitable fait accompli and remained neutral. P.C. Utaya and K.P. Karumbaiya opposed the motion and abstained from voting. The entire debate has been reproduced in the Appendix, verbatim, for those interested in knowing what transpired that day. The debate reflects a great deal about the activities in Coorg from 1952 to 1956.

Ultimately, a Kannada-speaking state was formed that included the princely state of Mysore, Part the 'C' state of Coorg, parts of the Bombay Province, parts of the Madras Province and parts of Hyderabad State (see figure 62). On 1 November 1956, Coorg became a part of the Vishal Mysore State—an event that was unavoidable, though not wholly welcomed. Many from the progressive princely state of Mysore too were not enthusiastic about this. Even after the reorganization, Coorg was the smallest district in the newly formed state. However, it is a fact that Coorg got neglected over the years after the merger.

A few conspiracy theorists continue to argue that the merger of Coorg could have been avoided and that it could have remained a separate state.[94] They cite the examples of Goa, Sikkim and Pondicherry, overlooking the fact that the merger of these three states into the Indian Union occurred much after the SRC report of 1955, and they had not been part of British India. Some union territories have also been formed because of

---

[94]Bopanna, P.T., *Rise and Fall of Coorg State: Kodagu's Loss, Karnataka's Gain*, Rolling Stone Publications, Bangalore, 2009.

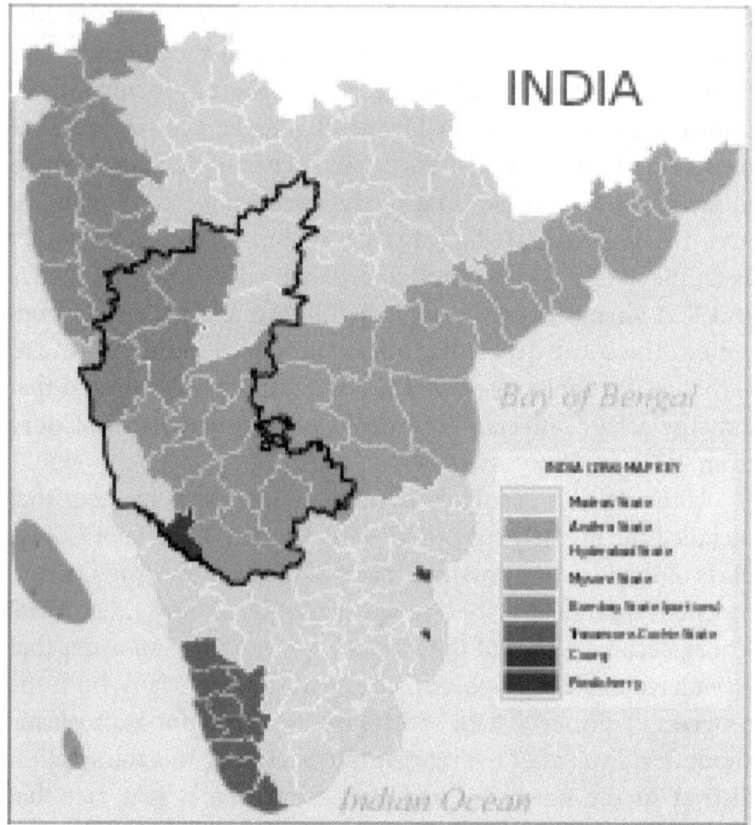

Figure 62: Map of Karnataka after the States Reorganisation Act of 1956.
Source: 'File:South Indian territories.svg', Wikimedia Commons, https://tinyurl.com/3retr7mv. Accessed on 24 February 2023.

their strategic and sensitive locations. Hypothetically, if Coorg were to be given statehood, there would have been similar demands from hundreds of other provinces in India, especially the 565 former princely states. The entire process of the states' reorganization would have been rendered meaningless. So, the central government was firm. Parallel demands in a few other parts of India were also overruled. Coorg had no other choice but to be a part of the Kannada-speaking state of Karnataka, despite some of the disadvantages.

The Coorg Government of the time was accused of not attempting to obtain special status for the Part 'C' state within the newly formed Karnataka state. In fact, a five-point 'safeguard' (see pp. 185–86) was proposed by the Coorg Government. However, only two of the demands were accepted by the central government: retaining Coorg as a separate district and safeguarding its identity, and continuing the Arms Exemption Act for those belonging to the Coorg race and to *jamma* land holders. Here, again, the problem for the central government was not encouraging too many exceptions, resulting in similar demands from other parts of the country, which would further complicate the process of states reorganization.

The population of India in 2022 stands at around 1.40 billion.[95] This figure is more than three times the population registered in 1947. This has made it necessary for some of the massive states, such as Uttar Pradesh, Madhya Pradesh, Bihar and Andhra Pradesh, to be split. As of October 2019, India has 28 states and union territories. By 2050, the population of India is projected to touch two billion. For administrative convenience, there might be a need for further bifurcation of states in the coming years.

---

[95]'India Population (Live)', WorldOMeter, https://tinyurl.com/4kfez3z7. Accessed on 12 February 2023.

28

POST THE REORGANIZATION OF INDIAN STATES

As mentioned earlier, Coorg received the moniker 'Tiny Model State of India' while being administered as a Part 'C' state. For the first time in its history, a responsible, popularly elected government ruled the province from 1952 until it was amalgamated with the Vishal Mysure State (renamed Karnataka in 1973) on 1 November 1956. Coorg was the smallest district of the state with the least population. Most of the demands in the resolution passed on 6 December 1955 in the Coorg Legislative Assembly (see the Appendix for the full text) were not granted. Coorg district was given three seats in the newly formed Legislative Assembly of Karnataka as opposed to the five seats they had demanded. As for the Lok Sabha, Coorg was not given any exclusive seats and was clubbed with the Mangalore constituency. The allocation of the Member of the Legislative Assembly (MLA) seats and Lok Sabha seats was in accordance with the formula that was applicable to all parts of India. Since then, further changes have been made and Coorg now only has two MLAs based on the delimitation brought in by the Election Commission. The Lok Sabha seat is currently shared with the Mysore constituency.[96]

---

[96]Ramachandrachar, D.B., *Avakashada Allegala Mele*, Sunanda Prakasana, 1990.

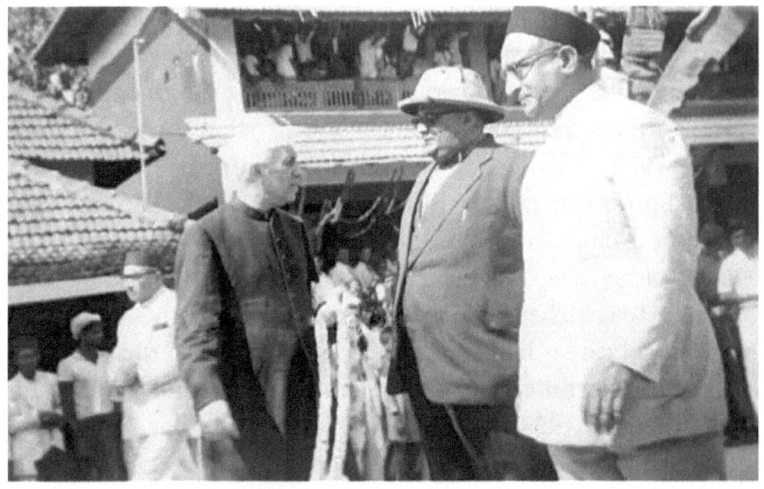

Figure 63: C.M. Poonacha with Prime Minister Nehru and Governor Wodeyar during their visit to Coorg in 1957.

Source: Author's collection

From 1 November 1956 to the elections held in 1957, all 24 members of the Coorg Legislative Assembly were retained as MLAs in the Karnataka State Assembly. B.S. Kushalappa was appointed the pro tem speaker of the House. C.M. Poonacha was appointed the home minister in S. Nijalingappa's cabinet.

In the first state elections held in March 1957, C.M. Poonacha, K. Mallappa and K.M. Devaiah, all from the Congress Party, won and became MLAs in the Karnataka State Assembly. Poonacha was appointed the minister for industries and commerce in the new ministry of Chief Minister S. Nijalingappa.

After the formation of the Kannada-speaking state of Vishal Mysore, the erstwhile Maharaja of Mysore, Jayachamaraja Wodeyar, who was the rajpramuk between 1947 to 1956, was appointed as the governor of the state.

In 1957, Prime Minister Jawaharlal Nehru visited Coorg. He

was accompanied by Governor Wodeyar and Vishal Mysore State Minister Poonacha. Prime Minister Nehru received a rousing welcome as he walked down the main road of Gonikoppal town along with the leaders and officials.

In 1958, Nijalingappa's short-lived ministry fell due to internal power struggles within the Congress. B.D. Jatti emerged as the new chief minister.

My father, aged 48 years at the time, did not get a seat in Jatti's cabinet. He returned to his coffee estate in Coorg believing that his political career had ended. However, Poonacha did continue as an MLA. Fortuitously for him, another opportunity presented itself when, in 1959, the then Central Minister for Commerce and Trade Lal Bahadur Shastri appointed him as the chairman of State Trading Corporation of India (STC), headquartered in New Delhi, for a term of five years.

The STC played an important role in the international trade of the country at the time. All the imports and exports, especially with the Union of Soviet Socialist Republics and the East European countries, were routed through it. Certain irregularities had been creeping into the STC and Shastri wanted a reliable and steadfast person to head the organization. So, he chose Poonacha to steer it, giving him a rank equivalent to that of a minister of state. One of the first letters Poonacha wrote to his boss was a detailed statement of his assets and liabilities. Shastri wrote back appreciating his voluntary disclosure.

In 1964, after completing his tenure with the STC, Poonacha was elected to the Rajya Sabha from Karnataka. In January 1966, Prime Minister Shastri appointed him minister of state for revenue and expenditure under the Ministry of Finance. A few days later, Shastri was in Russia for a summit meeting with Ayub Khan after the 1965 Indo–Pak War. India and the world were shocked when Shastri died inexplicably in Tashkent

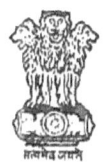

1925 - C/M/59

GOVERNMENT OF INDIA,
MINISTER, COMMERCE & INDUSTRIES,
NEW DELHI.

6th September, 1959.

My dear Poonacha,

Thank you for your letter of the 5th September 1959. It is so good of you to have sent a statement of your assets and liabilities.

Yours sincerely,

Lal Bahadur

(Lal Bahadur)

Shri C.M. Poonacha,
Chairman,
State Trading Corporation,
New Delhi.

'HRN'

Figure 64: Letter from Prime Minister Shastri to C.M. Poonacha, dated 6 September 1959.

Source: Author's collection

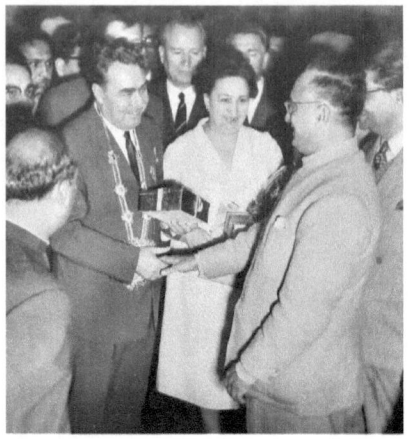

Figure 65: C.M. Poonacha receiving Leonid Brezhnev of erstwhile USSR visiting India, circa 1960.

Source: Author's collection

on 11 January 1966, a day after signing the Tashkent Declaration. Shastri had great faith in Poonacha's integrity and sincerity. The former's untimely demise devastated Poonacha.

Indira Gandhi, who succeeded Shastri, retained Poonacha in her cabinet as the minister of state for transport, shipping, and aviation. In the General Election of 1967, Poonacha contested the Mangalore-Kodagu Lok Sabha

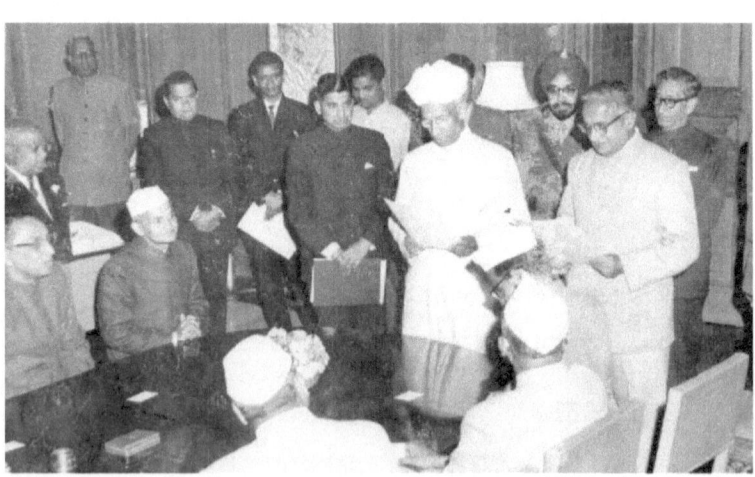

Figure 66: C.M. Poonacha being sworn in as a minister in Prime Minister Shastri's cabinet, 1966.

Source: Author's collection

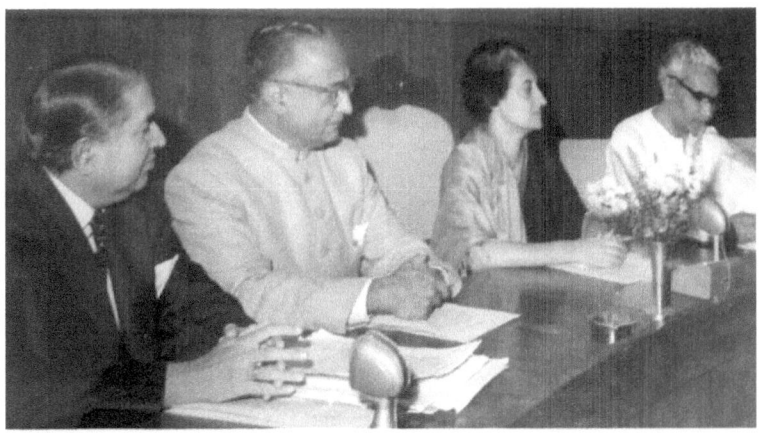

Figure 67: C.M. Poonacha as the union minister for railways in a meeting with Prime Minister Indira Gandhi, circa 1968.
Source: Author's collection

constituency and won. Indira Gandhi appointed him cabinet minister for railways.

In 1969, the Congress underwent a major split. The two factions that emerged were Indian National Congress (Requisitionists) (Congress [R]) and Indian National Congress (Organisation) (Congress [O]). Congress (R) was later renamed Congress (I), where the 'I' stood for 'Indira'. Poonacha was part of Congress (O), led by S. Nijalingappa, Kumaraswami Kamaraj, Morarji Desai, Neelam Sanjiva Reddy, S.K. Patil and others. Poonacha resigned from Indira Gandhi's cabinet in November 1969, even though she had not asked him to do so. In a letter written on 15 November 1969, Indira Gandhi accepted Poonacha's resignation and expressed her regret at his decision.

In the General Elections of 1971, Poonacha contested on a Congress (O) ticket from the Mangalore–Kodagu constituency and lost. Subsequently, he retired from active politics and settled down in Coorg.

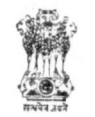

PRIME MINISTER

No. 1190-PMO/69   New Delhi,
                   November 15, 1969.

Dear Shri Poonacha,

    I have just now received your letter of November 15, tendering your resignation from the Council of Ministers. It is with deep regret that I have to advise the President to accept it.

    I earnestly hope that you will deeply ponder over the situation both within the party and the country. I have no doubt that when the dust of the current controversy has settled down, you will realise that our party has rejuvenated itself and come nearer to the people.

    I should like to thank you for your cooperation and support during the period I had the pleasure of having you as my colleague.

    With regards,

                   Yours sincerely,

                     (Indira Gandhi)

Shri C.M. Poonacha,
10, Akbar Road,
New Delhi.

Figure 68: Letter from Prime Minister Indira Gandhi to C.M. Poonacha accepting his resignation, 1969.

Source: Author's collection

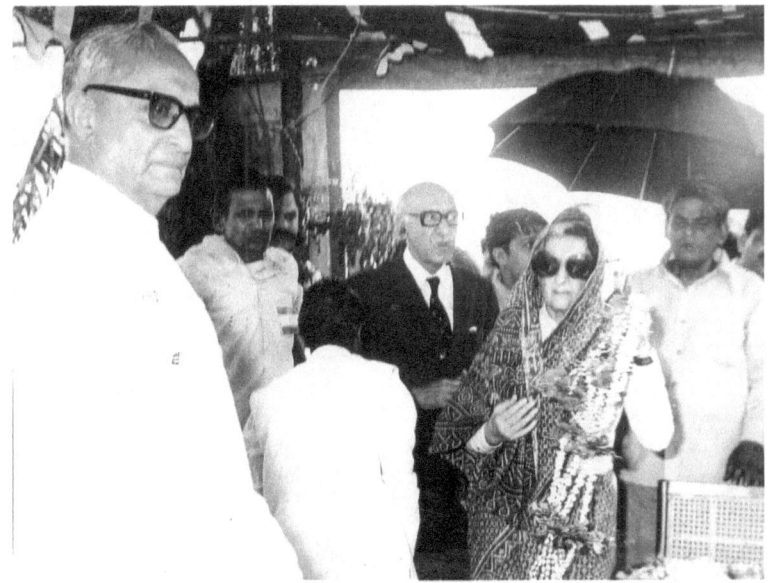

Figure 69: Governor C.M. Poonacha receiving Prime Minister Indira Gandhi during her visit to Orissa, circa 1981.

Source: Author's collection

In 1978, Poonacha was called to duty again when he was appointed governor of Madhya Pradesh by Morarji Desai's government at the centre while Sanjiva Reddy was president. When Indira Gandhi returned to power in 1980, Poonacha was shifted to governor of Orissa (now Odisha), where he completed his gubernatorial term in 1983.

Prince Charles (now King Charles III) visited Orissa in 1980 and was the state guest at the Raj Bhavan.[97] It was poetic justice, so to speak, for Poonacha to host the Prince of Wales, after having fought his ancestors during the freedom struggle.

---

[97]Ramachandrachar, D.B., *Avakashada Allegala Mele*, Sunanda Prakasana, 1990.

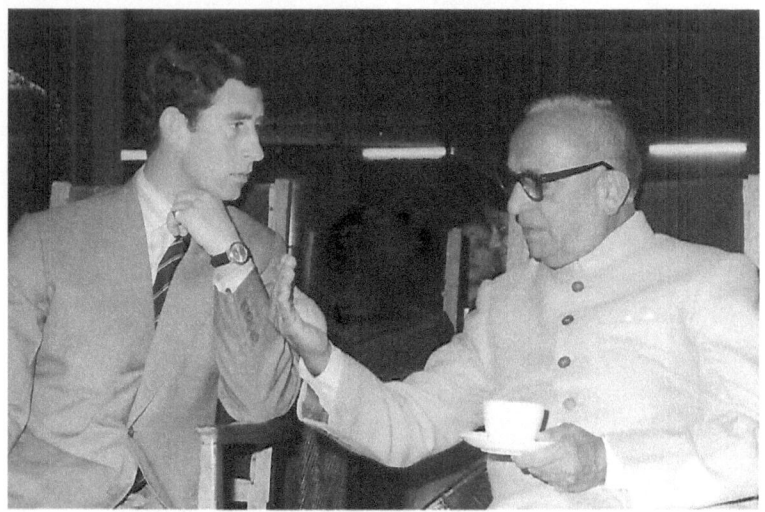

Figure 70: Prince Charles with Governor C.M. Poonacha during the former's visit to Orissa, 1980.
Source: Author's collection

Over the years, Coorg, which used to be a stronghold of the Congress since 1947, has gradually shifted to the Bharatiya Janata Party's (BJP) fold. For the past six terms, the two elected MLAs from Coorg have been from the BJP. Mysore–Kodagu, and earlier the Mangalore-Kodagu Lok Sabha constituency, too, has been with the BJP since 1991, except for the term from 2009 to 2014 when it was with the Congress.

The merger with Karnataka has been a mixed bag for Coorg. On the positive side, as Kannadigas, employment opportunities for people from Coorg increased manifold by the mid-1960s, with jobs in departments such as police, forest, revenue, state administration, banks, teaching, state government undertakings as well as in public sector undertakings.

This benefitted especially those with smaller land holdings

and enabled them to provide better education to their children, since there had been no great schools and colleges in Coorg until the 1990s. The merger opened up opportunities for higher education for the youth of Coorg. Otherwise, those aspiring for a degree, especially in medicine, engineering, agriculture and law, had to go outside Coorg, vying for one or two seats reserved for students from other states. After the merger, students from Coorg had equal access to higher education in Karnataka. Over time, Kodavas focussing on professional education for their children has led to many of them not only securing coveted jobs but also establishing successful enterprises and businesses.

A good number of Kodavas are working and living in the US, UK, Europe, Australia, New Zealand, Africa and the Middle East. In a significant development over the years, there has been a reversal of fortunes. The children and grandchildren of those who chose to live outside Coorg, especially in Bangalore and Mysore, after the merger in 1956, have achieved better economic standards than those in Coorg. Obviously, access to higher education has made this possible.

Not everything has been positive though. One of the major downsides of the merger has been corruption creeping into Coorg. It was unheard of in the region right from the time of the British administration till the merger in 1956. Another drawback has been the loss of political clout. Democracy, being a game of numbers, has rendered this thinly populated region devoid of a voice loud enough to make those sitting in the Vidhana Soudha take note of the local issues.

Corruption has led to the exploitation of Coorg's forests. This has adversely affected the pristine environment of the region. In the past three decades, the pattern of rainfall has perceptibly changed. Many wild animals have been displaced from their natural habitat and have been forced to roam into human settlements. Human–elephant conflict is getting worse by the day and there have been many fatalities. Agriculturists in Coorg live in constant fear of damage to their crops and threat to their lives by wild animals that stray into human settlements in search of food, fodder and water. Unfortunately, the government is not making a concerted attempt to address this issue.

Coorg suffered for want of good infrastructure, such as roads, communication and power, till the turn of the twenty-first century. While communication has improved because of mobile phones, power supply is still erratic. The condition of the roads has improved slightly. However, there is now fear of some major highway projects, benefitting only neighbouring states, passing through Coorg.

Similarly, a few years ago, about 50,000 trees were felled to lay a high voltage powerline for Kerala, a news story that was widely covered in various newspapers.[98] A railway track to Kerala cutting through Coorg has been proposed. If initiated, this process will destroy more than 100,000 trees and further disturb the pristine environment of Coorg. This railway project will not benefit Coorg in any way and will only further destroy the fragile ecosystem and cause problems for the people of the region.

On the brighter side, in the five decades of being a part of Karnataka, Coorg has not suffered economically. Plantation crops continue to be the mainstay of the local economy and the productivity has increased over the years. In the mid-1990s, the Coffee Board of India, which had a monopoly over marketing coffee, came under the central government's liberalization process. Growers were given the freedom to sell their crop in the open market. This helped coffee planters achieve better returns.

---

[98] '50,000 Trees to Face the Axe for the 400 Kv Power Line Across Kodagu', CoorgNews.in, https://tinyurl.com/452kpe4c. Accessed on 15 February 2023.

Unexpected increases in the international prices of coffee and pepper during the 1990s and early 2000s helped many agriculturists improve their properties and give the best of education to their children. A few private schools were set up in the region, making quality education available within Coorg. The past two decades have seen the establishment of professional colleges in Coorg, offering degrees in engineering, medicine, dental science and forestry. Unfortunately, the prices of coffee and pepper have dipped and stagnated since the past five years. At the same time, the costs of labour and other inputs have increased steeply, which has brought down profit margins.

Coorg has been on the tourism map of India for nearly two decades now. It is now a popular tourist destination with resorts and hotels mushrooming up all over the district. People flock to Coorg for its fresh air and to experience the pristine beauty of nature. The concept of homestays has caught on and is now a good source of additional income for many coffee planters. On the flipside, the influx of tourists is adversely affecting the very environment they come to enjoy. It is widely believed that the landslides in 2018, 2019 and 2020 were caused by several tourism-oriented construction and other activities.

As mentioned earlier, Kodavas take great interest in providing the best education possible to their children. Consequently, the highly qualified youngsters seek employment opportunities outside Coorg. This has led to Kodavas steadily migrating out of Coorg, drastically reducing their percentage in the region. It is a catch-22 situation—educate your children and enable them to fly out of Coorg!

The overall population of Coorg now stands at nearly 560,000, mostly consisting settlers from other states.[99] Those

---

[99]'Kodagu District-Population 2011–2023', Population Census, http://finyurl.

from the neighbouring states who have settled in Coorg invariably start a trade and their children join them soon after getting minimal education. People from other states have thrived in their businesses and their numbers are increasing. To make matters worse, the population of Kodavas is also dwindling because of compact families. The ideal birth rate to sustain any community is 2.1 children per couple.[100] The birth rate among Kodavas is around 1.5 children per couple.

Nevertheless, it is a matter of pride for the community, despite their sparse numbers, that they have achieved significant success in a variety of fields and are now spread all over the world. Most credibly, individuals have succeeded on their own merit. The contributions and achievements of the Kodava community in the defence forces are well-known.

As a micro-minority race in India, there has been an ongoing movement to obtain tribal status for the Kodavas. The community is currently classified as a forward community because of which many coveted posts in the government are out of their reach. Even though there are many highly eligible candidates from the Kodava community, they unfortunately lose out on account of the existing reservation policy.

One of the adverse outcomes of Kodavas moving out of Coorg is their ancestral properties in Coorg being sold to people from outside the region. Kodavas need to retain ownership of their land to safeguard the fragile environment of this area. The Western Ghats, of which Coorg is a part, are an eco-sensitive zone. Protecting this ecosystem is vital for the ecological stability of large parts of southern India. Coorg is the birthplace of the

---

com/yrw3vs73. Accessed on 24 February 2023.
[100] Smoak, Natahi, 'Fertility Rate' Britannica, https://finyurl.com/3vphc7e2. Accessed on 24 February 2023.

important river Kaveri. The emotional bond that the Kodavas and the *Jamma* landholders have for their land can save it from over-commercialization and exploitation.

An encouraging trend these days has been some of the successful Kodavas, whose parents and grandparents had parted with their landed property, coming back to buy land in Coorg. Many youngsters from the community have started diverse enterprises within Coorg, such as educational institutions, healthcare units, resorts, cottage industries, real-estate projects, agribusiness, ecotourism and adventure sports. There will be many more new opportunities in the coming years with digital technology growing by leaps and bounds.

Seventy-five years after India's Independence, the tiny province of Coorg has witnessed dramatic changes. There have been many progressive developments in the fields of agriculture, tourism and education. Coorg ranks quite high on most socio-economic indicators. At the same time, excessive commercialization has seriously impacted the environment. Coorg is at a crossroads, and a sustainable policy to protect the ecologically fragile district is urgently needed. The evergreen forest cover of the region has been rapidly shrinking due to encroachments, illegal felling, forest fires and landslides in recent years. Tourism, which was a welcome diversification for the economy, is posing a serious threat to the environment now. With unbridled tourism, one can see Coorg treading the treacherous path that places like Shimla and Ooty have taken. The Madhav Gadgil and Kasturirangan Committee reports have recommended various steps to safeguard the ecology of the Western Ghats. However, lack of political will and self-interest lobbies are endangering the environment for short-term gains.

APPENDIX

THE COORG LEGISLATIVE ASSEMBLY DEBATES

(Tuesday, 6 December 1955, Volume IX)[101]

Special Session to consider the Report of the States Reorganisation Commission

The Assembly met in the Assembly Hall, Fort, Mercara, at eleven o' clock. Mr Speaker, **Shri B.S. Kushalappa**, B.A., D.E. (London) in the Chair.

All the Members were present.

Resolution

Formation of Karnataka State

Shri C.M. Poonacha [Congress Party]: (Chief Minister) 'Sir, notice has been given about this Resolution...'

Shri P.C. Utaya [Separatist Party]: 'On a point of order, Mr Speaker, Sir, there was no notice of the Resolution at all as required by Rule 73 of the Rules of Procedure and Conduct of

---

[101] *The Coorg Legislative Assembly Debates (Tuesday, 6 December 1955, Volume IX)*, Government Press, 1955.
I would like to thank Kuppanda A. Chinnappa for lending me the original and only copy of the minutes of this debate.

Business of the Coorg Legislative Assembly...'

Mr Speaker: 'When did you get this notice?'

Shri P.C. Utaya: 'This morning.'

Mr Speaker: 'At what time?'

Shri P.C. Utaya: '8.30.'

Mr Speaker: 'So, what is your objection?'

Shri P.C. Utaya: 'We must have had sufficient notice.'

Mr Speaker: 'I personally feel that a Resolution like this, though according to the Rules requires sufficient notice, is on a matter which has been discussed and known to everybody. I do not think there is anything new in this. You also find that Shri A.C. Thimiah has sent a Resolution to the same effect. So, this is a matter which all the Members are aware. I personally do not feel that there is any case for postponement. But, if you feel that there was not time to study the Resolution, I have no objection for the House to adjourn till 2.30 p.m.

Shri P.C. Uthaya: 'Thank you.'

Shri C.M. Poonacha: 'May I submit Sir, the subject matter relating to today's discussion has already been indicated in the notice that has been issued summoning this Assembly. Naturally, the Government has a duty to initiate the debate here, and all that I propose is to initiate the debate in the form of a Resolution. Without a specific resolution, it would be difficult for me to initiate the debate. As such, Sir, I have preferred to move a Resolution myself and initiate the debate, in which the Hon Members can take the full opportunity of expressing their view-points.'

Mr Speaker: 'Any objections?'

Shri P.C. Utaya: 'The subject-matter may be a subject of general discussion. But, here this is a specific Resolution, and we must be prepared to answer specific matters arising out of the Resolution. So, we certainly want time.'

Mr Speaker: 'What the Chief Minister was suggesting was that he will initiate the debate now. Then, if the majority agree, we may adjourn till 2.30 in the afternoon today so that the Members may have enough time to think over the matter.'

Shri P.C. Utaya: 'Yes.'

Shri C.M. Poonacha: 'Sir, I beg leave to initiate the discussion on the recommendations of the States Reorganisation Commission by moving a Resolution which reads as follows:

'This Assembly, having considered the report of the States Reorganisation Commission, is of the opinion that the State of Karnataka, comprising of (1) Coorg, (2) The present state of Mysore including the whole of Bellary district, (3) The district of South Kanara including that part of Kasargod taluk lying to the north of Chandragiri river and Kollegal taluk of Coimbatore district in the Madras State, (4) The districts of Raichur, Gulbarga and the contiguous four taluks of Bidar district in the State of Hyderabad and (5) The districts of Bijapur, Dharwar, North Kanara and Belgaum (excluding Chandgad taluk) be formed.'

Shri P.C. Utaya: 'Mr Speaker, Sir...'

Shri C.M. Poonacha: 'This Assembly is further of opinion that having regard to Coorg...'

Shri P.C. Utaya: 'May I know, Mr Speaker, Sir, whether there is a comma after "Chandragiri River"...'

Shri C.M. Poonacha: 'No, Sir.'

Shri P.C. Utaya: Does it mean that Kasargod Taluk lying to north of Chandragiri River and Kollegal Taluk...'

Shri C.M. Poonacha: 'Sir, the areas which are now included in the State of Madras are (1) South Kanara including part of Kasargod Taluk lying to the north of Chandragiri River, and (2) Kollegal Taluk.'

Shri P.C. Utaya: 'So, there is a comma.'

Shri C.M. Poonacha: 'There need not be a comma. They are the two areas.

'This assembly is further of opinion that having regard to Coorg having been a separate unit for a century and with a view to maintain the present standard of progress in Coorg, the Government of India may kindly incorporate the following safeguards in the appropriate legislation to be enacted by Parliament in this behalf:

1. 'That the present state of Coorg be kept as a district as recommended by the States Reorganisation Commission.
2. 'That Coorg be given a minimum representation of five members in the future Karnataka Legislature.
3. 'That the present representations in the two houses of Parliament provided for Coorg be continued.
4. 'That the Second Five-year Plan programme as prepared by the Coorg State Government and approved by the Planning Commission be implemented fully; and
5. 'That the exemption so far enjoyed from the operation of the Arms Act by the people of Coorg be continued.

'Sir, the question of reorganising the component parts of the Indian Union under a Federal pattern has been engaging the attention of the Nation for a very long time. This has been the subject matter of keen discussions and inquiries from time to time. Several Commissions and Committees, both at official and non-official levels, were constituted to go into this matter in an exhaustive manner and give their recommendations. We have today a considerable volume of literature on this question wherein very useful data and information have been gathered. Prior to Independence, this question was not very seriously considered by the then Government of India for reasons well known to us. Though new provinces were created from time to time, the basis for such new creations was purely political than administrative. After Independence, the question became more lively and public opinion began to express itself in clearer and stronger terms. At the time when the Constituent Assembly was engaged in drafting the Constitution for Independent India, the question of reorganising the States on a rational basis was emphatically put forward by several sections and Government of India had to refer the same to a Committee, which is popularly known as Dhar Committee. The Dhar Committee had gone into the question of Reorganising the States of the Indian Union on a rational basis in great detail and its conclusions could not be brought into practice as there were several outstanding problems confronting the nations immediately after Independence. Partition of India, integration of the Indian States, the refugee problems, shortage of food grains, were all problems of unimaginable magnitude to which the Nation had to address itself for a successful solution. In that context, the framers of the Constitution thought it expedient to evolve a Constitution wherein four categories of States were created as Constituent Units of the Indian Union. These different categories of States were found necessary to meet the situation arising mainly out of the integration of 600 odd Princely States. I do not wish here to dilate on this question of integration of the Indian States between 1948 and 1951. That process was very ably brought to a successful conclusion by the outstanding statesmanship qualities of late Sardar Vallabhbhai Patel, the then Deputy Prime Minister of India. Thus, at the time of framing the Constitution at the first stage, a pattern was evolved to meet a particular expediency which was not final in itself. However, the question of reorganising the constitutional units of our Union Government still remained as an issue to be decided at a later stage after we had successfully tackled the more urgent problems of the Nation. Later, on 29th of December 1953, Government of India, by a Resolution, constituted a High-Power Commission to examine this question and submit its recommendations. That Commission toured all over the country, conducted detailed enquiries and has submitted its recommendations to the Government of India, which report was published on the 10th of October this year.

'Here in Coorg the future of Coorg has always been a live issue. Public opinion has been expressing itself differently, at times with a certain amount of emphasis in favour of amalgamation of Coorg with a major unit and at times, particularly during recent times, in favour of retaining Coorg as a separate unit. This question has been the subject-matter of discussions several times in the previous Legislative Council and in the Coorg Legislative Assembly, that is, in the March Session of this Assembly in 1954. If we carefully analyse the arguments that were advanced from time to time, whether for amalgamation or for separation, one would realise the fact that the question of merging Coorg in a bigger unit was invariably a hypothetical one, inasmuch as the Unit with which Coorg should be merged was never clearly defined or realised. At times some advocated merger of Coorg in Mysore and at times some sponsored the idea of merger of Coorg in the State of Madras and at times with the future

Karnatak Province which was not defined in precise terms. It is only now after the States Reorganisation Commission report that Karnatak Province has been more precisely defined and we are now called upon to give our views on the question of Coorg becoming an integral part of the Karnatak Province as envisaged by the States Reorganisation Commission. In the absence of a clearly defined Karnatak area, it was not possible to obtain a clear view on the point of Coorg merging with Karnataka. As such, public opinion in Coorg naturally laid greater emphasis on securing responsible Government to Coorg. This desire of the people was fulfilled by the passing of the Part "C" States Act of 1951, consequent to which this Assembly has been constituted with responsible Government.

'A further analysis of the agitation in Coorg regarding amalgamation or separation reveals that the matter was being considered only from the standpoint of Coorg alone without much reference to the All-India set-up. Therefore, the implementing authority naturally could not take a decision because they did not wish to tackle problems individually as they wanted to deal with these problems under a rational scheme of arrangements drawn up for the entire Nation. The States Reorganisation Commission has now placed before the Nation a scheme drawn up for the whole of India and in that they have made two important recommendations: (1) that there should be one category of States on a footing of equality as the constituent units of Indian Union, and (2) that the other categories of States, named "B" and "C" States should be abolished.

'The future of Coorg is directly affected by the abovementioned recommendations and in that context, we have to discuss the future of our State. It is no doubt a fact that at the time when the States Reorganisation Commission visited Coorg, people of Coorg in general and all the 24 Members of this House in particular represented that Coorg should be continued as a separate entity with the responsible set-up given to them by an Act of Parliament (Part "C" States Act of 1951). By doing so, we the representatives of the people have done our best to meet the aspirations of the people of the State. I wonder whether we could have made any representation in stronger terms than this in this regard. Having faithfully done that and also followed it up by our own acts of running the administration here on a progressive line to which fact the States Reorganisation Commission Report bears ample testimony, today we are required to review our position in the light of the scheme of things drawn up for the whole of India. It would be futile for anyone, in my opinion, to use this occasion to put the blame on anybody or try to find fault with anyone. We have done well, and we have acted in a united manner. It is now time for us to face facts in the context of the recommendations made by the States Reorganisation Commission. The Karnatak Province as envisaged under the States Reorganisation Commission recommendations has a bright future with immense potentialities for development. It has vast natural resources, good number of industrial enterprises and has many facilities for Trade and Commerce. It is but natural for a quiet people like the people of Coorg to feel a bit disturbed at the proposal of merging with a bigger unit. This temporary nervousness is only a passing phase and on careful examination and a will to work in co-operation with our brethren, I am sure we will be able to shake off the despondency. I earnestly request one and all here to give a whole-hearted support to the future Karnatak State which is sure to command a dignified position among the constituent units of the Indian Union and thereby enrich and strengthen our Motherland.

'Jai Hind'

Shri P.C. Utaya rose to speak.

Mr Speaker: 'You want the House to be adjourned till 2.30 in the afternoon? The House is adjourned till 2.30 in the afternoon.'
The Assembly adjourned at 11.19 a.m.

◆

2.30 p.m. after lunch

Mr Speaker: 'Honourable Members who wish to speak on the Resolution may take the opportunity of speaking.'

Shri A.C. Thimiah [Separatist Party]: 'Mr Speaker, Sir, although a Resolution was tabled by me about twenty days ago on an opinion regarding the acceptance of the States Reorganisation Commission Report, it seems to have taken the Government a very long time to decide and produce a Resolution before the floor of this House, the Resolution which I only received at 8.30 this morning. All I can infer from this is that we are dealing with politicians who cannot make up their minds but are fully prepared to sit on the fence and see which side they will turn. We are at the crossroads of history and the decision that we have to take is so vital in the interest of the State and its future. I know the local feeling, the inherited loyalty and the sentimental attachments of this Province, but we must be prepared to make this sacrifice in the larger interest of the State and India as a whole. The Reorganisation of States was a major problem, and our Prime Minister tackled this issue by placing the task in the hands of the three able men, viz., Justice Fazal Ali, Pandit Kunzru and Sardar Panikkar, one a distinguished Judge, and the other a distinguished leader, and the other, a great diplomat. These men were relied on to give their independent view of the problem. The task was by no means an easy one, and they have done a magnificent job in formulating the present Report.

'I listened very carefully to the Chief Minister's statement. He has, right through the course of his statement, not given one reason why Coorg should be joined on to Karnataka. When he made his statement, he merely mentioned of the various Commissions, and the States Reorganisation Commission, but has not shown why Coorg should be joined to Karnataka. The people today are anxious to know why? But those views have not been expressed.

'I was, at one time, a very ardent Separationist, and with the changing conditions of a nature, I have had to change my views. The original stand has changed in the light of the views of the Part "C" States expressed by the Commission and assessing the truth of those views by comparing them with conditions as they are practised in Coorg.

'One of the major problems is the administrative difficulty. We have most of our technical officers recruited from outside, which clearly shows that there is no scope or facility for young men of this Province which is isolated and unable to get the basic knowledge and professional experience essential for higher appointments. Let us look back to the period before responsible Government was introduced in Coorg. You have had people of Coorg in very high administrative and technical appointments in the outside Provinces in Mysore, and yet, since then, we have not been able to produce men to take over technical appointments in Coorg at much lower level! This clearly shows that this Ministry had no organised planning and foresight and were [sic] only prepared to carry on a day-to-day routine basis. These views have already been expressed by the Chief Minister himself before the Administrative Commission of Part "C" States in Delhi in 1951.

'The political background of this Province, though it started on a democratic basis, has become a personal rule with greater interplay of personal ambitions and jealousies mainly due to not enough work which has led to interference in administration, leaving little time for policy-making and strengthening the points of initiative, drive, and sense of responsibility in the Services. These aspects have been fully covered in the S.R.C. Report. The Members of this Legislature are fully aware of these points. They know that a true democratic set-up of government can only be run when the Party Rule ceases to exist.

'I would like you to consider the effect of separation on the youth of Coorg. Prior to 1952, it was comparatively easy for a young man to get vacancies in technical colleges. As you will agree, this is not the case now. They are finding it more and more difficult to do so. It is of interest to know that those of our young men who have had the [sic] education did not return to Coorg and found appointments elsewhere. This also is becoming more and more difficult, and unless Coorg is in a position to offer better prospects for these young men who cannot depend on land, Coorg must join a larger unit as has been suggested by this Commission. These young men who have proved themselves efficient outside Coorg when compared with other Indians, cannot be expected to stagnate in a small State. You have only to look back upon the achievements of the people of Coorg in the neighbouring State of Mysore prior to 1951. They have proved that efficiency is no bar. To prove my facts are correct, how many people have got any comparative position since we started this attempt for separation? There may be a certain amount of doubt as to the effect of amalgamation of Coorg on the Development during the Second Five-Year Plan. As you are well aware, our Prime Minister has made a statement to the effect that whatever finances have been allotted to the respective States as they stand today, will be utilised for their progress. Taking all these points in view, I find that we should all join Karnataka with a feeling of goodwill. I know the minds of everybody in Coorg regarding the S.R.C. Report. I would also like you to look at it in a dispassionate way. It will clearly show that politically, economically and from the point of view of our youth, amalgamation is the only solution. I would like to add that what I have stated is the problem as I see it. The people of Coorg are groping in the dark and they need guidance whether amalgamation or separation is better. I would welcome, and I am sure a statement by responsible Ministers on the issue would help clear any doubts that might exist. I have expressed the viewpoints, and I sincerely hope that the Members of this House, whether for or against amalgamation, will give their points so that people may have a clear view of the pros and cons of the issue.

'The Chief Minister during the course of his Address has said that the States Reorganisation Commission has praised the administration for its work. Well, I do not say that Coorg has not improved during the past four years. But I still maintain that all the progress that has been achieved in Coorg has been primarily due to the villagers and the small subordinate officers. They are the ones who have made Coorg what it is today. And as I said before, this government was governing the country on a routine basis. These plans were made in Delhi, and it was up to them to carry out those plans. The credit is to our Prime Minister and his worthy colleagues, who by their initiative and drive have made India what it is. We have been very snug and complacent. We have been only thinking of ourselves. In Coorg, we had all what we wished for. So, we were in a position to make the necessary improvements without any hindrance. Outside people were faced with famine, faced with rehabilitation problems. There was no food, and those problems were tackled with great efficiency, and today we can claim ourselves to be a Nation because these great problems were tackled and thus shown to the world that our internal structure is sound. I know, as I speak today, that the sacrifice of our people is great. In the course of my Resolution, I have said that "Although this Assembly is aware of the immense advantages to the people of Coorg, if Coorg is maintained as a separate State, the House realises that in the larger interest of the country as a whole, the recommendations of the Committee ought to be accepted and therefore endorsed and accepted." I accept the recommendations of the Commission, but I accept it with a very sorry heart. I love my country, and I know that the sacrifice is great, but I feel that we also will be contributing to a new India which is now taking a great stride into history for a social and economic revolution. Let us quit play-acting, get down to brass-tacks, work for implementing the provisions laid down in the Report of the Commission relating to the future of our Province. Let us look forward to a new era with hope and confidence, with universal brotherhood—live and let live—and work for the prosperity of the country.'

Shri M.D. Machaiya [Congress Party]: 'Mr Speaker, Sir, I fully support the Resolution moved by the Hon. Chief Minister. As we all know, the reorganisation or merger of this State has been before our people since many years. There was once an agitation to merge Coorg with Mysore during the year 1918 or so. This question received serious attention of the Indian National Congress during the leadership of Mahatmaji and consequently Congress organisation was organised on linguistic basis some years back, in which this State came under "Karnataka". This reorganisation was once more or less accepted by the people, but owing to one reason or the other, there has been an agitation against Karnataka since the last few years and in particular during the last general election. Since then, this question has been prominently engaging the attention of the people of this State.

'The Parliament of India found it necessary to appoint a Commission to go into this question. The Commission, after touring the whole of India, has now submitted its recommendations, wherein they have included Coorg in the future Karnataka which is the proper place for this State under the present set-up.

'At the time of the stay of the Commission in Coorg, the opinion of the people was ascertained, and this Assembly not only passed a unanimous Resolution, but also submitted a memorandum to the effect that the State be kept as it is. Since the publication of the Report of the Commission, the Congress organisation of this State sent out a deputation to find out the possibilities of keeping this State as it is. These efforts also failed, and therefore, we have no other democratic way than the acceptance of the Report of the Commission. This Commission has also made it clear that in the future set-up, there will be only one form of States and Centrally Administered Areas, thereby completely eliminating "B" and "C" States. Our "C" State has no place to remain as a State in the future set-up and consequently there is no alternative for us but to join the adjacent State. As far as Centrally Administered Areas are concerned, I wish to point out that such administration would amount to autocratic rule of one man, of which we had had sufficient experience since the past so many years.

'There is some agitation in south Coorg to see that this State is integrated and a part of the same merged in Malabar. This is a very unhealthy move and dangerous in the interest of the people. It is not impossible that such a move may not bear fruits in due course, should this State remain as it is for some time more.

'The Working Committee of the Indian National Congress has also recommended that in the interest of this State, acceptance of the Report is advisable. This advice comes from the great National Leaders of this country. These are the Leaders who sacrificed their everything for the cause of independence of this great and ancient country and whose advice and guidance is really reasonable and dependable, and therefore, in the real interest of the people and in the interest of this small State. I have full faith in this leadership and, therefore, I fully support the Resolution that is before us.

'Jai Hind'

Shri P.K. Channaiah [Congress Party]: 'Mr Speaker Sir, in welcoming the S.R.C. Report, I place before the House a few of my own ideas.

'Ever since 1928, a cry from good many persons were [*sic*] heard that linguistic province, i.e., Karnataka State, should be formed. Recently J.V.P. and Dhar Committee were set up for forming this Karnataka State. The valuable recommendations of these Committees were submitted to the Government, but they were not accepted and implemented.

'After our Congress government came to power, the S.R.C. was set-up on 22nd December 1953 for promoting the welfare of the people of every part of Bharat.

'The S.R.C. toured in all parts of the country, met all people and examined the question on population, finance, area, welfare of the people, administration, future progress and language and some defects and drawbacks therein were pointed out in this report produced by them for which they have to be thanked.

'But considering the culture, language, the financial position, the present administration by the Honourable Ministers, the developmental works carried out in the country, the unity among the people and the co-operation they offer, it is my desire that Coorg should have remained separate and should have been administered by the Ministers. It was the desire of the people throughout the length and breadth of Coorg.

'A report on the opinion of the public and the Members of the Legislature was submitted to the S.R.C. sometime back.

'The wishes of the political parties, the people, social workers, journalists, representatives of municipalities and notified areas and individuals on the future of Coorg was placed before the Commission.

'Noted persons of the Central Government have expressed their appreciation of the speciality of Coorg among the "C" States of India and its efficient administration, the developmental works done in the State and the confidence of the people in the Government. Because of this, our beautiful Coorg has gained a place of distinction. The Central Government has great love for our distinguished State.

'Believing that even in future Coorg will get great help from the Centre considering the welfare of India as a whole, I give my whole-hearted support to the resolution moved by the Honourable Chief Minister.'

(A Pause)

No Member rose to speak.

Mr Speaker: 'If you keep the House in suspense like this, I think it is better that I call the Honourable Members in the alphabetical order.'

(A Pause)

Shri P. Lakkaiah [Congress Party]: 'Mr Speaker, Sir, I welcome the S.R.C. Report and express my opinions. The Britishers ruled our country before our Congress Government came into being. They divided India into several provinces and ruled. Even then the leaders of our country fought for reorganisation of the provinces, and it was in vain. Then the Congress Government was established in India. Immediately there was a change in the whole of India. At no other time in the history of our country were so many items of work undertaken and completed in so short a period. Meanwhile, the S.R.C. was set up and it surveyed every State. When they asked Coorg, all the 24 representatives of the people of Coorg expressed the same opinion, namely, that Coorg should remain separate. Though the Members belonged to different parts, there was no difference of opinion on this issue and all the 24 Members gave a unanimous statement that Coorg should remain separate. But the S.R.C. has examined all the States including those which are equal to districts and those which are equal to big countries and have decided that such States should not continue and to remove their defects and drawbacks they should be reorganised into conveniently large linguistic States. Our leaders have a great desire to improve the States. We yield to this but wish that there should be a good representation to Coorg in the future Karnataka State. Saying that if such a representation is given there will be no doubt that even in future Coorg will maintain a high standard of efficiency, I support the resolution moved by the Hon'ble Chief Minister.'

Mr Speaker: 'I am making a list in the alphabetical order and I will call the names.'

Shri C.K. Calappa [Congress Party]: 'Mr Speaker Sir, when the States Reorganisation Commission came here, we all placed before them our unanimous opinion that Coorg should be kept separate. But they did not agree to this and they have given in their report several reasons for this. But the way they have referred to Coorg in their report makes us proud. In para 252 of page 71, they have said "of the nine [actually, 10] Part 'C' States, six have legislatures and Ministers; and of these only one, namely Coorg, has been in a position to carry on so far, a reasonable system of administration without Central assistance.'

'This is a thing which all the people of Coorg may be proud of. The S.R.C. have placed before us their report keeping in view the welfare of the people of India as a whole. Dividing India into linguistic States has been one of the aims of the National movement of India. When politicians have upheld that opinion for the last 40 years, it does not seem right to side-track the issue now. The Commission have deeply considered all aspects of the problem, the historical background, the present state of affairs and presented their report.

'Today the government has placed before us a resolution. We are now guided by the present context and we should act accordingly. There is no use putting up a sandy dam across a speeding flood. It is prudent to act according to the circumstances we are placed in and it is inevitable.

'The resolution moved by the Honourable Chief Minister is quite suitable to the occasion. I beseech the Central Government to comply with the requests contained in the resolution without any exception. The amount allotted for Coorg in the Second Five-Year Plan should be spent in Coorg. There should be at least five representatives from Coorg in the Karnataka Assembly. The concessions in Coorg under the Arms Act should continue. In addition, the 'Jamma' tenure should also continue forever. Requesting that there should be representation for Coorg in Lok Sabha and Rajya Sabha maintaining it as a separate district, I completely support the resolution.

'Promotion of unity and security of the whole of India should be the chief aim of any step taken in the name of reorganisation. Any agitation that brings about disunity in the country will ultimately be dangerous to all the parties in India. Any step, in reorganisation which results in intricacies and breach of peace will be a blow to the feeling of oneness of the people of India and any such thing should not be allowed.'

Mr N.G. Ahammed [Separatist Party]: 'Mr Speaker, Sir, I strongly support the resolution moved by the Leader of this House for the formation of Karnataka State. There is no doubt that we will be losing our individuality as Coorg State, but we the Members of this Assembly feel that our main objective is to see that the people of Coorg prosper and have all the amenities which are enjoyed by the people in a well administered State. All the members of the House are aware of what improvements have come up in our tiny State during the last five years. This is all due to the strenuous work put in by our Ministers and further if all the safeguards proposed for enactment are approved, I can definitely say that even then our Coorg District will be one of the best districts in the whole of Karnataka. We are not joining with foreigners. They are our brothers, and with mutual help we will prosper further, and the time is not far off when Karnataka will have a very important position in the Union of India.

'Jai Hind'

Shri P.I. Belliappa [Separatist Party]: 'Mr Speaker, Sir, I do not wish to speak.'

Shri K.M. Devayya [Congress Party]: 'Mr Speaker, Sir, I regard that today is the most important day in the history of Coorg. We have to discuss the recommendations of the S.R.C. and carve the magnificent future of Coorg and hence the progress of the Indian Union. If we review the history of Coorg for the last 40 or 50 years, the future of Coorg was taxing the minds of people of Coorg even when it was under the British rule and has been so after Independence and the advent of the people's government. The future of Coorg is a question which has been occupying the most important place in the political field of the thinking people of Coorg. We have seen that several groups of people of Coorg have spent thousands of rupees on their visits to Delhi and Bangalore keeping this question at the Centre.

'Sir, my intention in giving this introduction to the subject is to show how important the question of the future of Coorg is to the people of Coorg. At this crucial moment when we are to discuss this important question, we have to review, discuss and come to a definite conclusion with the recommendations of the S.R.C. in the background.

'We all know that when the Britishers left our country, the map of India was not in a condition capable of promoting the good of the people. On the one side there were 600 feudal States, on another, States having a mixture of several languages and cultures and still on another side, petty provinces. Thus, it was a confused mixture. Only a few years after attainment of Independence, the unparalleled thinker of India, the late Vallabhbhai Patel uprooted the 600 feudal princes and created a new map of India. As a result, the States of Rajapramukhs were given birth to. This was the first step in the politics of India. This change resulted in the formation of three types of States–"A", "B" and "C". The administration in these three types of States was not alike and several knotty problems arose. By this interim change, the people of India gained valuable experience in the democratic form of government.

'The lack of uniform method of administration in the several parts of Independent India caused a set-back in the economic, cultural, political and democratic growth of the country and the Lok Sabha which realised this, set-up the S.R.C. The most experienced wise men of India were appointed as members of this Commission. The total number of representations, telegrams, etc., from the many political bodies and individuals received by this Committee was 1,52,250. They have with them the opinions, memoranda, and suggestions from more than 9,000 institutions and individuals of the country. These great persons have very carefully reviewed and examined these. They have regarded the unity and all-round development of the Union of India as their yardstick in examining these.

'The important features of this report are the abolition of the posts of Rajapramukhs and "C" States and giving equal status and complete independence to the people of all the States under the democratic set-up. It is very good of the Commission to have done away with the invidious differences among the "A", "B" and "C" States and formed states having the same status. While forming such States, the unity and progress of India as a whole have been given importance. This report founded on the security of the Union of India has gained appreciation of the Central Government. This report has been already accepted by several States of India. Though this report has not satisfied all the people of India, it has satisfied a good majority.

'I am one of the persons who have realised that our Coorg can remain as a separate State having the required facilities to stand on its own legs. But the reorganisation should not be viewed from the standpoint of the welfare of only one State. The security of the Indian Union and historical and cultural background of a unit should be the criterion. The report might have disappointed many people of Coorg. But we should place before us the map of whole of India, keep down our selfish desires and examine the question today. When we do so, we notice how our neighbouring State of Mysore has accepted the recommendations keeping the unity of India in view. We too should have the same view and accept and welcome the recommendations. We shall be a part of the Karnataka State and by being so we shall hope for the progress and all-round development of the Indian Union.

'Whatever be the problems staring before us, we shall try to examine them coolly causing no disturbance to the unity of India, avoiding selfishness and holding up to the whole world the torch of peace and sacrifice. We shall therefore decide selflessly and peacefully that it is one of our duties today to welcome the recommendations of the S.R.C.

'Jai Hind'

Shri K.K. Ganapathi [Separatist Party]: 'Mr Speaker, Sir, I first of all thank the States Reorganisation Commission for having spoken well of Coorg in their report. Among other States some have accepted the report and some others have criticised. I thank the Hon'ble Chief Minister for having moved this resolution. Thanks for having moved that Coorg should be kept as a separate district in the proposed State of Karnataka. When we have to merge with Karnataka, he has at best asked for a separate district of Coorg and therefore he should be thanked (*laughter*). It is with the idea that it is not possible to keep separate such small States like Coorg that they have recommended that Coorg should merge with Karnataka. But practically it is not impossible. When Sardar Patel removed petty princes and combined several small feudal States into "B" States, many small States disappeared. But there were examples of States even smaller than Coorg running their own administration. It is not proper to make any remark on the smallness or bigness of administration. From the point of the Government and people, it is better to have smaller States. It is more convenient to improve such small provinces like the Chief Commissioner's provinces. It is convenient to the State and to the Government. Poor people will get the help they want easily, we know. From this point of view, it would have been better if Coorg had remained separate. Those who want to accept the recommendations of the States Reorganisation

Commission in support of the formation of Karnataka with the welfare of India in view, want to show to the others how to implement the schemes as we have done in Coorg by working with the same earnestness. We could have shown this. If the Central Government had allowed us to remain separate at least for another ten years, we could have been a model to the others by working out our schemes successfully. Because the income of Coorg is sufficient to enable it to stand on its own legs, it is a model to the whole of India. The Hon'ble Chief Minister said that they tried sufficiently but they could not succeed. But I feel that proper attempt was not made. I was very happy when we gave a unanimous report to the States Reorganisation Commission when they visited Coorg. Coorg can, however, join Karnataka. All favour the move. But thereby the poor *ryot* and the worker will be hit hard. It is not enough if we look to the welfare of India. We should look after our welfare first. If every State in India can run its administration well, it is better to be separate.

'There is no way for us to remain separate. Coorg has left our hands. If all the 24 members had joined together and convinced the Central Ministry the other day that we could stand on our own feet, we would have succeeded. I feel—some people still feel—like that. Many feel with me that it is better to remain separate.

'I have actually seen many people not heeding their suffering, coming from long distances, and meeting our Chief Minister. Many still wish to keep Coorg separate. It may be difficult. Many want all the 24 of us to try to keep Coorg separate.

'Even then I, in a way, say again and again that Coorg should soon merge with Karnataka. There is a particular difficulty if we have such a small State. Many are already feeling that they should join a bigger province. They create all sorts of trouble in a small State setting up parties and groups. We won't have such difficulties if they are at a distance. It is better to join bigger States. Those who wanted to remain separate have changed their opinion and want to join bigger States. You might have seen in papers. Many articles and statements have appeared. If you go to the village corners, the difficulty of the people...'

Shri P.M. Nanamayya [Congress Party]: 'You must give some specific instances, who has given statements, and in which paper? This may be made clear.'

Shri K.K. Ganapathi: 'Some have published their names, and some have not. Shri Nanamayya...'

Shri P.M. Nanamayya: 'Please specify the article and state who is dissatisfied and who are all that have suffered. There is no use in beating about the bush. Who has sacrificed whom?'

Shri K.K. Ganapathi: 'I did not say that any one is sacrificed.'

Shri P.M. Nanamayya: 'I have an opportunity of answering them and I shall answer them.'

Shri K.K. Ganapathi: 'From this point of view...because Shri Nanamayya interrupted, I forgot what all I thought *(laughter)*. From this point of view, I want Coorg to merge with Karnataka as early as possible. With these words I support the resolution moved by the Hon'ble Chief Minister.'

Shri B.K. Kala [Congress Party]: 'Mr Speaker, Sir, I have nothing to speak.'

Shri K.P. Karumbaiya [Separatist Party]: 'Mr Speaker, Sir, I should think this is the saddest day in the history of Coorg, for, we have got to discuss a motion very seriously, purported to efface from the map of India the separate entity of Coorg, which we all loved so much till now. In moving the motion before the House, the Leader of the House has traced the conflicting opinion in the State, at least during our generation, as to the existence separately or as a part of a major adjoining State. I should think that if there were any conflict, if the wishes of the people to go into a major State having not materialised in the past, to my knowledge in the year 1918 to go with Madras or subsequently with Mysore, it was not because the adjoining State was not in its full working condition or was not a State whose boundaries were not demarcated or a State which was very uncertain to go with. If at all the people have kept back from going to a major State in the past, it was because there was some sort of bickering and difference of opinion as to their continuance to exist as a separate entity. There was a harmonious compromise to run or continue as a separate entity. To my knowledge, it has been a sad feature that ever since I became Member of Coorg Legislature in the year 1941, there was hardly a year when we did not have the discussion as to the future of our State. It looked as though there was some sort of insecurity or uncertainty as to what we are going to be. In the year 1949, the matter became very serious. All the same it was with the good grace of the Government of India we were allowed to remain separate for some time till future orders changed our status quo. Fortunately for us in the year 1951, the Part "C" States Act came into being and it has given us the popular Ministry. Though many of our protagonists of merger of the State with an adjoining State were chafing under some sort of uncertainty or uncomfortableness as to the successful working of the popular Ministry on account of various difficulties such as finances, and administrative capacity, etc., I was very happy to find that the Popular Ministry, according to me, was a success, and I was very happy that the people of the country shed their doubts as to the possibility of remaining a separate entity and united themselves to see that Coorg continued as a separate entity as it has been hitherto, without any sort of interference, so far as the status quo was concerned. Accordingly, there has been further evidence, Sir, of an unanimous Resolution passed on the floor of this House during the Budget Session of the year 1954, and that Resolution to my great surprise, was moved by my Hon. Friend Shri A.C. Thimiah and supported by every Member of this House to the effect that Coorg should continue to remain separate. There, before recording the votes, the Government of the day— our Ministers—refrained from voting for reasons known to themselves best. But an amendment was moved by my friend Shri C.A. Mandanna that all the 24 members of this House should unanimously sign a memorandum to be presented to the States Reorganisation Commission and submit it as an operative part of the resolution. Though the Hon'ble Ministers refrained from voting for or against Resolution, I am so glad that they too signed the memorandum and thus fulfilled so far as the operating part of the Resolution was concerned, unanimously. So, it was a happy augury for us all and I felt for myself that the future of our State was certain because we as one man had signed the memorandum and made a very clear case before the States Reorganisation Commission that our State could exist hereafter as it has existed hitherto a separate entity and a component of Indian Union. Even in reply to certain questions orally asked by States Reorganisation Commission—"Whether we could not go with Mysore or Samyuktha Karnataka", we categorically replied that our State could remain as it had been hitherto as a separate entity as a component of Indian Union, because it has got all the ingredients that warrant the existence of a separate State. We made a case that on account of historical reasons, the compactness of area, financial viability, economic progress, administrative convenience, distinct individuality and for several reasons that make a small but steady State, we can run and can continue as a separate State. I, for myself, felt no reason to change that very healthy decision that the country as a whole had come to through its representatives on the floor of this House and as represented to the States Reorganisation Commission, by a memoranda.

'Even when the Report of the States Reorganisation Commission was published, I gathered that certain representatives from this country went as far as the Government of India to impress upon them the necessity of not interfering with our status quo. Till yesterday, Sir, I for one felt that the Coorg Legislature as a whole would not allow themselves to deflect from what opinion they gave before the States Reorganisation Commission just sixteen months ago. We have listened very carefully to the observations made by the Hon'ble Members of this House, particularly from the Congress Benches, during the last Budget Session, that our State, our Popular Ministry has been functioning very efficiently, that we have been having something like a paradise here in this State, today, and that has been due to, among other factors, to Coorg remaining as a separate State. So far as I am concerned, last evening when I got the agenda of the Government supporting the merger of Coorg to the future Karnataka, I was surprised, and I do not know what are the reasons, what are the considerations that have heavily weighed on the Government of the day and also the ruling party of the country to depart from the decision we unitedly took some months ago. I for one would strongly feel, Sir, that so far as our recommendations or the case we have made before the States Reorganisation Commission, the States Reorganisation Commission has not categorically refuted our claims, our capacity and right to remain as a separate State. While making comparisons of "C" States as institutions in this country, they have paid, I should think, an approbation or encomiums on Coorg having functioned better than other "C" States. So far as we are concerned, they have said that of all these "C" States, in the country, or at any rate, out of the nine Part "C" States, Coorg is the only State that has not gone with bended knee to the Government of India for doles. It is the only State which has been remaining on its own feet so far as the finances are concerned. It is the only State, at least it is implied in so many words that the popular Ministry has been as much a success as it ought to be proud which we feel to note, Sir. If that is so and if the States Reorganisation Commission has stated categorically that every State is something like a limb of the Indian Union, what is there to prevent us from saying that we are like one of the five fingers of the hand and what does it matter whether one finger is longer or stouter than the other and as long as these limbs are there to strengthen the full structure or organs as a whole. I cannot personally see any reason whatsoever why a limb, because it is short or stouter than the other, should be cut off from the main organ or at any rate could have been selected to be put an end to and obliterated, when we see both small and big States existing side by side elsewhere as organs of Unions.

'So far as this Resolution as it stands, Sir, it favours the merger of Coorg with Karnataka, comprising of the various Kannada speaking areas. Even there, the Leader of the House feels that all may not sail well. He even feels that if we go with Karnataka, at any rate, he is not probably complacent or feeling it at ease to say that we can, however, swim or sink with them. He wants some safeguards. Of course, he has referred to, as recommended by the States Reorganisation Commission, that Coorg will continue as a separate District. Even there, the States Reorganisation Commission has respected our views by reason of our individuality that Coorg should be kept as a separate

District in the future. Certain other safeguards that the Leader has sought for are of course "Exemption from the operation of the Arms Act and five seats in the Provincial State Legislature and two seats in the Indian Parliament". Of course, so far as I am concerned, if the Government of India is out to bring about some sort of unity, if the Government of India thinks of prescribing seats in the Indian Parliament "Lok Sabha", at one seat could be given to a State which has a population of seven and a half lakhs, and if our State continues to be a District of one of the big State "Karnataka", I have got my own doubts whether the 2,29,000 people would be given one seat in the Lower House and another in the Rajya Sabha and constitutional guarantee could be given to Coorg. At the same time, to my knowledge, I find that so far as Mysore Legislature is concerned, they have provided one seat for a population of 75,000 and if that is the calculation on which seats have got to be allotted in the future Karnataka, I do not know whether for a population of 2,29,000 we would be entitled for five seats. In the States Reorganisation Commission Report itself, a comparison has been drawn between Coorg and Malabar and other States so far as the number of electorates are concerned. They have said that 24 members in a small State like ours is too many. They have said one Minister for an electorate of 45,000 is too much compared to other States. If that is so, I am sure in these days when no discrimination could be made between man and man, between citizens and citizens as per our Constitution, any preference or any weightage would be given to us, and I would be the happiest man if the claims of this House or the people of the place are complied with by the authorities concerned, and the same incorporated in an Act of the Parliament in the future.

'So far as the exemption from the operation of the Arms Act is concerned, I submit, I am not very keen to have that, for these reasons. These are the days when every citizen is allowed to hold a gun, is allowed the free pass to hold a gun if it is found necessary. Every Indian is being and ought to be trained in the art of defence. So, only one community to exercise that privilege, means asking for perpetuation of a privilege in these days of equality and I am not very keen so far as the pressing of the particular safeguard is concerned. But, in the interest of our economy, in the interest of the peasantry, I would go a step further and say that the eligibility to the continuation of the inalienability of land tenure could be retained somehow or other, if at all we are making a claim for any safeguard, that safeguard could be sought to see that our peasantry is not rendered landless. And further, the Hon'ble Members are aware that so far as Coorg is concerned, we have got some sort of statutory exemption from the sale of immoveable properties are concerned in the execution of personal decrees in a Civil Court and if any statutory provision is made available to that effect that would certainly be a blessing in disguise so far as our rights in the State are concerned.

'Anyways, Sir, so far as the Resolution as a whole is concerned, this is a Resolution which I have got either to vote for or against. Pleading my grievances as they are, I should say that I am one of those who have sought election to this House during the last election in the year 1951–52, election on the specific issue that our State should remain separate. The mandate that the people of the country have given me is that I should go there and see that our State prospers and that the continuation of the State as a separate entity is ensured. If that is the mandate, I have been able to get from the 26,000 votes i.e., out of about 62,000 and odd that had participated in the polling, I have no right on the floor of this House to go and exercise my vote freely and see that the separate entity of the State is effaced from the map of India. I, therefore, cannot vote for the resolution. So far as my other friends are concerned, I do not hold brief for them. At any rate, it is but fair that our ruling party of the country which replied to us when we made a specific issue of the future during the last general election, that this issue did not arise at the time, should ponder over their stand. As per the letter of the Leader of the Nation, Pandit Nehru, which the ruling party read before the electorate at the time, the future of this State did not arise for the very simple reason that the Part "C" States Act was only then passed and that immediately after the passing of an Act like that for the Popular Ministry to function, the question of the future did not arise. I therefore felt that so far as the electorate of the country was concerned, they had not been given the right lead on the specific issue. But, all the same I am very happy that even those members of the ruling party in the year 1954 passed a resolution unanimously that Coorg should remain separate, and further as an operative part of it, they unanimously signed a memorandum presented to the States Reorganisation Commission pleading that Coorg can exist separately, and must continue to be separate, that its future must be ensured so far as the future set-up of the country in the reorganisation scheme is concerned. Therefore, I feel that we have got all the reasons that we have pleaded before the States Reorganisation Commission just sixteen months ago, even now, to keep Coorg separate. We feel that the welfare of the people must be the paramount issue so far as the changed set-up of Government is concerned. Therefore, if you have made a case for finding the way to self-sufficiency, if you have made a case because this is a small unit, that the administration is more efficient, if you have made a case that our finances could further be augmented, there is no reason to make a departure from that wholesome stand now as the various Chief Ministers met in a conference, and it was pleaded on behalf of the Part "C" States that the Government of India must concede to a portion from the divisible pool of Income Tax and Central Excise Duty under Article 264 of the Constitution to all "C" States and must be made available to the concerned "C" States, also were only kind enough to press that, if you were unanimous so far as that position is concerned that would have further augmented our revenues required for overall development. I am sure that any decision the Government of India or the Indian Parliament would have taken under those circumstances cumulatively in respect of the implementation of the recommendations of the States Reorganisation Commission relating to our State would not have gone against the wishes of the people of the State or the aspirations of the people. I am sure we have not exhausted all the means that are at our command to see that the people's wishes and aspirations are fulfilled, and it is a matter in evidence even so far as today is concerned that some people who fought to see that Coorg is [a] separate unit have come all the way from all the corners of Coorg out of sheer depth of feeling and love for Coorg to impress upon us and remind us of the promises we held out to them during our electioneering so that we may not deflect from the path of our duty to see that the State as hitherto continues still further as a separate entity, as the continuance of the State as a separate entity would be certainly promoting the welfare of the people of this State as a whole. For these reasons, Sir, I feel that it would not be possible for me to go counter to the wishes of the people who have returned me to this Legislature, and it would not therefore be possible for me to vote for the motion. All the same, I would make a last appeal in my life that there is still time for the Members of the House to reconsider their position and to see that in a compact area of Coorg where the finances are being developed and improved day by day, in an area the ambition of every man of the ruling party and also the Opposition has been to make this a model State, as "Rama Rajya" as given expression to by late Sardar Vallabhbhai Patel, that the separate entity of Coorg is not effaced from the map of India.

'These are the few observations, Sir, that I have got to make.'

Shri G.M. Lingarajaiah [Congress Party]: 'Mr Speaker, Sir, welcoming the States Reorganisation Commission Report, I wish to offer a few remarks. I support the Resolution moved by the Honourable Chief Minister. Meanwhile, the Britishers who were the ruling leaders of India, were asking for the reorganisation of the provinces of India. But it did not materialise. When the power was transferred to our leaders and Swaraj was granted, the Central Government set up a committee to reorganise the States. They toured the country, and they submitted a report to the Central Government recommending the division of the country into 16 States according to the languages and customs and manners of the people. The Central Government published the report. People in some States have been suspicious about the report. But when the Commission visited States, the people of each State placed their opinions before the Commission, and they had all these in their mind when they produced this report. This is a body set up by our Central Government and it is natural that we should accept their recommendations.

'The Central Government, considering that ours is a Malnad area, have helped our State in several ways to improve our State. It is reasonable to accept their decisions now. I give a wholehearted support to the Resolution moved by the Hon'ble Chief Minister and request the House to pass the Resolution. Moreover, I thank the Committee for having caused the materialisation of the dream of a unified Karnataka.'

Shri C.A. Mandanna [Congress Party]: 'Mr Speaker, Sir, in supporting the Resolution moved by the Leader of the House endorsing substantially the recommendations of the States Reorganisation Commission for the formation of Karnataka State including Coorg, I may submit before this House that ever since the States Reorganisation Report was published, I have been watching the rise and fall in the barometer of public opinion in Coorg. I must admit, the immediate reaction was against the merger of the State with the proposed Karnataka State. Of course, when a State, which has remained separate for over a period of hundred years, in a State in which people have certain advantages, when it is proposed to be merged, it is but natural that the people should immediately react. But, since the publication of the Report, the people have been watching the development in the various Legislative Assemblies outside Coorg and also the reports in the Press. They have also dispassionately considered the Report, and I must say the reactions have been considerably boiled down. I may add that I have also been consulting the opinion of the various responsible gentlemen, and I must place before the House that I have been persuaded, perhaps over-persuaded, not to agitate against the merger of the State, but fully endorse the opinion of the States Reorganisation Commission to merge Coorg with Karnataka. I may also mention that in the stand I have taken, I have the consolation of feeling that I have bestowed considerable thought over the matter and have been fully convinced that the only place for Coorg in the new set-up is "Karnataka". I hope, Sir, nobody will challenge my loyalty to my people. I love my people and my State, and if anybody would challenge, I should state, with all the vehemence at my command, with all the courage of my conviction that in the love of my people, I stand second to none.

'Sir, analysing the different shades of opinion in the country, we find that a section of the people have been expressing that the State should have been kept separate for at least a period of five to ten years. They argue that for the implementation of the various developmental schemes and for working the Second Five-Year Plan, the democratic Government—the present set-up of democratic Government—should have been given another chance. Thus, in principle they agree that at some future date the State must merge with Karnataka. The only answer to them is that they must not be agitated over the working of the Second Five-Year Plan Programme, because we have the assurance from Government of India, and also as recommended in the Commission, that whatever monies have been allotted to a particular area, would be spent in that area. There is another section of the people, particularly among the younger generation which says that the educational and occupational careers would be ensured in the larger set-up, and if Coorg remains separate, there would be no scope for their future. Of course, this is the opinion with which we should also subscribe. It is also said by some that if we had waited for a couple of years—a few more years—we would have agitated for the merger of Coorg with Malabar. Of course, this opinion obviously is by a section of the people who have just now come down from Malabar. Considering the various opinions which we see in the country, we find, or I feel that those who advocate separate existence of Coorg constitute a very small minority. My appeal to the people is to those people who still maintain that Coorg should be kept as a separate State is that they should look at the problem of reorganisation dispassionately and devoid of all emotional feelings and come to a correct conclusion, a conclusion which is in the best interest of the unity of India and solidarity of the Nation.

'It may be asked as to why, having secured—having fought—for securing democratic government and having worked the democratic government successfully, I should now endorse the opinion in favour of merger. Sir, the answer to this question could only be appreciated in the light of the reasoning advanced by the States Reorganisation Commission. These able statesmen who were appointed as Members of the States Reorganisation Commission were appointed after due consideration of their abilities, their statesmanship, and they have given it as their considered opinion that all Part "C" States should go. In considering the Reorganisation of States, relevant factors such as unity of India, national security, administrative convenience, not only of any particular State, but also of the nation as a whole, have been taken into consideration. In the Reorganisation of India in the new pattern of Government that is proposed to be set-up, it would be futile for anyone to agitate to keep any State as a Part "C" State. I need hardly state that as much as 3,50,000 square miles of Princely States, with a population of 59 million people have been reorganised. As I said, it would be futile on our part to agitate any further to keep Coorg, a tiny State such as this, as a separate entity.

'We see that the Resolution also contains certain safeguards. I must, on behalf of the people, in the first place, thank the Commission for having recognised the fact that Coorg has some distinct individuality of its own, and to have recommended that Coorg should be kept as a separate District. The other safeguards are only very modest. My appeal, not only to our Karnataka brothers, but also my request to the Government of India is that these small considerations which may act as a solace to the people of Coorg may be given.

'So far as my Hon'ble friend, Shri Karumbaiya, is concerned, he suggested that certain local laws should be maintained. I think it has been recommended by the Commission that the local laws existing in the merged States should not be disturbed in so far as they do not affect the people in the State in which it has been merged. Anyhow, I request the Government to place this matter before the Government of India and to see that the unalienable system of land, the *jamma* system of land, the protection from attachment of immovable properties by personal decree-holders could be retained. There may be differences of opinion whether people have gained anything in keeping the *jamma* lands. I still say that if among the *jamma* holders there is not one single beggar today, it is because he was able to maintain the land all through. I do not know why such a system of land should not be maintained.

'Sir, my Hon'ble friend, Shri Thimiah, while supporting the Resolution made certain observations. I was rather surprised that he should have made a very uncharitable observation against the administration. It looked as though it is only because it is impossible for him to get on with this administration that he is making out a case for merger. At the same time, looking at the Resolution that he has tabled, a portion of which says that if one Karnataka is not formed and if two Karnatakas are to be formed, Coorg should be retained as a territory...'

Shri K.P. Karumbaiya: 'On a point of order, Sir, it has not been raised in the course of this debate. It has not even been moved...'

Shri C.A. Mandanna: 'I am just expressing an opinion as to what opinion that he was holding...'

Mr Speaker: 'That has not come to the consideration of the House.'

Shri C.A. Mandanna: 'It has been placed before the Members.'

Mr Speaker: 'But, he has not raised that question now.'

Shri C.A. Mandanna: 'It is not so much for the purpose of discussing the Resolution. I am not asking the House to vote for or against the Resolution, but I am only submitting what opinion my friend was holding. I am very sorry that that Resolution has not been moved in this House...'

Shri P.M. Nanamayya: 'May I know, Sir, whether it has come to the notice of the House at least?'

Mr Speaker: 'No. It has not been moved in the House.'

Shri C.A. Mandanna: 'Apart from the Resolution, Sir, I have heard it said that my friend Shri Thimiah, has been going about telling in the country that if there is going to be two Karnatakas, he will fight for keeping Coorg separate, even as a territory under a Chief Commissioner...'

Shri A.C. Thimiah: 'Mr Speaker, Sir, that statement is not quite true.'

Shri C.A. Mandanna: 'I do not know, Sir, whether the information I got was not correct...'

Shri P.M. Nanamayya: 'My submission only...'

Mr Speaker: 'Let him finish.'

Shri C.A. Mandanna: 'Anyway, I submit whether the House is in possession of the Resolution or not, the Resolution is there, it speaks for itself. My friend, Shri Thimiah, to whom it has been impossible to carry on under this administration, criticised the Government. He said that party rule should cease to exist for any democratic Government to thrive. I leave it to the Members of the House to understand the meaning of these statements. How can there be democracy without a party? I remember, Sir, that as soon as our new democratic Government was set-up, some people went and represented to the Chief Commissioner that he should be made a Minister, not knowing that in a democratic set up it is the party which elects the Ministers. My friend, Shri Thimiah, I am afraid has not understood the implications of a democracy when he said that party rule should cease to exist. It is obvious that my friend would welcome rather the Chief Commissioner's Rule than party rule. Probably he is reminded of the old days when Coorg was a "Planter's Paradise."' *(Laughter)*

Shri A.C. Thimiah: 'Mr Speaker, Sir, even that I object because I never said that I would prefer Chief Commissioner's Rule.'

Shri C.A. Mandanna: 'Anyhow, whatever may be the uncharitable remark which my friend has made, I have the consolation of knowing that other Members of his Party, particularly Shri Karumbaiya, was pleased to state that Coorg is a "Paradise". He was pleased to praise the administration. I know nobody holds brief for another among the Hon'ble Members sitting to my right. But there should be some sort of consistency, at least it should not appear that one is criticising the Government just for the sake of criticising. I do not know how when one could say that Coorg is a "Paradise", that the administration is good, the other could describe the Government as "Hell". I do not know how we can reconcile ourselves, how we can approach the people and represent to them as to what the Members are doing.

'Sir, I do not wish to make any further observations. I fully realise the sentiments expressed by my Hon'ble friend Shri Karumbaiya. I have also been thinking for some time why the State of Coorg should be merged for the mere pleasure governing language. What is wrong in Coorg? But, as I stated already, considering the whole matter objectively and devoid of all emotional feeling and in the best interest of the Nation as a whole, I have come to the conclusion that I should support the Resolution moved by the Leader of the House.'

Appendix: *The Coorg Legislative Assembly Debates* 221

Shri G.M. Manjunathaiya [Congress Party]: 'I do not wish to speak, Sir.'

Shri H.T. Muthanna [Separatist Party]: 'I have nothing to say, Sir.'

Shri P.M. Nanamayya: 'Mr Speaker, Sir, while supporting the resolution on S.R.C. report moved by the Hon'ble Chief Minister, I wish to offer a few remarks. Our friends who spoke before me on the subject have given sufficient details. Therefore, I do not want to waste the time of this House by referring in great detail to its previous history. Still, I have to state one or two points.

'The Britishers were ruling India before Independence. Even during those times our country was divided into several provinces. On what basis? They based it on their administrative convenience only. While doing so, the satisfaction of the people, their moral outlook, cultural life etc., were not considered. With some ulterior motive they divided the country into provinces clubbing together people speaking different languages and having different problems. This took place in their regime. There was not much awakening among the people then. As people realised more and more that the continuance of the provinces in the same way would not give place and facilities to the people. As a result, the Congress which represents the people, also felt likewise and only 35 years ago our leaders decided that our Indian States should be reorganised in the interest of the country, language, culture and administration etc., in a more suitable manner to bring permanent peace to the country. The responsibility of implementing the same decision was borne by the Indian Parliament which represents the people, and the Central Government appointed the S.R.C. This Commission toured all-round the country and have presented their Report to the Government.

'While expressing his opinion on this, Shri Karumbaiya said that, that opinion of our people was not recorded properly. Therefore, that was not the free opinion of our State and that our people would not agree to this. Shri Ganapathi also expressed the same opinion. The Commission has visited 105 places. They have interviewed people from all walks of life. Likewise, they have elicited the opinion of the Assembly Members and private persons. To say that the Report does not represent the public opinion is not right and that opinion cannot be accepted. They have referred to the Kannada speaking areas in their recommendations. That is, that the Kannadigas suffered most with their area split up into bits. Therefore, they want to rectify it and all the Kannada speaking people wish to form a unified Karnataka. They have suggested that the Karnataka State should include Coorg, Mysore, North and South Canara districts and it is only then that the people of Karnataka can prosper. They have given sufficient explanation for it. Any Kannadiga who has reviewed this suggestion should welcome it. If you keep in view the all-round development of the people of Kannada areas, every Kannadiga should accept this. Shri Karumbaiya said: "Our Government and Ministers had a particular opinion till yesterday. But today while seeing this terrible resolution, it is not understood why they had to change their opinion. Sufficient attempt has not been made." It looks as though he feels that we should agitate. We may agitate. We should not follow the "frogs in the well." The report prepared by the very wise men after eliciting the opinions of the whole of India has been accepted by the bigger States and greater people with very little modifications. What have the great persons said? They have not said that they would not accept. They have suggested slight modifications. It is not proper that the people of Coorg should fight. If we do so, it would not be a constructive suggestion. If we do, people of Coorg will be considered as "frog in the well". This is a time when we should welcome the Report prepared in the interest of the all-round development of the whole of India and as a part of this try to secure for our own people our due share of facilities for improvement. There is no use of our doing anything else at present and our problems will not be solved by making demonstrations in the street. We should put our next step in the right direction. We should not abuse our power. In the interest of the country as a whole everything will be done. We should not act otherwise and be ridiculed. Whatever should happen will happen. The safeguards and conveniences that we want will be obtained if we attempt to get it in the proper way. The Hon'ble friend should examine what our Prime Minister has said, what our Congress leaders have said and what Pandit Govind Vallabh Pant has said. When they are reorganising the bigger areas like Mysore State and Bombay Presidency, small States like Coorg can never remain separate. It may have a sound financial security. Our State has not been considered on the footing of financial security or efficiency of administration.

'Our friends were telling before as follows: "Our expenditure on administration is mounting up. After the advent of the Ministry in Coorg, they have increased the expenditure very much. It should be reduced". Now, when the Central Government wants to introduce a small scheme, they impede it. They talk as if "the snake should not be killed, and the stick should not be broken". This is only to criticise, and it is of no use. We should reduce the expenditure and we should bring prosperity to our people. Considering this, it is but necessary, just, and reasonable, that we should have a unified Karnataka. Some of us may be frightened on account of the formation of a united Karnataka. There is no room for such fear.

'Shri Ganapathi tells us that it would be very difficult for us if Coorg, which has been a separate State merges with Karnataka. It is a human weakness. The strength lies in readjusting ourselves. Even a graveyard is pleasant if we get adjusted to it *(laughter)*. There is no room for fear or anxiety. We will have better facilities and greater benefits. We have now put up two dams, one across Lakshmanathirtha and the other across Harangi. Unless our neighbouring States agree, we cannot do it and the people will not be benefited. On the other hand, when we form part of Karnataka, the people of Karnataka will be benefited by these and therefore there is no doubt we will succeed.

'While Shri Thimiah gave his opinion on the subject, he has criticised our government. He has brought certain charges against our Ministers themselves. He has accused them of having sat on the fence and turned to the side which was convenient to them. We must know how far it is correct. The recommendations of the S.R.C. are before everyone in the House. Who is sitting on which fence? Our Ministers are not sitting on any fence. They are real statesmen. They have to understand things, weigh the pros and cons, find out what is precedent and act accordingly. We have an old proverb meaning "adjust yourself according to the times." If they sit quiet, we will not be satisfied. Under the circumstances, they have been doing what is most beneficial to our State. I have already said that they are very good statesmen. Shri Thimiah may not realise that. Instead of that it will not be incorrect if it is stated that Shri Thimiah tries to seize the opportunity. His opinion itself is evidence for this.

'He said further, "If we remained separate, before 1952 we were getting something in technical colleges which we are not getting now and the Ministry..."'

Shri A.C. Thimiah: 'Technical appointments, I said—not technical colleges.'

Shri P.M. Nanamayya: 'Technical appointments—let us accept. Our government had to get men from outside for technical appointments. He has not told us what all technical appointments. Our government has brought some technical experts from outside. Because when we have to implement the developmental schemes under the Five-Year Plan, we have to consider whether we should not bring them from outside when we don't get the experts we want in our own State. Now that we have to undertake the Barapole Project—should we sit quiet till we get our technical personnel, or should we get them from outside and undertake the work? We should either implement the scheme or not? If we have to, we have to get experts and technical staff from outside and get it done. Why should we entertain the idea that the Mysore Government is different and Madras Government is different? The Government is lending men to the All-India Services. That feeling of "outside" and "inside" should not be there. The statesmen who are responsible for the administration of a State should not have such feelings.

'Shri Thimiah said one more thing. He agrees that the State has improved after the establishment of the Ministry and says that it is on account of the villagers and the petty officials. He has not understood correctly. It is owing to great leaders that any good work is done. Shri Thimiah gets the work in his estate done by mazdoors. Whatever income he gets is the result of the labours of these servants. Master does not work. Therefore, it means that the estates belong to his servants. It is not so. Work is done only when the master and the servants co-operate. Similarly, our leaders, people and petty officials have all joined together and done good work. It is only a good leader who can lead the people along the right path. Our Ministers are such leaders and they have done such good work. He puts salt in his mouth and says that it is tasteless. Shri Krishna has said in the Bhagavadgita "..." It is their own attitude. Once Shri Krishna told Dharmaraya "..."'

Mr Speaker: 'If it is too long, we shall not have it.'

Shri P.M. Nanamayya: 'Duryodhana could not get a good man in the whole of his country. Dharmaraya could not get a single bad man. Similarly, it is according to one's own attitude and outlook. He said: "Plans are prepared and sent from Delhi. They approve them there and send them. Our government has to do what they ask them to do". It was said our First Five-Year Plan prepared before the Ministry came to power was to cost ₹73 lakhs only. But our Ministers revised them to cost two crores and six lakhs of rupees. These were implemented. All these have to be implemented. All these have to be implemented by the State Government after taking the sanction from the Central Government. Our government has likewise. This was implemented and completed within three years after our Ministry was set up. It is only in the two States in the whole of India that schemes have been implemented so quickly. One is Saurashtra and the other is Coorg.

'If we do as our friend Shri A.C. Thimiah wants to, we cannot implement any scheme. It is only efficient State Government that can implement such schemes. "A husband who does not like curds, picks stones in his curds". When Shri Mandanna replied to him suitably. Shri Thimiah perhaps does not know what Dr Panjabrao Deshmukh stated in his address to the All-India Apiculture Conference. He has stated: "There is not such a model State like Coorg anywhere. Its government has prepared their schemes keeping in view the improvement of its people". The representatives of other States will do well to visit Coorg and prepare their schemes in the same manner. Let Shri Thimiah agree or not. We don't force him. We had an opportunity of meeting Pandit Pant when we visited Delhi. Even he said that in no other State has progress been so rapid as it is in ours. Several other Ministers have visited our State. Shri Alageshan and Shri C.D. Deshmukh have come. Everyone has heard the speeches delivered by them. Even then people say all sorts of things. God has given a tongue and he can say all sorts of things. Shri Srikanth had come. He visited Nehru Colony at Ponnampet. Then our friend invited him to visit Krishna Colony. What did they say? "I have toured through all the States in India before visiting your State. I actually see that your schemes have spread to all the corners of your State". Our friends in the front bench do not believe all this. There are so many things like this. There is no use in telling all that.

'Our friend Shri Ganapathi, said, "I am well. Inform me about your welfare". This is to be said by a *sanyasin* wearing saffron-coloured clothes. There is vast difference between a wise man and a *sanyasi*. Wise men say "All should be happy". But *sanyasis* say, "Pious persons should be happy". This is the opinion of the party in front of us.

'I do not want to take more time, Sir. Viewing from every aspect, it is good for us to accept the recommendations of the S.R.C. as our great persons have said. It is our duty to adjust ourselves to the circumstances and secure for ourselves as many safeguards and conveniences as possible.

'Another point. There is a cry that our Ministers should resign. At this crucial hour when so many schemes have to be undertaken, instead of trying to get through this Government as many safeguards as possible, some want to overthrow the existing Government. There are many things to be said on this point. But there is no time for all that.

'Every inhabitant of Coorg should agree to join unified Karnataka in the greater interest of India and at the same time try to get certain securities, safeguards and conveniences. We should agree and fight for the grant of facilities. Shri Karumbaiya has said that we cannot get five seats in the Assembly of Karnataka. What is said in Gita? *Karmanye vadhikarasthe mapalesha kadachma.* "Take care of duty and the result will take care of itself". We must try to get as many facilities as possible. Sir, I give my full support to the Resolution moved by the Hon'ble Chief Minister.'

Shri H.A. Nanja [Separatist Party]: 'Mr Speaker, Sir, when our country was free from the shackles of the foreign rule, the Congress Party came into power. A Commission was set-up to examine the question of reorganisation of the States in India which was divided into bits. The Commission have prepared a report after visiting all places keeping in view the welfare of the country and its people and I welcome it.

'Though there may be some defects in the recommendations, in the interest of the country as a whole the report may be accepted.

'I therefore fully support the Resolution moved by our Hon'ble Chief Minister.'

Shri P.D. Subbiah [Congress Party]: 'Mr Speaker, Sir, I welcome the report of the States Reorganisation Commission and say a few words supporting the resolution moved by our Hon'ble Chief Minister. The future of Coorg has often been discussed during the last 28 years in the Council and in the present Assembly and everyone knows it. Whatever might be our differences of opinion on other matters, all the 24 Members of this House expressed their unanimous opinion in the year 1954 at the Assembly before the States Reorganisation Commission, when they asked for our opinion. It would not be wrong to say that this satisfied our people. The Commission which has studied the question in all its aspects very minutely has recommended that Coorg should form a district of the proposed Karnataka State considering its administrative set-up, economic condition etc.

'We can see from their Report what all reasons they have given for the formation of Karnataka. Our Prime Minister Nehru and the All-India Congress Committee have been convinced that the recommendations of the States Reorganisation Commission are suitable to the present conditions, and prepared after having considered the languages, the administration and population of each State. It is intended to make India a great power second to no other nation. The Commission appointed by the Government of India has examined every question and they have produced a detailed report with no intention of wounding any one and without any bias of any sort. It has been placed before the Central Government.

'When we see all this, we feel that the Rama Rajya, which Gandhiji wanted to build in India, has already begun in every corner of India. The people of India were expecting this for a long time.

'We have remained separate till now. We had a happy time under the able administration we had, which satisfied everyone and made everyone happy and comfortable. It is, therefore, quite natural for everyone to feel that we should continue to be a separate State. But considering larger interests, it is but right to spread this happiness to the backward people in the neighbouring areas taking them to our fold and giving them the benefits of our experience in good administration. For this we should have a larger State.

'A question arises whether "C" States cannot continue. But when it is intended to abolish all "B" and "C" States and have only "A" type of States, everyone can see that it is futile to agitate for keeping Coorg, one of the "C" States as a separate

State. Coorg, which is one of the "C" States like other "C" States, should merge with the neighbouring Kannada areas like Mysore, South Kanara, North Kanara and other areas mentioned in the resolution moved by our Hon'ble Chief Minister, and it is one of our most important duties to help the formation of the unified Karnataka State. On the other hand, if we fight for a separate existence, we will be depriving our people of what facilities they might otherwise get. We should give up that attempt with "B" States and we should all join a "A" State, which is wanted by everyone. People from all parts of India have submitted memoranda that they should all be treated alike. The same thing has been decided at the Conference of the Chief Ministers of States. When the Chief Ministers of "A" and "B" and "C" States who attended the Conference have joined hands in taking a decision, there is no meaning in maintaining that our small State, that too "C" State should remain separate.

'Even before there was a desire that the whole of Kannada speaking area should form into a single State and accordingly the Commission recommended that it should be so. The All-India Congress Working Committee have also agreed to this. The Conference of Chief Ministers of States have accepted the recommendations. And now we should go with the wind, and it is dangerous to go against it.

'I remember that our friend, Shri A.C. Thimiah in his speech agreed for the formation of Karnataka only because he was disgusted of our present administration. But such an opinion is not good in the interest of the Nation as a whole. It is wrong and meaningless. I remember a proverb which I shall say with the permission of the Chair: "Does not matter if the daughter becomes a widow, but the son-in-law shall die". I am of the opinion that what he said was similar to this. We should get rid of this separatist tendency. "Karnataka State or no Karnataka

State, let the administration go—whether for good or evil". This opinion is wrong. My Hon friend, Dr Nanamayya has very ably criticised this view and I do not want to repeat what he said, and I don't wish to comment upon further on the criticisms of Shri A.C. Thimiah.

'Shri Karumbaiya said one thing: "I stood for election on the issue of trying to keep Coorg as a separate State. I have been returned to the Assembly on that issue. I have been elected to this Assembly with the support of 16,000 people. I, as a representative of these 26,000 people, do not agree for this merger of Coorg with Karnataka," he said. If he represents those, it would have been better if he had stated as to how many of them have participated in today's demonstration. Shri Ganapathi is a separationist. He said that a number of people came to Madikeri today and met the Chief Minister. If so, 16,000...'

Shri P.M. Nanamayya: 'It is not 16,000, Shri Karumbaiya said it was 26,000.'

Shri K.P. Karumbaiya: '26,000.'

Shri P.D. Subbaya: 'Out of these 26,000, I don't know how many joined the procession today. Is he really having the support of so many people?'

Shri C.A. Mandanna: 'Perhaps they did not come as they could not meet the bus charges.'

Shri P.D. Subbaya: 'We should not try to put any one opinion but try to shape the opinion of the people in such a way as to do good to the country. But if we induce them to be narrow-minded, the benefit and facilities that we might get in future may even be lost. It is not right to create such a situation. They think that we have not placed before all the people and elicited their opinion before taking the step we have taken. It is not correct. We should educate our respective constituencies to understand the present situation and advise them as to how best they should act under the present conditions and try to get as many concessions and benefits as possible. We should not make them say "Our cock only has three legs."

'We have debated upon this point sufficiently. In supporting the resolution moved by our Hon'ble Chief Minister, we have expressed our individual opinions and incorporated in the resolution the special benefits that we want to ask for. It is now the duty of our Hon'ble Ministers and the people to strive to get all the conveniences mentioned in the resolution and join the unified Karnataka. Let our Ministry struggle hard to win in their attempt and win fame even in future Karnataka. Wishing all prosperity to our people, I support the resolution and bring my speech to a close.'

Shri G. Subbaya [Separatist Party]: 'Mr Speaker, Sir, I have nothing to speak.'

Shri P.C. Utaya: 'Mr Speaker, Sir, my position has become difficult. I have been returned on an anti-merger ticket by my constituency. At that time, the Congress also issued a manifesto that when the question of the future of Coorg came up, they would rather resign their membership of the Assembly and make room for a plebiscite than continue as Members. Subsequently when the States Reorganisation Commission was appointed in 1953, the Chief Minister together with the Member of the Lok Sabha, Shri Somanna, went round the country and collected the opinion of the people and they found that the country was overwhelmingly in favour of retention of Coorg as a separate unit. In pursuance of that, in the Budget Session of March 1954, several Members sent up Resolutions urging the retention of Coorg as a separate unit, and finally, it was passed unanimously by this Assembly. When the States Reorganisation Commission came to Coorg about June 1954, all the 24 Members of this Assembly were called together by the Leader of the Congress Legislative Party, differences were promised to be made up, and it was urged that all of us should send up a memorandum jointly, without any dissension. Accordingly, we presented a memorandum and all of us without any dissension pleaded for the retention of Coorg as it exists now. The States Reorganisation Commission published its Report and to our surprise it was found that they had recommended Coorg to be included in the new Karnataka, which was to be formed. Even after the publication of the Report, the Coorg District Congress Committee, together with most of the Assembly Members met and decided to send up a deputation to Delhi to plead for the retention of Coorg as it is today as a separate unit, and it was hoped that when the Assembly met to consider the Report, all of us would unanimously give the same opinion that we had given in the memorandum we had submitted. What transpired in between is not known. I am told that there is a directive from the High Command that the recommendations of the States Reorganisation Commission should be accepted but that is not binding on this Assembly...'

Mr Speaker: 'The directive of the High Command, whatever it may be, it is not binding on the Assembly.'

Shri P.C. Utaya: 'That is what exactly...'

Shri P.M. Nanamayya: 'May I know from the Hon'ble Member to which party he belongs?'

Shri P.C. Utaya: 'I am not going to supply information here.'

Shri P.M. Nanamayya: 'We want certain information, Sir.'

Mr Speaker: 'Let him proceed.'

Shri P.M. Nanamayya: 'I wanted to know whether the Member is a Congress Member or not.'

Shri P.C. Utaya: 'In any case the present attitude has rather taken me by surprise. Only this morning I got the Resolution moved by the Hon'ble Chief Minister, supporting the States Reorganisation Commission Report. I have listened to the various speeches by most of the Members, and what I gathered so far was they have all pleaded for the retention of Coorg as a separate entity. But they say that in the larger interests of the country they are prepared to abide by the Report. Nobody has stated anything about what the "Larger Interests" are that would suffer by our remaining as a separate entity…'

Shri P.M. Nanamayya: 'Then he has not heard the speeches of the members. If he had!'

Mr Speaker: 'Please do not disturb.'

Shri C.A. Mandanna: 'On a point of information, Sir, does the Speaker propose to close the debate…'

Mr Speaker: 'I will decide. I shall see how long Shri P.C. Utaya takes up the time.'

Shri P.C. Utaya: 'In any case, I do not know how any directive would be such as to compel people to give up the opinion they already hold and abide by what the S.R.C. Report enjoins, for, there have been Congressmen elsewhere, particularly in Himachal Pradesh, Bihar, Vindhya Pradesh and Maharashtra where they have not abided by the recommendations of the States Reorganisation Commission. I heard one of the Members say that we have to do our duty and not think of what the result would be.

'With reference to what Shri Karumbaiya spoke about the latter portion of the Resolution asking for seats, one Member said that we would do well to ask; whether we get it or not is not for us. They could have taken the same view and pressed their opinion in support of the stand they had already taken, namely, to keep Coorg separate. Now, the Report itself says:

'No change should be made unless it is a distinct improvement in the existing position and unless the advantages which result from it, in terms of the promotion of "the welfare of the people of each constituent unit, as well as the nation as a whole"—the objectives set before the Commission by the Government of India—are such as to compensate for the heavy burden on the administrative and financial resources of the country.

'So, when taking the larger interests of the country as a whole, how the separate units stand are also to be taken into consideration. Merger with the major unit—Karnataka—is certainly detrimental to the Province as it stands. Financially it suffers, because we are going to States which are financially not in so favourable a position as we are. Then, do we gain anything? Is there any economic gain, or does our remaining separate come in the way of the economic expansion of the neighbouring States? It does not. On the other hand, it might come in the way of our own development, of our own resources, for, in an equitable distribution of the revenues, some of the projects which we can ourselves take up immediately will have to be postponed indefinitely. For instance, the Barapole Project, which if left to ourselves, there is a chance of this being worked up, but may be indefinitely postponed because the reorganisation is such that those people who would benefit from the project most would be cut away from us—I refer to Malabar, and they would be forming a separate State by themselves. Moreover, does it impair the unity and security of the country as a whole by this tiny Province remaining separate? On the other hand, I should think that the creation of bigger States—huge States like Uttar Pradesh with over 69 million people—would be more a menace to the Centre than a tiny State like the State of Coorg, for, having all the resources in a big area, they could, if they choose, even defy the Centre, because the Centre has to depend for its support on the contribution made by the various Provinces. Whereas a manageable, an easily more compact unit will have all its resources at command to defy the Centre. It is, I think, Rajaji who suggested a Unitary State, the country being redistributed into several districts with Regional Commissioners to supervise them and the State itself having direct control. So, the question of Coorg being too small does not arise in the re-set-up of States. After the integration of the various Princely States, Coorg has come to remain as a small unit. It has within its own sphere done as good work as any other bigger State, and the Report itself has accepted it. Such being the case, where is the need for Coorg to be joined to Karnataka? The reason given to us do not appeal to us. "The affiliations of this State are predominantly with Karnataka. Kannada-speaking people form the largest linguistic group in the State, accounting for 35 percent of its population; Coorgi or Kodagu, which is spoken by about 29 per cent of its people is akin to Kannada". It is akin to Kannada, it is akin to Malayalam, it is akin to Tamil and it is akin to Hindi, for some of the words, I suppose, must have started from the beginning when people began to see the phases of the moon and count the days of the week. We do not say, *Somawara*—Monday, *Mangalawara*—Tuesday, *Budhawara*—Wednesday; but *Thingalache, Chavvache, Padanache, Belache, Bolliache, Chaniyache* and so on. Is that Kannada? What I mean is...'

Shri P.M. Nanamayya: 'Sir, it is Kannada, He must know it...'

Shri P.C. Utaya: 'What I mean to say is that whatever investigations have been made by the Commission, they have not been thorough. "Culturally, Coorg has had more links with the east, which is mainly Karnataka country". Even there, I refute that statement. If anybody were to go to Virajpet side and look into the villages there, he will find that they are based mainly on the village system prevailing in Malabar...'

Shri K. Mallappa [Congress Party]: (Home Minister) 'What about Somwarpet and Kodlipet?'

Shri P.M. Nanamayya: 'Mr. Speaker, Sir, I would like to know which are those features which are akin to Malabar?'

Shri P.C. Utaya: 'I am not talking of the future, but the features.'

Shri P.M. Nanamayya: 'What do you mean by that, please let me know.'

Shri P.C. Utaya: 'May I tell you one example? What is the type of house in which you are living?'

Shri P.M. Nanamayya: 'That depends upon the carpenter, Sir. Perhaps my friend depended on a Malabar carpenter for a design.'

Shri P.C. Utaya: 'So Coorg has become a composite State though we have taken Kannada as the regional language due to historic reasons, and for matters of convenience. The various communities have been living together without any hitch over language. If you go to the shops, you will see that some people are maintaining their account in Urdu, others are maintaining their accounts in Malayalam and still others are maintaining their accounts in Tamil. In the Courts, there is Kannada as well as English. So, just because of certain superficial observations, to classify us as Kannadigas and recommend this State as a part of Karnataka that is to come into being, is an injustice done to us...'

Shri C.A. Mandanna: 'On a point of information. Has my friend given this opinion before the States Reorganisation Commission?'

Shri P.C. Utaya: 'I did. When they said that this Kodagu language is akin to Kannada, I said, "No".'

Shri C.A. Mandanna: 'Orally, but not in writing.'

Shri P.C. Utaya: 'Yes, not in writing. I had no chance to present an independent report. We all presented a combined report.'

Shri C.A. Mandanna: 'Did my Hon'ble friend give any dissenting note on the combined report?'

Shri P.M. Nanamayya: 'In writing, he agreed with the Members.'

Shri K.P. Karumbaiya: 'Are the Members abided by the Report of the States Reorganisation Report?'

Shri P.C. Utaya: 'It is true that they have abolished Part "C" States, but the reasons for doing away with the Part "C" States did not appeal to me at all. The other Part "C" States have been a drag on the Central Administration, inasmuch as nearly 50 per cent of their revenues had to be met from the Central Revenues to run, even in some cases, the day-to-day administration. We had not merely funds to run our day-to-day administration, but we had funds also for development purposes. So, I do not know why we should have taken the defeatist mentality and say that the States Reorganisation Commission has suggested the inclusion of Coorg in Karnataka and the four-man High Power Committee has also suggested the acceptance of the Report and so we accept it. What could we do? That I think, in my opinion, is not what we should have done. We should have said that it should continue as a separate entity...'

Mr Speaker: 'Why do you bring that into this discussion. It is just a party affair.'

Shri P.C. Utaya: 'No. What I surmise is that...'

Mr Speaker: 'You speak on surmise?'

Shri P.C. Utaya: 'After all, I may be allowed a little margin to surmise also with things we imagine. In any case we could have left it to constitutional experts to find a way out to retain this as a separate unit in case they were not retaining any Part "C" States. Various drawbacks have been shown and some people have suggested that the opinion in the country after the publication of the report, has been favouring the acceptance of the report. One would have noticed that immediately after the publication of the report, the country was in a torpor. It was only after that they woke up from it, and I presume that torpor was due to the fact that due to the prevalence of almost a personal rule after the popular Government came into being, there was such a feeling among the people that they did not care whether Coorg remained separate or merged, for, some of them at least did not find that happiness they anticipated by being free. But, after some time, opinion revived. After all, every country whenever there is a new set-up, there have been instances like this. It is only a passing phase. What we would lose permanently was the institutions that we so dearly cherished and of which there was the likelihood of effacement. Opinion began to grow fast and today if one goes round the country, he would find everybody feeling so sad that the Commission has recommended the merger of the State with some bigger unit.

'Coming to the Resolution itself, I agree with Shri Karumbaiya that either we asked for this State to be kept separate or when we go out and merge with others, we merge with them on an equal footing. We do not want to claim any concessions, for, the claiming of concessions would be on the part of people who feel themselves weaker than those with whom they are...'

Shri P.M. Nanamayya: 'I would like to know whether it is his personal opinion or the opinion of the people of Coorg State.'

Mr Speaker: 'It is his personal opinion.'

Shri P.M. Nanamayya: 'That is what I wanted to know.'

Shri P.C. Utaya: 'So, instead of these concessions being asked for, I would rather take things on an equal footing with others and fight it out than remain a "Favoured Child", because the effect of being a "Favoured Child" brings an inferiority complex which we should not be prepared to feel. It would be much worse if we had asked that so many posts of Ministers also should be reserved in the new State to come. I feel that on the whole the wishes of the people of this little place have not been heeded to and as a Congressman, I am not allowed to vote so long as I have got conscientious objections and I shall remain neutral.'

Shri C.M. Poonacha: 'Mr Speaker, Sir, I am very much obliged to the Members of this Hon'ble House for having given a very fair and sympathetic consideration to the Resolution I have moved this morning. On the whole the debate revealed that there is a general acceptance of the Resolution, and even those who had their own reasons to disagree with the Resolution, did in a way to express their feeling against certain recommendations of the Commission. In making a few observations, there has been a few jarring notes and in that some Members thought it fit to fling some uncharitable remarks against the Government. I for one hoped that this would not be used as an occasion for such uncharitable observations. However, Members did think it fit to make those remarks. In any case, we as the Government here and the party—Congress Party—cannot adopt either of the methods or the languages that are used by other parties.

'My friend, Shri A.C. Thimiah, started his speech saying that I perhaps as a politician was sitting on the fence and was not able to come to a decision within the time he expected. My friend, Shri A.C. Thimiah, lives in "Green Hills" and I, Sir, stay in "Fair View"! I have got to take a fair view of things before my friend could take a leap from the hills'!

Shri C.A. Mandanna: 'Once the Chief Minister was living in "Crystal Palace".'

Shri C.M. Poonacha: 'That is a fact, Sir, and people who lived in palaces are now taking a very fair view of things.

'Whatever it is, Sir, whether one stays in "Fair View" or lives in "Green Hills", my earnest prayer is that our fair view need not get blurred, or the green hills become barren tops. In any case, Shri A.C. Thimiah found it reasonable to accept the Resolution that I have moved and in that he said that he had come to the conclusion because of some bitter experience. He felt that initiative was practically killed in this State and personal rule was in vogue. At the same time, he said, that what little progress this little State has achieved during the past three or four years has been mainly due to the initiative of the people in the villages and our subordinate officers. I am unable to find the reasoning between these two statements. If the initiative was killed all-round, I wonder how, of all persons, the villager could be enthused to such an extent as to make our programmes a success. Much more, how our subordinate officials, of all persons, could be enthused in a task of this magnitude. That means to say, initiative has not only been maintained but has been enthused at the bottom, at the lower level, at the foundation itself. It might be that this all-round initiative that might have disturbed a few, perhaps, the politicians. Because, as he was making those observations, I was reminded of a remark made by one of the senior officers of the Government of India, Mr Vaghaiwalla, I.C.S., who was connected with the Community Projects Administration and who is now in charge of the Indian Administrative Service Probationers' Training College at Delhi. He, on his visit to Coorg, after a thorough inspection, wrote the following few lines, and I would like to read it out for the benefit of the House. He, among other things said:

"'This reveals an extremely satisfactory state of affairs for which this tiny State deserves all credit and congratulations of the Community Projects Administration. Comparisons are odious, but as contrasted with its next-door neighbours, Mysore, which has spent hardly 3½ per cent of the budgeted expenditure in the same period, Coorg has already spent 25 percent. This, in such a fashion as to show a record of achievements of which any State in the country, large or small can be proud" *(hear, hear)*. "The primary causes for this extremely happy state of affairs are that the entire State machinery from the Chief Commissioner with his Cabinet colleagues down to the Gram Sevaks as also the public of Coorg has been working as a team which is to be seen to be believed" *(applause from the Treasury Benches)*.

'He further proceeds, this is the wording he used:

"'If actual concrete achievements be any criterion for success in political life and if gratitude any consideration in receiving votes and for securing public offices, the present Cabinet of Coorg appears to lay solid foundation for ensuring a permanency of tenure for themselves" *(applause from Congress Benches)*.

'I know that in having functioned with the support of the people very successfully, the coming General Elections if held keeping Coorg as a separate State, is bound to give a certain verdict over which quite a number of people are now very much alarmed! And it is for this reason that a few have been telling or advocating "Well, let it be merged. After all it is not going to give us any chance." If such a frustration has come upon the minds of anybody, I do not think there can be any cure for it. But, here, we have to take a constructive view of the facts and calmly deliberate over the pros and cons and come to proper conclusions. It should certainly take some time and thought, which we have bestowed calmly, over the problems that relate to the question of future of Coorg.

'He [Shri Thimiah] also referred, and my friend Shri Utaya repeated the statement, over which I feel very much hurt. They said that a sort of personal rule was going on in Coorg. Yes, we did take the task that was given to us—I and my colleagues— personally and we have not spared ourselves to exert the most to fulfil certain programmes that were given to us. No doubt we did take personal interest in ever so many things. I am here to say and to substantiate before this House that we have not resorted to any kind of autocratic rule as was suggested by my Hon'ble friends on the other side. This negative approach or this sense of frustration should be given up at the earliest. We should not live under a sense of frustration any longer. My friend Shri Thimiah felt that he would find salvation by adopting a negative attitude of saying that let Coorg be merged because none of these people will be found in places of position. As he was making that statement, I was reminded of a few observations made by his father [Shri Chengappa] in the Legislative Council in the olden days. On a similar question, which was being discussed in the Legislative Council in the 1935, he said:

'"I had the fortune or misfortune to be on one of the deputations to go and wait on Mr Montague and Lord

Chelmsford. From that year it has been the common cause of all people in Coorg to fight out the Government to give us necessary reforms suited to the condition of the country. Our prayer was practically shelved, and we were given after two years the Legislative Council in name, but in fact it is only an Advisory Body."

'And so on, he narrates how the country was disappointed as the Government of India had not conceded the demands of Coorg for reforms. But merely on that account he did not think it fit to adopt a negative attitude. He always maintained a positive attitude. In this I am reminded of a beautiful piece in our epics, wherein, the faithful *Dwarapalakas* of Lord Vishnu—Jaya-Vijaya—when asked by Lord Vishnu as to how they would like to have *Moksha* (salvation), whether by becoming *Asuras* and adopting a negative attitude, jealousy and hatred or by becoming *Suras* by adopting a positive attitude of devotion and sacrifice. The negative attitude had a shorter term of three years, while the positive attitude had a longer term of seven years to attain *Moksha*. Jaya-Vijaya said, "We would rather adopt the negative attitude and find salvation more quickly" and later on took their births as Hiranvaksha and Hiranyakashipu, Ravana and Kumbhakarna, and Sishupala and Danthavakthra. Similarly, while late Shri Chengappa adopted a positive attitude, my friend Shri Thimiah seems to have chosen the negative attitude of the *Asuras*.

'He had also mentioned that in the interest of the youth of the country amalgamation has become necessary. I am only trying to draw his attention to certain facts, and I do not want to give my opinion on that now. I would again like to ask him to read the proceedings wherein his revered father has given an opinion. He says: "Leaving that aside, let us face facts. The main idea of the present population of Coorg is that our educated young men have no footing in our Province, and since the principle of each province is to work for its own benefit, our young men will not get a footing in the Madras Presidency or elsewhere. At present, the Madras University produces, on an average, about five to six thousand graduates every year, out of which Coorg is producing a couple. What is the percentage of appointments that the whole Madras Presidency can give in a year for those graduates, and where are we to find a place among the six thousand?" Naturally, students who are really very bright and intelligent will have the scope in the various public services as the candidates are to be chosen through competitive examinations. That means to say that merely by merging, young men are not going to get jobs. Let me make it clear to our educated young men in this country, that they are not going to get jobs on the mere fact of Coorg merging in Mysore. They have got to qualify themselves for it, merit the appointments, and if they have merit and qualifications, definitely they will get opportunities to enter Government service wherever they be, whether in Coorg or elsewhere. So, merger by itself is not going to produce a miracle. That is what I wanted to mention in referring to the argument put forth by my Hon'ble friend.

'He also referred to the question of Party Rule. My Hon'ble friend Shri Mandanna also referred to that. Party Rule is an inescapable element of democracy. My Hon'ble friend who is known to have been educated in a country where democracy is very mature, to have made his observations to say that "Sooner the Party Rule ceases the better"—seems to me that my Hon'ble friend is yet to have a good grasp of the principles of democracy. However, after having said all that, he has supported my Resolution in the same way the epical faithful servants of Lord Vishnu did. He now feels that he could only find salvation in supporting my Resolution by arguing from the negative side.

'Shri Karumbaiya made an eloquent speech, of course disagreeing with the Resolution I have moved, and he, as is quite usual to him, put forth certain cogent facts which have given the direct lie to what my friend Shri A.C. Thimiah has said. He said that the Government has done very well, and this could be continued, in case Coorg is kept as a separate Province. I realise the sentiments, and I want to submit that we have now got to take a broader view of things. It will certainly be helpful to the people of Coorg to allow them to manage their affairs in a way best suited to them. But that is not all that is indicated in the Constitution that we have adopted to [sic] ourselves. Social justice, equality of status and equality in the economic enjoyment are all things which are assured not to one or a few living in Coorg, but to everybody who is a citizen of this vast sub-continent. We should not feel very much disturbed by merging with a State like the proposed Karnataka Province. As I mentioned in my speech earlier, it has great potentialities and still greater scope for economic and industrial development.

'My friend Shri P.C. Utaya was trying to argue that what the S.R.C. has recommended is not quite correct. He was trying to emphasise that Coorg was not strictly a Kannada-speaking area and people of Coorg did not have affinities and affiliations with Karnataka. He also said that the Coorg dialect was more akin to Malayalam, Tamil and what not. The position is now as to what Coorg would be in the light of the recommendations of the States Reorganisation Commission. They have said that there shall be one category of State with equal footing, federating at the Centre as constituent units of the Indian Union. After all we have to argue on that. Then the position would be that Coorg, if it is not akin to Karnataka or has not got affiliations with Karnataka, should find its place in such other neighbouring unit which it legitimately belongs. It may even be said, if Coorg is different from Karnataka, it can go with Kerala. I do not think my Hon'ble friend held that view. Therefore, if it is a composite State and that it should remain as such, then, the position would be that it will have to become a Part "A" State. We cannot argue in between. My Hon'ble friend has not thrown any light on that point...'

Shri P.C. Utaya: 'I have left it to constitutional experts.'

Shri C.M. Poonacha: 'That is perhaps to shirk responsibility. The matter is absolutely clear to us. If we can hope to see that our State is maintained as a Part "A" State, that is a different question; if it is the idea that we may be continued as a territory, then it will be a different thing. As far as I am concerned, I can never support the idea of Coorg becoming a territory. In my opinion, no self-respecting democrat would ever entertain an idea of that nature. It would be a negation of democracy and it will be a most retrograde step and we will be marching backwards and not a step forward. Whether it is possible in the light of the recommendations of the States Reorganisation Commission to claim the status of Part "A" State is a point that should be considered. I do not think it requires any constitutional expert to give an opinion on that, as it would be futile to expect a small area, however well-administered it maybe to be given all the paraphernalia of a Part "A" State, which would unnecessarily involve heavy expenditure and waste of public money without much tangible benefit. Therefore, the States Reorganisation Commission have rightly come to the decision that Coorg should form part of the future Karnataka State.

'Some mention was made with regard to the big projects that we have in view for execution, particularly the Project [sic] like Barapole Hydro-Electric Project. I do not see any difficulty so far as the Barapole Project is concerned. The Barapole Project has been recognised and accepted to be a Project to serve a region and not a particular State. It is to serve a particular region where there is now acute shortage of electric power. Whatever may be the result after the implementation of the States Reorganisation Commission, the working of the Barapole Project as far as I am able to make out, will not be affected and I still hold that it has all the bright chances of being taken up for execution as early as possible. So also, the other developmental programmes envisaged in the Second Five-Year Plan Programmes drawn up by this Government. If that programme, after its being executed would raise the economic standard of the people of Coorg, I for one do not feel any hesitation over the consequences after merger. After all, we have to look into the interests of the common man and to serve the interests of the common man certain schemes have been drawn up, accepted and agreed to be worked. If those schemes are going to be worked up, which I am quite sure will be worked up, the common man need not be worried. It will be to his interests also and in the interest of the people as a whole that we agree to become part and parcel of the Karnataka Province which, as I said earlier, has a very bright future. With the will and with a firm and fervent desire to co-operate and work, we will be able to realise very soon that Karnataka Province has fulfilled our desires and given sufficient opportunities for the people of Coorg, both for the educated men of Coorg, and may I say, Sir for the ambitious politician too.

'Sir, with these words, I conclude.'

When the Resolution was put to vote, Messrs. K.P. Karumbaiya, P.C. Utaya and A.C. Thimiah remained neutral, and all the other Members voted in favour of the Resolution.

The Resolution was declared *carried*.

Mr Speaker: 'Shri Thimiah, do you wish to move your Resolution?'

Shri A.C. Thimiah: 'No, Sir, I am withdrawing my Resolution.'

Shri K.P. Karumbaiya: 'So also my Resolution.'

Mr Speaker: 'The House is adjourned sine die.'
The Assembly adjourned at 6.05 p.m.

[Note: One of the MLAs, Shri Yeravara Belli (Congress Party), was apparently absent.]

APPENDIX

The following resolutions which were tabled by Shri A.C. Thimiah and Shri K.P. Karumbaiya were withdrawn by them before moving.

Shri A.C. Thimiah:

Acceptance of the States Re-Organisation Commissionm Report

This Assembly is of the opinion that the recommendations of the States Reorganisation Commission be noted and that although this Assembly is aware of the immense advantages to the people of Coorg, if Coorg is maintained as a separate State, the House realises that in the larger interest of the country as a whole, the recommendations of the Commission ought to be accepted and therefore endorses and accepts, the recommendations of the Commission for the formation of a United Karnataka.

Coorg Not to be Merged in the Event of Two Karnatakas

This Assembly notes with concern the demand for two Karnatakas and is of the opinion that should the Parliament decide on the formation of two separate Karnataka States, the State of Coorg be maintained as a separate entity without being merged with either Mysore or the residuary Karnataka.

Coorg to be Centrally Administered Until the Formation of the United Karnataka

This Assembly is further of the opinion that in the event of Coorg State being kept as a separate State, it should be governed as a Centrally administered area till such time as the formation of a United Karnataka Province envisaged by the Report of the Committee.

Shri K.P. Karumbaiya:

Coorg to be Separate

This Assembly is of the opinion that the recommendations of the States Reorganisation Commission favouring merger of Coorg as a District of Karnataka are far short of the wishes and aspirations of the people of Coorg and therefore urges upon the Government of India to desist from implementing the recommendations and interfering with the status quo of Coorg, having due regard for the composite nature of its population, compactness of its area, administrative convenience, financial viability and economic progress and thus ensure the promotion of the welfare of the people of this State.

ACKNOWLEDGMENTS

This is my fifth book with Rupa Publications. My grateful thanks to their Managing Director, Kapish Mehra, for the support and encouragement he extended to me in pursuing my passion for the written word. I thank Saswati Bora and Sneha Bhagwat for their sound advice in editing the manuscript and improving its presentation.

My profound thanks to Dr Nima Poovaya-Smith for her help in improving the contents of this book. Readers will find references in the book to the valuable support I received from Dr Poonaya-Smith in promoting the story of Victoria Gowramma in the UK.

A number of my friends and family members helped enhance the essays by readily providing photographs, documents and references. My thanks to all of them. Specific contributions have been acknowledged in the body of the book.

A few of the essays in this book have appeared in some form or the other in newspapers such as *Deccan Herald*, *Star of Mysore*, *Coffeeland News*, and on P.T. Bopanna's popular website: www.coorgtourisminfo.com. I am grateful to all the respective editors.

My wife Aruna, son Vikram, daughter-in-law Dechu and grandsons Ved and Veer provide me with all the inspiration to chase my dreams. I am most grateful to them.

BIBLIOGRAPHY

Ganapathy, B.D., *Swathantra Horata: Kodagina Kathe*, Kodagu Press, 1965.

Jeaffreson, William, *Coorg & Its Rajahs*, John Bumpus, London, 1857.

Krishnayya, D.N., *Kodagina Ithihasa*, University of Mysore, 1974.

Login, Edith Dalhousie, *Lady Login's Recollections: Court Life and Camp Life, 1820-1904*, Smith, Elder & Co., 1916.

Mögling, Hermann, *Coorg Memoirs: An Account of Coorg and of the Coorg Mission*, Wesleyan Press, 1855.

Private Letters of Marquess of Dalhousie, William Blackwood & Sons, 1910.

Ramachandrachar, D.B., *Avakashada Allegala Mele*, Sunanda Prakasana, 1990.

Rice, Benjamin Lewis, *Mysore and Coorg: A Gazetteer Compiled for the Government of India*, Mysore Government Press, 1878.

Richter, Georg, *Manual of Coorg: A Gazetteer of the Natural Features of the Country and the Social and Political Condition of its Inhabitants*, B.R. Publishing Corporation, 1870.